LOBBYING
CONGRESS

LOBBYING
CONGRESS
How the System Works
Second Edition

Bruce C. Wolpe

Bertram J. Levine

With Case Studies
By the Editors of Congressional Quarterly

Congressional Quarterly Inc.
Washington, D.C.

CQ Press
A Division of Congressional Quarterly Inc.
1414 22nd Street, N.W.
Washington, D.C. 20037

(202) 822-1475; (800) 638-1710

www.cqpress.com

Copyright © 1996 Congressional Quarterly Inc.

Printed in the United States of America

05   04   03   02   9   8   7   6

♾ The paper used in this publication meets the minimum requirements of the American National Standard for Information Sciences—Permanence of Paper for Printed Library Materials, ANSI Z39.48-1992.

Library of Congress Cataloging-in-Publication Data

Wolpe, Bruce C.
  Lobbying Congress : how the system works / Bruce C. Wolpe, Bertram J. Levine ; with case studies by the editors of Congressional Quarterly. -- 2nd ed.
      p.   cm.
    ISBN 1-56802-225-5
    1. Lobbying--United States.   2. Lobbying--United States--Case studies.   I. Levine, Bertram J.   II. Congressional Quarterly, inc.   III. Title.
    JK1118.W64   1996
    328.73'078--dc20   96-24721
                                                        CIP

TABLE OF CONTENTS

Table of Contents

PREFACE

Congress is an institution given to hyperbole; mere acquaintances are "dear friends," ordinary acts of legislating are "courageous," and routine problems constitute "impending crises." For lawmakers and the media who cover them, this kind of exaggeration seems more the norm than the exception. It is not surprising, then, that when polls closed on November 8, 1994, and it became clear that Republicans had gained control of both the House and Senate for the first time in forty years, the Washington press corps would proclaim that an "earthquake" of monstrous proportions had rocked the city, or that cartoonists would depict the Capitol building as shaken to its very foundation and the nation's political leadership as running either for cover or to seize power.

While most Americans took some level of interest in these rantings and rumblings, one group had special reason to speculate about what it all meant. This group was the thousands of lobbyists whose livelihoods depend on knowing the lawmakers who control process and make policy in Congress. For them the inversion of party roles—Republicans to the majority and Democrats to the minority—was truly an "earthquake." And "monstrous proportions" was not hyperbole.

It is easy to understand why such an extensive change in congressional leadership would be considered cataclysmic by lobbyists. Gaining a favorable legislative result frequently depends on close relations with particular—usually powerful—members of Congress. A change in congressional leadership is a change in the tools of the trade. When the change occurs, instantly removing from power more than 150 committee and subcommittee chairs, these lobbyists must master new ways of providing service to their clients.

Beyond inverting party status in Congress, the 1994 elections brought on even more fundamental changes in Washington: when Newt

Gingrich assumed the Speaker's chair, the power equation that had existed between the executive and the legislature was altered, perhaps for years to come. Much of what had been understood about decision making in Washington during the twentieth century began to appear dated—not necessarily obsolete, but not as functional as it once had been. It seemed undeniable that Congress was prepared to play an even more aggressive role in the policy process than it had in recent decades. And this change is likely to endure for many years, regardless of which party controls Congress and which party occupies the White House.

The change in the congressional-executive power equation is important to lobbyists on two accounts. First, lobbyists must understand how much impact an administration can have on Capitol Hill. If history is instructive, we know that presidents and their administrations have considerable tools for influencing legislation. But we also have learned that this influence is seldom static—even during the course of a single presidency. It varies by chamber (House or Senate), committee, issue, and time. For lobbyists it is important to detect and respond to these changing patterns. Astute practitioners will know when an administration is able to have its greatest effect on legislative outcomes and when Congress is determined to follow its own lead. They will frame their strategies with these fluctuations in mind.

The second reason that the change in the power equation is important to lobbyists has to do with understanding exactly why it happened. During the early months of the 104th Congress, leadership in the House of Representatives took on many characteristics normally attributed to the executive branch. By creating a legislative platform (the Contract with America) and exercising close control over the selection of committee chairs, the Speaker forged a strong link between his policy preferences and his "management" team. In essence, he centralized policy direction and decision making on the major issues. He left details to the committees— as long as those details did not damage the leadership's broader objectives. He reinforced his control by heightening his own visibility which, while his personal popularity remained strong, aided his ability to market political concepts directly to the public.

Of these innovations, the notion of a congressional party platform will be the most difficult to duplicate in future years. It is unlikely that a combination of such determined leadership, party cohesiveness, and national mood will come together more than a few times in a century— if at all. What seems more certain to endure is the movement of at least some legislative authority from committee chairs to the House leadership. Indeed, the reforms adopted by the House in 1995 may permanently alter the seniority system and other traditional levers of power and influence in Congress.

It would make perfect sense then to argue that the fundamentals of lobbying Congress—certainly the House of Representatives—have changed significantly. But the game is still the same.

For lobbyists seeking to influence broad policy directions—the sorts of matters that congressional leadership is best equipped to deal with—a more powerful Speaker's office may offer an additional avenue to pursue. During the first one hundred days of the 104th Congress, Speaker Gingrich demonstrated that unified congressional party leadership could control the legislative agenda and much of the policy outcome in the House of Representatives. But that was for a brief period in one chamber and mostly confined to broad-based policy issues; most lobbying deals with matters far more specific and technical than the items that were included in the GOP Contract. This circumstance is not likely to change. Congressional committees will continue to write the majority of laws that affect the day-to-day interests of most citizens and most lobbyists.

What is more, members of Congress will always be subject to personal political pressures; they will need to satisfy their constituencies, mount reelection campaigns, and be faithful to their own sense of what is right. Sooner or later most members will define their own policy directions, thus giving lobbyists ample wriggle room to ply their craft, even on broad-based "party" issues.

So the structural reforms of the 104th Congress, should they become permanent, will not substantially change the fundamentals for lobbyists representing their clients in both bodies of Congress. The changes may add to the scope and challenge of the job, but they will not alter its core—and that core will remain focused on the individual legislator and his or her district and committee assignments.

This book recognizes and is premised on that reality, a reality that acknowledges that much of what we read and hear about professional lobbying is based on myth—more a product of Washington hyperbole and less the result of dispassionate evaluation. Stories that depict superlobbyists as controlling the course of public events are exciting to tell and eagerly consumed by an audience whose political heroes worry aloud about the corruption of power and the insidious effects of faction. But such mythology glamorizes and overstates both the means for and the extent of lobbying influence. It ignores the difficult, often mundane, work that is essential to thorough preparation and hard-won credibility—the marks of most successful lobbyists.

That there are exceptions to this view of lobbyists is without question, but the overwhelming majority of lobbying is done by honest citizens—sometimes professional, sometimes amateur—who believe in what they say and who, at one level or another, make a positive contribution to the quality of public debate by honestly arguing an issue held with conviction.

The chapters that follow focus on what is true about lobbying. There is no political or cultural dogma here; the book is a straightforward discussion that applies with equal salience to political and economic positions of the left, right, and center. Although some chapters are presented in the context of commercial activity, the core tenets can easily be extrapolated and made applicable to public-interest groups and organizations with purely political agendas.

Part I examines the essentials. This section seeks to fulfill the purpose that motivated the book when it first appeared in 1990: to explain, in generic terms, how lobbyists work. It provides a manual for the practitioner of the craft. Most books on legislation and lobbying in Washington recount stories about important legislative battles and the personalities involved, with the reader drawing lessons and inferences for the future from the experiences of the past. Part I creates a reverse template: it presents a framework that readers can apply to the legislative and political problems they are managing. If lobbyists read what follows and can find strategies, tactics, and perspectives of value to their work and the objectives they are trying to achieve, these chapters will have fulfilled their purpose.

Part II examines specific lobbying venues and techniques used in the profession. It gives close attention to opportunities and problems that often escape the observation of those who do not know the profession firsthand. This part builds on the foundations established in Part I and demonstrates their relevance to a variety of settings—strategic and organizational. Whether a lobbyist is working for small businesses or large, as part of an association or individually, whether attempting to enlist the support of a career service employee or a committee counsel, the essentials do not change: honest presentation of the facts, attention to detail, and consideration for the special needs of elected officials are the elements of success.

The case studies that make up the second part of the book help the reader understand the application of lobbying essentials and techniques discussed earlier. These studies, prepared by freelance author Colleen McGuiness from reports prepared by Congressional Quarterly editors and writers, cover a number of important political issues that Congress has debated in recent years. They were chosen to show a range of lobbying efforts.

Throughout this book we hope to provide an outline of what constitutes "good" lobbying. Stories of heavy-handed lobbying, strategies that backfire, and self-defeating behavior are legion on Capitol Hill. To date, the rules of the game, as it should be practiced, have been anecdotal, developed over time in the manner of the common law. We have set out to catalogue definitively what works—what should be done in what settings, or what should never be done, and why—and propound a principled approach to lobbying.

Republican control of the House of Representatives has been accompanied by allegations of a new politicization of lobbying—of especially close ties between elected officials and representatives of certain industries and causes, of the leadership dictating the flow of political contributions, of lobbyists directly writing legislation and major amendments to bills. Whether based on fact or the product of mere suspicion, such reports have increased the public's cynicism about lobbying and lobbyists.

Our view is that such distortions in the political system, to the extent they exist, will not long endure because they are at variance with fundamental values in our democracy. This is a time of political reform. Practices that are substantially out of step with the public interest in good government will not withstand scrutiny.

For students, observers, and analysts of Congress, we hope that by dispelling myth and focusing on what is real, the book will shed light on the distinctive role lobbyists play, and can hope to play, in the legislative process.

ACKNOWLEDGMENTS

T he first edition of *Lobbying Congress* was (and remains) a succinct and insightful discussion of what workaday lobbyists must consider in going about their business. As a lobbyist-turned-teacher, I found the book to be the perfect teaching vehicle—virtually everything that was important to say about the profession was within its covers. For this reason, I am especially thankful to Bruce Wolpe for allowing me to horn in on his project; his wise counsel and good humor made preparation of the second edition as much a pleasure as it was hard work.

When writing a book, it is not a bad idea to be married to an English teacher—especially the one I married. Thanks to Shelly for commenting on endless numbers of drafts. Her feel for the written word and innate good sense were almost as important as her patience.

Thanks also to David Tarr of CQ for his confidence, accessibility, and sound advice on the best direction for this new edition; Liz Helfgott for her impressive editing skills; Stephen Gettinger for his meticulous work on the glossary; Maggie Walsh for her pre-editing; my academic role models Stan Brubaker and Mike Johnson; Phil and Nancy Newfield, Joel Goldberg, Robin and Matt Freeman, and Mike Levine for reading and critiquing drafts; and Laura Firmin for helping to put the manuscript in readable condition.

Finally, thanks to Charles, Ruth, and Saul—I miss you all.

BJL

Bert Levine has brought to life this second edition of *Lobbying Congress,* and I am sincerely appreciative, professionally and personally, for his unstinting support for the book from its first appearance six years ago. The new work is a collaboration of the best kind, and Bert made it possible.

Acknowledgments

I am grateful to those who have educated me best about politics, public policy issues, and the management of public affairs. Their wisdom continually informs my thinking; they are a permanent inspiration and guide to me. I wish to express my appreciation to Henry Waxman, Anne Wexler, Bob Schule, Will Ris, Phil Schiliro, Steve Ricchetti, Pat Griffin, Jack Valenti, and Tamera Stanton.

David Tarr has always backed this book, and he and his colleagues at Congressional Quarterly have given us the very best support throughout the writing and editing.

This book would not exist without the support of my wife, Lesley Russell, whose love makes possible all the richness of life.

BCW

Introduction

WHO LOBBIES?

L obbying, like law, medicine, journalism, or virtually any other profession, is practiced in a variety of settings. The range of people, organizations, and causes demanding service is as complex and diverse as the country itself. With this understood, it is possible to identify a few broad categories that encompass the vast majority of venues, forms, and forums in which professional lobbyists conduct their business.[1]

"Contract" Lobbyists

The first, and probably most pronounced, demarcation is between those who lobby for a fee and those who are on salary. Not every organization needs or can afford a full-time Washington representative on payroll. And even those that do have their own lobbyists occasionally need some special expertise or other benefit—such as a tie to an important committee chair—uniquely available through an outside individual or organization. "K Street" law firms (the Washington, D.C., counterpart to New York's Wall Street law firms) and high-powered government relations specialists are the most visible and, frequently, most effective among these. The senior partners—the marquee names—and many junior partners and staff are well known in Washington insider circles. Most have served in Congress as members or staff and others have held prominent executive branch positions. They (the good ones) know issues, people, and process and understand how to get things done.

---

1. We do not attempt an exhaustive typology here. The intent is to present a brief profile of the most common lobbying organizational arrangements. Others—single issue groups, social welfare and civil rights groups, organizations representing farmers—could be considered hybrids of the categories we enumerate.

Corporate Lobbyists

Many of the nation's largest corporations maintain government relations offices in Washington. These range from one-person outposts to teams of well-paid, well-connected professionals. The essential difference between these people and their contract brethren is that corporate employees work on salary and represent only one organization: their employer. Also, it is not uncommon for corporate lobbyists to have "come up" the corporate ladder—marketing, sales, general counsel's office—as opposed to the government route. In addition to managing their own caseloads, corporate lobbyists are responsible for recommending when and if their company should retain outside (contract) lobbying services.

Business and Professional Association Lobbyists

The District of Columbia telephone directory contains more listings for government relations-oriented associations than for any other category of business. While they can be vastly different in organization, membership, and function, these associations all have one thing in common: each represents the collective interests of an industry or group of industries. They can be separated into three not-so-distinct categories: *peak associations,* which represent broad business interests and may count other associations among their members (the U.S. Chamber of Commerce, the National Association of Manufacturers, and the Business Round Table); *trade associations,* which represent one industry (the Motion Picture Association of America, the National Automobile Dealers Association, and the Health Insurers Association of America); and *professional associations,* which represent the interests of practitioners in law, the healing arts, accounting, and other professions.

Virtually all of these associations are either headquartered in Washington or have government affairs offices there. Regardless of size, the majority of associations seek to provide their members with an array of services. Prime among these are: information on legislative and executive branch policy directions; a forum for reviewing and commenting on proposed regulations; advice on how to comply with existing federal requirements; and a forceful mechanism for participating in the legislative process—in other words, lobbying. As few members of Congress can afford to ignore the views of a credible association, the groups' obvious political advantage is collective action.

Public-Interest Groups

Public-interest groups are defined as organizations seeking policy objectives that do not "benefit selectively either the membership or activists of the organization." [2] In a sense these groups are the antithesis of business and professional associations: other than in a very broad context, they protect no specific economic interests but rather their definition of the public interest. Their organizational structures and economic support bases range from mass membership organizations that rely on thousands of donations and subscriptions to much smaller organizations that are funded by foundation grants, a limited number of individual benefactors, and public funds, if and when available.

The sophistication with which these groups pursue their goals has grown immensely since their emergence in the 1970s. Today they are far from ragtag, though they can present that image when useful. They have become the recognized masters at coordinating legislative objectives with supportive press coverage, direct mail campaigns, and grassroots lobbying. Their political strength is in the perceived selflessness of their commitment, the appeal of their positions, and, in many instances, the numbers of people they can claim to represent. This is strong political stuff. They know it and use it well.

Public-interest groups also have moved across the political spectrum to the point where, by the mid-1990s, conservative citizen action groups had eclipsed—in influence, membership, revenues, and effectiveness—those identified with liberal and left causes.

Labor Unions

Labor unions combine five elements that define political power in Washington: money, people, information, organization, and, perhaps most importantly, a willingness to use these assets in support of legislative and political objectives. Members of Congress know this: they are aware that labor's grassroots communicators are active, tenacious, and plentiful. They also know that unions, better than most other organized interests, remember and support their friends at election time. From political action committee (PAC) money to campaign volunteers to delivering votes at the polls, participation by labor is a valued component in many

---

2. Kay Scholzman and John Tierney, *Organized Interests and American Democracy* (New York: Harper and Row, 1986), 29.

congressional campaigns, especially for Democratic candidates. Labor is nevertheless at a crossroads, as declining union membership raises questions regarding the degree of power and influence the movement can bring to bear on the outcome of legislative battles.

Explanation of Terms

Words and phrases in *italic* type in Part I, the Elements of Lobbying, are explained in the Glossary, page 180.

Chapter 1

THE MYTH OF MYSTERY IN POLITICS

T here is no mystery or awe to the federal legislative process. The dance of legislation, as it has been called, is complex and convoluted, but it is not an enigma. Outsiders are nevertheless extremely wary of dealing with, or becoming involved with, Congress. Indeed, the very existence of the modern-day profession of lobbying—the so-called hired guns and superlobbyists who have emerged so visibly in Washington over the past two decades—is a function, in part, of the sense that the inner workings of Congress are opaque and impenetrable, and that specialists are needed to understand it and make it respond to outside interests.

To the contrary, the House and Senate readily yield their secrets to those who care to study and understand and participate in how Congress works. The myth of mystery in politics, if it ever existed, has fallen away, and with it the mystique of lobbyists, their power, and how they operate.

Congress is more open to public scrutiny even as the perception exists that the House and Senate are out of control, "captured" by powerful and secretive special interests who render the institution unable to make decisions in the interest of the nation as a whole, as opposed to each parochial interest. Campaigns of interest groups, corporations, and constituencies are waged fiercely throughout the halls of Congress, but the fact is we know more about them than ever before.

This openness is being driven by several factors. First, there has been a vast increase in the numbers of people employed to lobby Congress. There are more than fifteen thousand registered lobbyists listed in *Washington Representatives*, the phone book of the lobbying business. This is due in part to the centralization of political power in Washington, a trend that began to pick up steam during the presidency of Franklin D. Roosevelt and then virtually leaped forward in the 1960s and 1970s. And while that trend may now be stalled—perhaps even reversing—it remains indisputable that Washington has supplanted much of the province and authority exercised in earlier decades by city hall and the state legislature. The role of the federal government is so pervasive in everyday life (affecting, for example, taxes, housing, communications, health care, environmental protection, and the rules of commerce) that it is imperative to participate in it. To observe the government and try to make it respond to their needs, organizations of all kinds have established listening posts in Washington. An explosion of representation, from the largest corporations in the United States (and many from abroad), to the smallest conceivable constituencies, has reverberated throughout the capital.

Second, the revolution in technology has made the processes of Congress more accessible and temporal. There is now instantaneous electronic access to and broadcast of political information, ranging from nationwide cable coverage of debate on the House and Senate floors and in committee hearings (via C-SPAN and Cable News Network), to the now-ubiquitous armies of lobbyists equipped with cellular telephones that enable them to report, within seconds of a vote, to their home offices or to Wall Street in time to affect market forces that day. More than one thousand trade publications and newsletters service the new legions of organized constituencies by tracking in minute detail the most arcane issues for the benefit of their subscribers.

Perhaps the most dramatic technological advancement has been the Internet and the World Wide Web. Every citizen who can afford, or has access to, a computer and a modem can "pull up" bills, amendments, committee schedules, hearing rosters, and even the *Congressional Record* almost as quickly as these are made available to members of Congress. What is more, they can make their views on the content of these documents known without ever leaving their computer screens. All they need is an E-mail account.

Third, Congress continues to open its formal processes to public scrutiny. At the beginning of the 104th Congress new rules were adopted in the House of Representatives that made it more difficult for committees and subcommittees to do their business in "executive" (closed) session. The new standards require that national security, law enforcement considerations, or the possibility of doing serious damage to some person's reputation be at issue in order to justify moving legislative business behind closed doors.

Even if members attempt to work around "sunshine" rules by conducting business in informal gatherings or through off-the-record negotiations, accurate and detailed accounts of who stands where are available from multiple staff and member sources.

Even the smallest legislative details do not escape public notice. Hidden, discrete legislative provisions designed to protect or benefit a parochial interest rarely stay secret for long. Legislators opposed to the stuffing of special breaks into massive bills, or those angry because their favored amendments failed to be included by the committee, or reporters hot on the trail of legislative favoritism, demand and release lists of these *transition rules*, all duly reported by the press. Specialized media services obtain and publish verbatim copies of elusive legislative documents in time for lobbyists to digest them and act upon them before many legislators and staff are fully aware of what is happening.

Only the highest officials in the government—the president, the Speaker of the House, the majority leaders of both the House and Senate—have the ability unilaterally to launch initiatives in a very short period of time, under great secrecy, with sweeping and profound implications (and then most often in the area of foreign policy). But those actions are the exception, rather than the rule, and they must inevitably be scrubbed and reified by the legislative and political process, which is in the open. It is true that terribly important matters can be decided, usually late in the session, in closed *conferences* among senior members of House and Senate committees. But what is decided is almost always defined by parameters drawn weeks before by legislative and political activities that have shaped the bill under consideration.

There are, in short, more people than ever before watching Congress, and fewer secrets that can be kept hidden. The work of Congress is more than ever before a public enterprise, and information about what is happening, and why, is readily available to those who know how to obtain it. It is precisely the very openness of the process that makes Congress so susceptible to influence by lobbyists.

All lobbying on Capitol Hill begins and ends with the members whose support and votes are needed on any given issue. The singular prerequisite to a lobbyist's success and effectiveness is understanding the members of Congress. As public officials, legislators are rarely hidden; they are plainly visible. They were elected by expressing themselves, which they thoroughly enjoy, and they continue to do it in Washington, and back home in their states and congressional districts, with a vengeance. (Indeed, the city's main product—what people in Washington create, organize, manipulate, and respond to—is words: legislation, floor statements, resolutions, proclamations, speeches, legal briefs, court decisions, newsletters, reports, press releases, and so on. The network news from Washington is really about what was said that day; when Congress or the president does something, it is with words.) Lawmakers are almost always on display every day Congress is in session, and they almost always have something to say. In expressing themselves, legislators reveal their hopes, world views, aspirations, frustrations, and objectives. They also expose their character (something that is ultimately imperative for a lobbyist to understand, because the essential element of character in politics is trust). And they disclose, by what they say, what they want to accomplish and what is at stake, as they see it, in the legislative process. Once a member of Congress is understood in these terms, a lobbyist can craft a strategy to enlist that legislator's support or neutralize his or her potential opposition.

The essential task of the lobbyist—in addition to being able to marshal political influence and power outside the Capitol and have a decisive effect on events inside the Capitol—is to make it as easy as possible for a legislator to support an issue or request. The optimum measure of leverage on behalf of a lobbying objective, the elemental standard that must temper every legislative strategy, is maximum political gain for the minimum expenditure of political capital.

With more lobbyists following legislation, more media coverage of congressional activity, and members who are more public and visible, the legislative process in Congress is no longer driven by backroom deals. Lobbying is less the application of behind-the-scenes arm-twisting than bread-and-butter execution that covers all dimensions of the process. There is no mystery about it; lobbying is the straightforward implementation of political strategy.

For the lobbyist these dynamics place a premium on three threshold practices:

First, an attention to details no less than to the big picture. Certainly, the overall political context of a measure is pivotal: Is it a spending bill in a time of fiscal restraint? Is it a civil rights initiative in an era when such proposals are under assault? Does the bill change precedent when the constituencies for such change have not matured? But it is even more important for a lobbyist to focus on the details of legislative activity. To succeed, lobbyists have to make things happen. Daily attention must be given to which lawmaker is taking the lead, which staff are involved, and who is opposed and why. Lobbyists have to stay current on related developments all over the city, in Congress, the executive branch, and the courts, and be informed about what their opposition—members, staff, and other lobbyists—are doing. The lobbyist's worst enemy is not political opposition but ignorance of what is happening that will affect his or her interests.

Second, touching all the political bases pertinent to the outcome of the issue. It means little to have support among a handful of majority party members only to face opposition from a united and vigorous minority. There is only small gain in passing a bill or amendment in the House if no groundwork for it has been laid in the Senate. Support in an *appropriations* subcommittee can be enhanced if the relevant *authorizing* committee is informed and on record behind the program. It is useless to succeed in an authorizing committee only to have the provision ruled ineligible for consideration on the floor. Success in committee can be cemented if the leadership agrees your issue is a priority—and your proposal can be consigned to oblivion if the leadership is opposed. It is impossible to operate without building a base with every faction that will influence the process. Each must be cultivated.

Third, following through on commitments. As words are the currency of Washington, they can suffer tremendous inflation in their value. Talk becomes cheap. Commitments extended in the legislative process are worth something only if they are fulfilled. If a member requests information on an issue, it must be provided. Promised questions for a hearing must be delivered. Informing and activating the grassroots back home must be carried out. Messages from one political party to the other must be transmitted and received. Just as trustworthiness as a character trait is essential to politicians, so it is for lobbyists. If they cannot be trusted to meet the responsibilities they have set for themselves in the presence of legislators and staff, they will never be trusted again in a legislative battle.

To thrive and triumph in the environment of Congress, lobbyists must understand the rules of the game, the fundamentals of lobbying, and the informal constraints that govern the political art of lawmaking. Lobbyists must adapt to the prevailing rigors and mores of the institution. The mysteries of Congress and legislation have been steadily stripped away. With Congress more open, accessible, and accountable, with even the most private personal and political matters now prominently chronicled on the front pages of the newspapers, lobbyists accustomed to operating in the shadows are today at a disadvantage. As there is no mystery to how Congress works, so there are no great secrets to what makes a good and effective lobbyist, or to what must be done if one is to have a chance to succeed.

Chapter 2

THE FIVE COMMANDMENTS

The game for the lobbyist is to get the votes. There are five basic commandments of this game. They are simple, straightforward, and obvious, but if one fails in a legislative task it is usually because one of these commandments has been broken. These rules must be employed every time contact is made with Capitol Hill.

Tell the truth.

Lobbying is the political management of information. A lobbyist is only as good as his or her word; your words are bonds upon which all subsequent judgments are premised. Everyone knows not to lie. Liars are discerned quickly and are never trusted seriously again. So overt lying is not the issue. Language, which is so important to politics, is filled with nuance, shading, and subjectivity. The challenge of truthfulness for the lobbyist is not simply to be straight, but to be honest in representing an issue and the political environment in which it is being played out.

Truth is not only stating the factual but also avoiding the omissions that materially impede an accurate understanding of the situation. If you fail to convey the truth, in its fullest sense, a legislator can proceed on your behalf without either full factual knowledge of the issue or a full appreciation of the obstacles ahead and could suffer the worst personal and political consequences if called to account by others. Be it through ignorance or stupidity or willful omission by the lobbyist, such adverse consequences for the legislator will come home to haunt the lobbyist and harm his or her prospects on this and other issues. A lobbyist asks a legislator to do battle. If a lobbyist chooses not to arm a proponent with as much information as possible (and with the same information on which the lobbyist is making decisions) the legislator is handicapped by the lobbyist from the start. Information is power. Truthful information has the greatest power.

Never promise more than you can deliver.

The extravagant promise is the easiest temptation. It is criminal to promise a legislator that the votes are there on an amendment when they are not, or at least an embarrassment with lasting consequences. Similarly, promised commitments of support from other potential allies must be delivered. If an assurance is made that labor support is in hand, for example, it must be forthcoming. If grassroots results are promised, the telephone calls, faxes, and letters must be generated in the amounts, and to the targeted legislators, as outlined. If the head of your client's company is expected to make a phone call to ask a legislator personally for assistance, that call had better be made.

The strategy of the battle plan (who will be approached on your behalf, and how; which constituencies might be motivated, and when) should always be shared at the outset with your legislative champion, whose personal imprint can then be grafted onto the plan as it unfolds, and who can take into account the degree of progress that is in fact being made.

The success of all tactics depends on an accurate sense of the resources that can be deployed to achieve the objective. Promised resources are effective only when they are in hand. It is always preferable, however, to understate your capabilities on obtaining votes and marshaling constituent pressures and to let the power of their effect, once unleashed, speak for itself.

Know how to listen so that you accurately understand what you are hearing.

Nowhere in American life is language so baroque and pregnant with meaning and shades of meaning as in politics, and especially in politics as practiced on Capitol Hill. There are the arcana of the rules of the House and Senate, the stilted legal phrasing of legislative draftsmanship, and the studied politeness (essential to avoiding fisticuffs) of debate in committees and on the floor. All of these must be known, and they can be understood only with careful attention and applied discipline over an extended period of time.

Success in lobbying hinges on understanding the messages one is hearing from staff, from members, at *markups*, and during floor debate. There is too often the temptation to believe that a legislator is on your side—something the legislator wants you to believe at certain moments—before, in fact, a commitment of support has been given.

Accordingly, it is critical to comprehend and discount expressions such as:

"I want to be with you on this."

"I fully share the concerns you are expressing to me."

"I think we should do something about this."

"I want to help you."

"This is also important to me."

"I believe you have a good case."

"I could accept what you want."

"I support you—but does the chairman?"

In every such instance there is a desire to be helpful, but in fact no commitment to supporting your cause has been extended.

At times members will make what seems to be a solid verbal commitment and then vote differently in committee, on the floor, or in conference, often pleading changed circumstances at the moment the vote was cast. A legislator is not immune from such changes of heart even when written pledges have been made to constituents, although such departures are rare. Legislators always want the ability to exercise an "out" if one is made necessary by factors such as the emergence of pressure from the leadership or the packaging of one provision with another, overriding matter that a legislator must oppose. All such possibilities have to be anticipated.

Lobbyists are hardly the only victims of political auditory impairment. In any seriously contested race for a leadership post in the House or Senate, the total of all commitments made to all candidates prior to the final, secret ballot regularly exceeds, by a substantial margin, the total number of members voting in the caucus.[1] Knowing how to listen is a prerequisite to knowing how to count, and knowing how to count is essential to victory.

The strength of any commitment is, in the end, your judgment of the legislator's credibility, something that can be known and acted upon only on the basis of personal experience over a period of time. When expectations and desire cloud perception, the result inevitably is miscalculation and disappointment. Knowing legislators and staff at first hand,

---

1. Former Senate majority leader Robert Byrd, Democrat of West Virginia, said it best: "I read a person's eyes, how he says what he says. My credo was if a Senator has not actually said he was for me, even if he said things like, 'I see no problem,' or 'You don't have to worry about it,' then I had to count him against me in my tally." (The *New York Times*, "Washington Talk," September 21, 1988.)

observing them in action, weighing their rhetoric against their votes—all will guide the value a lobbyist can place on the words: "I'm with you."

Staff are there to be worked with and not circumvented.

The credibility and trust that is built between lobbyists and members must also be constructed in the first instance between lobbyists and staff. All lobbyists cherish and value the personal relationships they may have with representatives and senators, and they relish their ability to speak directly with members on important issues. But legislators, of course, depend overwhelmingly on their staff for judgment, guidance, and assistance. It is impossible for any member, each of whom is most likely sitting on at least two committees[2] and many more subcommittees, to be fully informed, on an up-to-the-minute basis, of all the issues under his or her immediate jurisdiction, much less all matters on the floor that day, all events in the district, the latest crisis with Moscow or the Middle East, the newest twist in a regulatory fiasco at a regulatory agency, or that day's Supreme Court ruling on a case initiated three years ago. And so staff are the first lines of defense for any member, the first persons that they turn to in figuring out what happened, why, and what should be done about it.

Staff also tend, over time, to take on the traits, instincts, outlook, and judgment of the members for whom they work. This is both a natural function of their affirmative choice to work for a person of a certain political alignment and temperament, and their success in building trust between themselves and their member. Congressional offices eventually will fully reflect the style and character of their leader; the signals of desirable and acceptable staff behavior come from the top and are absorbed throughout the member's office. Winning the confidence of staff—and maintaining it thereafter—is a prerequisite to an ongoing, successful political relationship with any political office.

Staff are differentiated over functional lines. Although there are idiosyncratic variations in each member's office, there is a standard staff structure. The administrative assistant (AA), who acts as chief of staff, is usually the member's political alter ego. Generally a veteran of the member's election campaign, the AA is involved in all key political and issue deci-

---

2. House members serving on the Appropriations, Ways and Means, Rules, or (for Republicans only) Commerce committees are the exceptions; these are "exclusive" committees, with no additional assignments on other legislative committees permitted for members on these panels.

sions. Legislative assistants have line authority over legislation and are usually assigned separate responsibility for each of the committees the member sits on and other issue areas. A member's executive assistant or personal secretary is responsible for scheduling, appointments, and travel.

The structures of the committee and subcommittee staffs are more varied. But two factors are crucial. First, at least one staff person is assigned to each issue area under the panel's jurisdiction and is the in-house expert on that topic. Second, although the committee staff is supposed to serve, on an objective basis, all the members of the committee, the staff's first loyalty is to the chair, and they speak for and act on behalf of the panel leader.

Staff therefore gradually develop a measure of expertise over many issues, the players and politics of the committees, the legislative process, and the interest groups and constituencies involved with legislation. They thereby become an indispensable resource to the members and to lobbyists. Because of this symbiotic relationship, it is a mistake of the first order to circumvent the staff and exclusively approach a member directly on an issue.

 An end-around serves no purpose. First, the staff will be alienated because you did not trust them at the outset. Second, the staff will be blindsided when the member asks them for advice and they are unprepared to respond because you have not contacted them. Third, you will have lost an opportunity both to get guidance on how to most effectively approach the member on your behalf, and to have the staff on your side when the member asks for staff advice, as will inevitably happen. Members will almost never make a flat commitment before consulting with their staff. Fourth, when the member asks the staff for help, the staff will contact you for further information, and no time has been saved by ignoring the staff in the first instance. Staff, then, must be cultivated no less than the members themselves.

If one makes an enemy of staff, through neglect or ignorance, through an act of commission (deliberately evading the staff) or omission (not informing the staff of a matter of material relevance to the member's legislative or political interests), the costs to yourself and your clients will be high. It is true that personal ties to a member—through friendship or campaign fund-raising, or because of the primacy of your client in the state or district—can be established, and maintained, outside the staff. But these ties can be leveraged even further with the active solicitation of the staff.

Spring no surprises.

Politicians hate the unexpected, and especially any news that is adverse. They want, and need, to have relevant information in a timely fashion and to be in a position to act on it, rather than react to it. Legislators must not be misled, willfully or inadvertently. It is therefore essential to assess the element of surprise in any lobbying strategy.

Members and staff need to know beforehand the source and degree of opposition—and support—for any bill or amendment or agency action you are seeking. Before committing themselves, they will want to know whether an initiative is supported or opposed by labor, the business community, public-interest groups, key corporations, the committee leadership, and leading legislators; or whether a matter has been endorsed or flailed by local or national media; or whether it affects a pet project of an influential member (on or off the committee of jurisdiction). Members and staff need to anticipate which interest groups will be engaged for or against the proposal, and how high a priority it is for them. All significant facts and arguments must be made available, with a full outline of the debate that will unfold, both its general dimensions and specific twists.

It is especially important to anticipate and outline the criticisms that will surface against your proposal, and to share them fully. This permits the legislator to hear such arguments first from you, and it allows you to shape the counterarguments that will serve as the primary line of defense. By being the first to get your message to key legislators and staff (especially by notifying them of an adverse development), and placing it in the best possible context, you can defuse the volatility of surprise, enabling your allies to discount the opposition from the beginning.

Representatives and senators also need to know of material events affecting their constituents, particularly actions that have a bearing on the local economy. Large corporations and their employees are often the most important economic, political, and social forces in any local community, and legislators care deeply about their welfare and future. Lobbyists must ensure that the congressional delegations who represent their clients have an ongoing knowledge of their client's activities. Although good news needs to be shared in a timely fashion—a plant expansion, a union contract, a government grant, favorable action by the state legislature or city council, a philanthropic community program—it is bad news about an unsettling development that must be shared immediately, before it becomes a public issue. Corporations especially are often loathe

Hang a lantern on your problem

to undertake such notifications. But plant closings, hostile takeover attempts, layoffs, the initiation of controversial legal action, or a challenge to a regulatory agency are matters where it is in your interest to get your story out as quickly as possible and in the most favorable light. Those affected adversely will turn immediately to your legislators for help. Unless the relevant legislators have the benefit beforehand of your knowledge and perspective on the action that has been taken, there is a much greater chance that their public reaction will be unfriendly toward you.

Ideally, lobbyists should plan for such contingencies by determining, in advance of a public announcement, which congressional offices need to be contacted, at what levels, and by whom. In addition, all people making calls and visits must have "talking points" to guide the discussion and written information to leave with the person visited.

All too often corporate executives in particular pay attention to their immediate constituencies—management, employees, shareholders, and the media—and ignore the political dimension of their actions. Such inattention and neglect unwittingly play directly into the hands of opponents who also wield political influence. The general rule of thumb should be: If a matter is important enough to bring to the attention of securities analysts in New York, or if it merits a local press announcement, it also is worthy of briefings for or notices to members and staff in Washington.

Legislators never get involved with issues only when you want them to. They are responding to innumerable stimuli from their communities, their colleagues, and the media. They will become involved when you are most vulnerable. Removing the element of surprise, by anticipating events and acting first, can neutralize the opposition you will inevitably encounter.

Chapter 3

LOBBYING: THE FUNDAMENTALS

T he fundamentals of lobbying constitute a day-to-day regimen that must guide a lobbyist's contacts on Capitol Hill. The rules of the game must be applied to every lobbying strategy.

 Define the issues in any lobbying visit. Determine at the outset what you want.

Lobbyists often confuse means and ends, and they are susceptible to trying to play out the last moves in the legislative chess game even as the first moves are under way, and while the shape of the chessboard itself is changing. Each lobbying exercise must begin at the very beginning, and then advance one step at a time. In any lobbying visit, the basic question that will define the task is: What is the purpose of the contact? Is it to give information or get information? To elicit support for a particular position? To encourage opposition to an unfolding event? To provide an alert (with your perspective on it) in anticipation of future events? Or to get a vote?

Definition is crucial because of the relatively narrow temporal focus of legislators and their staff. Because they are overloaded by the press of daily events, it is hard to keep up with breaking issues, let alone with long-term strategy. (Planning sessions are an integral part of nearly every office, but rarely are they ever fulfilled over any given year. The planning activity politicians know best, and that they regularly execute, concerns electoral survival—endlessly calculated, calibrated, and implemented.) The most effective contacts, therefore, should be timed with breaking events, or those that will take place in the immediate future. Providing advance knowledge of what is coming is especially valued; those privy become insiders, and hence privileged, and wield the power of being informed.

Legislators and staff are therefore geared to focusing on the immediate tasks at hand. This cycle of activity usually means that most legislators and interests working on an issue tend to be involved at the same time, creating an air of freneticism, pressure, and harassment that is inevitable when literally hundreds of political vectors are converging on one point—a committee markup, an agency meeting, an *oversight hearing*, a session of the White House Council of Economic Advisors. Under such pressures the premium is on specified, targeted information and suasion: that request, suggestion, or provision of information that will elicit the most positive, efficient, and directed response. Accordingly, it is counterproductive to take precious time with members and staff to discuss floor strategy when the matter is still in committee, or to lobby the Senate when the item has not passed the House, or to press for binding commitments on a matter to be resolved in conference when such a joint meeting is ten weeks away. (But a lobbyist must always be thinking about such future events and preparing to influence them.)

Lobbyists must know and appreciate what is occurring on the Hill outside of their parochial concerns. A member cannot be expected to be responsive to your needs on a morning with a heated markup in another subcommittee or an urgent foreign policy debate on the House or Senate floor. You need to know when such conflicts are on the agenda, and guide your contacts accordingly. Lobbyists are most effective when they provide information and political resources that meet the needs of the moment. To the extent they demonstrate their relevance to the decisions of the day, they will be approached for similar help in the next rounds.

Organizations, trade associations, companies, and interest groups obviously have long-term needs and carry out long-range agendas. The congressional calendar contains numerous slack periods throughout the year when such matters can be discussed quietly and extensively, when visits for the legislator in the district or state with affected constituents can be arranged, when there is time for members and staff to read lengthier briefing materials. The key is to anticipate the rhythms of the Congress and the political calendar, and then to choose the moment when your message can be heard with minimal distraction and maximum sympathy. Your objective can be achieved only through sensible tactics sensitively employed—a pattern of execution built on a full appreciation, developed over time, of the conflicting pressures and demands confronted by legislators and staff every day.

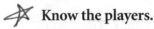 **Know the players.**

Effective lobbying, in its Washington (as opposed to its grassroots) dimension, is a function of interpersonal relations: who politicians are, where they are from, what motivates them, and where they stand and why in the political firmament. Every lobbyist knows to consult the *Almanac of American Politics* or *Politics in America*[1]. But to make a difference lobbyists have to bring those informed profiles and descriptions to life for themselves and their clients. Lobbyists must understand the concerns and perspectives of the legislators who are important to the issues they care about. They must grasp every such politician's world view: what he or she wants to accomplish. And lobbyists must perceive the style and pattern of politics as practiced by their targeted legislators. Again, information and the comprehension of its implications are fundamental.

There are no easy answers or shortcuts. Study, reflection, analysis, and direct involvement and participation in the legislative process are all necessary. Because politicians are public creatures, their record is amply available: votes, speeches, press conferences, statements in committee and on the floor, and public correspondence. Each piece helps fill out the mosaic. The best way to get to know them is to observe them directly, particularly in committee or on the floor. It is there that the outlines of political character begin to be discerned. By what is said on a particular issue, the nature of their political beliefs becomes evident. By what is said over time, certain patterns of consistency in political direction emerge. By how votes are cast, and for what reasons, nuances in thinking and strategy are revealed. By how much is said on how many different types of issues, the range of interest on policy matters is outlined. By discerning the tone of political dialogue, and the effectiveness of interaction, between a politician and his or her colleagues in committee or on the floor, you can make judgments about the degree to which the legislator is respected, liked, or despised—and how much you would want him or her on your side of a legislative battle. A lobbyist must ultimately conclude how effective a politician is in building the personal trust essential to commanding respect and winning votes, and the degree of confidence that can be placed in that politician on the matters of concern to you. Ultimately, each legislator presents a political personality and character, all of whose attrib-

---

1. These are the standard reference books, published every two years by National Journal Inc. and Congressional Quarterly Inc., respectively, with lengthy political and personal profiles of all members of Congress.

utes and deficiencies must be taken into account in approaching that legislator and in calculating how that legislator can best be used, or neutralized, to your advantage.

Your understanding of each politician's personality—ideology, character, world view, interests, and motivations—will dictate your strategic approach to him or her. Knowing what arguments will appeal to a politician will determine the particular shading of your argument. Lobbyists also must resist the temptation to stereotype politicians or to disregard subtleties in political thinking and relationships that can provide crucial opportunities for tactical advantage. Every issue is different and has the potential for the creation of new, and winning, coalitions. The conservative Democrat who regularly votes with the Republicans may also want, at certain moments, to cement a better relationship with his or her leadership. A panel chair, in devising strategy on a bill you support, may be amenable to limited concessions designed to win a swing vote. A legislator who is conservative on foreign policy and national security issues may be more liberal on civil rights and the environment. A liberal legislator who champions federal welfare programs may hold uncharacteristic free-market beliefs, shared by conservatives, on the deregulation of certain industries. Under certain circumstances, therefore, it is possible to unite members from the extreme left and the extreme right, providing fertile ground for the construction of a powerful alliance. But such opportunities can be exploited only if they are perceived and their potential grasped—an ability derived solely from knowing the players and how they think.

 ## Know the committees.

Committees are the most important venue in which legislators operate. As the most intimate legislative forum, they are a fulcrum of activity and they provide the most intense setting for the expression of personal political identity and power. As the first step in the enactment of laws, the decisions reached there usually determine the contours and dynamics of subsequent activity. If you lose in committee, it is harder to win on the floor; a victory in committee creates a precedent and momentum that place a heavier burden on those seeking to reverse at the next stage of the process. What happens in committee is almost always the single most important determinant of success or failure.

Accordingly, understanding the committees with jurisdiction over your issues is as important as knowing the players. Lobbyists must learn how the committees work: <u>politically, legislatively, parliamentarily</u>. Their processes and politics must be mastered no less than their members and staff. Ideally, one should become a student of the committees with which one is primarily engaged.

The political character of a committee is decisive. It flows from the chair and is modified by the members. Is the chair strong and authoritarian, or weak and passive? Confrontational or a consensus builder? A setter of the agenda or reactive? What is the role of the subcommittee chairs? Do they tend to be forceful and independent, or under the effective domination of the full committee chair? How strong is the staff and to whom do they have a sense of allegiance? Over the past several years congressional leadership, committee chairs, subcommittee chairs, and the ranking minority members of committees and subcommittees have had different levels of authority for hiring staff. It is essential that the lobbyist know who has the power to hire and fire staff. It also is important that the lobbyist be tuned in to the tone of the political debate. Is the committee usually split along partisan lines, with the majority always prevailing, or is the panel collegial and generally bipartisan?

Each committee is different, and House committees differ sharply from their Senate counterparts because of the substantially different parliamentary rules in the House and Senate and the distinctive styles of the two chambers. Lobbying tactics will be dictated by such differences. <u>In general, House committees are more partisan than Senate panels</u>. In the House, certain key committees—such as <u>Ways and Means, the tax-writing panel</u>, and the *Rules Committee,* <u>which controls the flow of legislation to the House floor</u>—have an <u>artificially high number of members of the majority party</u>. This is to assure, to the extent possible, adequate control of critical procedural and policy matters by the House majority leadership. The partisan breakdown of other committees is generally in proportion to the party ratio of majority to minority in the House as a whole.

When the House is under the firm control of one party it is difficult for a minority member to prevail in committee without significant support from the other party, which is not unusual on some committees. The Commerce (formerly Energy and Commerce) Committee, for example, usually attracts aggressive and independent members from both parties, who often form legislative majorities that cross party lines. The House Banking and National Security (formerly Armed Services) committees were engulfed throughout the 1980s in contentious relations between their chairs and

24

their members, limiting the binding nature of votes taken in committee and thereby providing greater opportunity for reversal on the House floor. The House Transportation and Infrastructure (formerly Public Works and Transportation) Committee, responsible for multibillion-dollar highway and construction projects so coveted by lawmakers for their districts, has had a history of incestuous bipartisanship, with the members generally protecting each other's pet projects.

While pressures to achieve a balanced budget, together with what some see as a tendency toward increased partisanship in the House, may reduce the incentives and the willingness for members to "reach across the aisle" for support, it is a safe assumption that this will be a short-lived phenomenon. The history of the House of Representatives reveals many swings of the political pendulum—between Democratic and Republican control, between more and less powerful leaders, and between heightened and diminished degrees of partisanship. While these swings may influence the way in which members conduct their business at any given time, they do not change the fundamental elements of committee politics: getting enough votes to report legislation to the floor, and addressing each member's need to respond to his or her constituency. Given these realities, bipartisan coalitions always will be a feature of the House committee process, though perhaps more ingrained in the culture of some committees than in others.

Senate Committees

The differences in style among Senate committees are similar but less intense, primarily because of the Senate's rules. Senate parliamentary practices enshrine the right of unlimited debate, or *filibuster*, by each senator—a right that can be revoked only by a special procedure known as *cloture*. Thus, each senator has the potential ability to frustrate, by resorting to unlimited debate, the orderly imposition of majority will. Consequently, there is a higher value in the Senate and its committees to achieving consensus through efforts to accommodate, when possible, each senator's particular concerns. Votes are rarely along strict party lines, except on the most highly charged and politicized issues, such as the budget, major presidential nominees, significant foreign policy issues, or campaign finance reform (in which the outcome may affect each party's financial, hence electoral, potency, with implications for deciding which party will control the Congress). In these instances, votes often become referendums on the policies of the president or a political party. The enlistment of any one senator from either party can, if effective enough, ensure that your issue will at least be heard. A lobbyist therefore has greater leverage on an issue in the Senate than can be expected, at the outset, in the House.

Appreciating how your issue might fare in a particular committee, and be mediated by the structure and politics of that committee, is only the beginning of the work involved. Understanding the committee's character is the key to unlocking the winning votes.

Essential to understanding the committees, and discerning which members can be your strongest allies on any given issue, is a dispassionate view of the process. Lobbying and single-interest politics are virtually synonymous. Lobbyists want to personify the very clients and causes they represent: Mr. Realtor, Ms. Public Broadcasting, Mr. Securities Industry. Recognition of your identity is important, but being discounted is harmful. If you are known or understood or perceived only on the basis of your issue, your effectiveness is diminished, if only because of the predictability with which you are greeted.

Such distortion impairs the lobbyist. Issues are indeed paramount. A lobbyist evaluates first and foremost where each legislator stands on those issues. The House of Representatives and the Senate can become, in their most elemental form, a tally sheet of votes for, against, or undecided, with a lobbyist's approach to each member guided by his or her position on that issue.

But viewing the world through such a lens causes an astigmatism— a shortsighted prescription for decreasing effectiveness, to the point where one is only heard, not listened to.

Public policy issues often have common themes, even though they cut across different interest groups in differing legislative contexts.[2] Lobbyists must understand what is happening to other industries, constituencies, and interests in the very committees they are tracking as well as in other, parallel arenas, in order to fully appreciate the dynamics that will control their personal issues. The same legislators are making choices in these other matters, and they will use those experiences in reaching judgments on your issues.

---

2. In the 1980s, for example, the Reagan administration strongly advocated less government intervention in the private sector and greater reliance on free-market forces as opposed to federal regulation. Many industries, such as broadcasting, trucking, and airlines, were deregulated. Government-owned assets were "privatized," or sold to the public. User fees for marine services and for the processing of licenses and applications at regulatory agencies were imposed on business to help defray costs to the government. These changes were enacted by numerous committees, involving hundreds of legislators, over several years.

If you observe how these other debates unfold, parallel strategies and opportunities may suggest themselves. A legislator's interest in one area can be harnessed to yours if framed through a similar appeal. But these openings, and your appreciation of how they can be exploited, exist only if you see the world neutrally and realistically.

This can best be gained by attending committee meetings and listening to floor debate when you have nothing at stake. The political process can then be observed dispassionately, its color viewed without the polarization of self-interest. Strategic options will suggest themselves. One learns to appreciate the peculiar strengths and weaknesses each legislator can bring to bear, the abilities of staff, the networks that the players have used (and that might be available in the future), and the pattern of argument and sentiment.

There is another virtue of being present in committee when you have no ax to grind: You are not asking for anything at that moment. You can share ideas, pick up information and gossip, and commiserate on events without any pressing or obvious motive. The lobbyist will be seen in a different light: as someone interested in more than what he or she is paid to follow, as a student of the process. And the realization may dawn on the legislator that such a person might be a resource on matters beyond the parochial—ultimately to their mutual benefit.

Know what the public policy rationale is on the issue.

Members of Congress thrive on issues. Issues drive legislation, hearings, press coverage, analysis, debate, editorial opinion, and government action. All of Congress is geared to the management of issues. Every conceivable facet of activity, public and private, is under some form of congressional jurisdiction; literally every issue in the universe, from surrogate motherhood to the exploration of space, can ultimately be translated into a matter under the control of one or more congressional committees. All issues addressed by Congress eventually evolve into debate on the legitimacy—the public policy justification—of government action or inaction.

All of Congress's being is devoted to the purpose of considering whether legislation is warranted. As a general rule Congress never justifies legislation on the basis that it may reward a private, special interest. The public benefit is the formal, overriding rationale, no matter who or what the proposal helps or hurts in the end.

Every legislative proposition must be rooted in a respectable and defensible public policy argument. Public officials cannot be expected, and must never be asked, to do otherwise. To do so would risk compromising the integrity of all involved. Congress simply does not award millions in grants or tax breaks or transition rules to private entities simply for the sake of doing so, or to appease greed. In every instance there is a public policy justification framing the action. And if it is a measure that cannot stand the light of day, a provision whose rationale is not credible, it will not be adopted or will be subsequently repealed, or the legislator will avoid being placed in such a position again. The reason for any request for official action, or introduction of a bill, or sponsorship of an amendment, must be cast in terms that are reasonably related to the underlying public policy debate on the issue. If a lobbyist cannot pass this "red face" test, the effort is doomed.

To the public, and even within Congress, long-standing fights between, for example, the broadcasting and cable industries, the banking and securities industries, or the local telephone companies and long-distance carriers have been viewed as all-or-nothing battles between warring private interests. But all arguments advanced by each side are tinged with the veneer of benefit to the public and consumers (for example, competition, diversity, access to services, or costs). Members of Congress do not justify their taking sides with the explanation that they favor the wealthy and powerful; rather they argue that the advocated policy will redound to the public interest.

Lobbyists need to follow the ebb and flow of public policy debates to best match their issues with the requisite public policy rationale. The nation moves through cycles of ideology, and legislative priorities of the moment reflect the changing themes. The programs of the Great Society and of the civil rights, environmental, consumer protection, and human rights movements of the 1960s and early 1970s gave way under the Reagan presidency to retrenchment on domestic spending, an expansion of military power, deregulation, and tax reform. The effective lobbying issues of the 1980s and the early 1990s were those that cost little or no money, assisted the military-industrial complex, called for no government regulation, could be accomplished by private business, or did not require tax incentives. As we have moved further into the 1990s "devolution"—the process of returning program authority (and budget responsibility) to the states—has further extended this policy trend. In any Congress, proposed initiatives that do not conform with the prevailing ideological regime bear a higher burden of proof in the legislative process.

Public policy justifications also must be artfully drawn to span, if possible, conflicting poles of political power. Legislative advocates must be sensitive to the priorities and cues of the major figures in Congress: the leadership and the committee chairs. Particularly in a divided government or a divided Congress, when party control between the executive and legislative branches is not uniform, as in the 1980s and mid-1990s, the party not in control of the White House will try to thwart administration initiatives, creating a treacherous operating environment. A lobbying message designed to be responsive to congressional leadership will fall on deaf ears in the White House. Choices must be made with the risk of alienating one powerful branch of government or the other. Success in legislation is, in the end, a function of the success in finding a consensus. When possible, the political edges of an issue should be smoothed out, their partisan character blunted, and their consistency with precedent emphasized. Any lobbying initiative must therefore be sensitive to the prevailing balance of political power and its ideological atmosphere, and be shaped to present a pragmatic opening to all sides.

The pragmatic opening that best transcends ideology is one based on constituent appeal. When something becomes important to voters in a legislator's district or state, it cannot be ignored; it will be addressed in some manner. The success of constituent appeals depends most often on the extent of countervailing political pressures and where they are located. A legislator often will support a compelling local need in defiance of strenuous White House or agency opposition, even if they are of the same party. But if one interest in a community is pitted against another—for example, the environmental movement against the coal industry—the interaction will often induce paralysis. The deadlock can be broken, however, by arguments designed to demonstrate that without that legislator's intervention the "greater good" of the state or district will be sacrificed, something tangible to the community will be lost, or a wrong will go unrectified.

The legitimacy of a lobbyist's argument, and its intellectual strength in the political process, is derived from the public policy rationale that undergirds a political or special interest. Without it, the proponent stands naked and utterly vulnerable to indifference and humiliation.

✄ Prepare materials. *Memos*

The power of persuasion lies in clarity and concision. Mastering the art of the one-page briefing memorandum is essential. Behind every issue is a morass of detail and nuance that must be reduced to a central theme leading to one unyielding conclusion: support for your initiative is the right choice.

On the Hill each member receives, from his or her legislative staff, a floor folder for the day's votes. The materials include a cover memorandum identifying all scheduled measures and capsule summaries of major amendments, and the support for or opposition to them. Staffs' understanding of these amendments is derived from an endless flow of paper: *"Dear Colleague" letters* from the sponsors, allies, opponents, and interest groups; letters from constituents; views from affected agencies; and others. Staff and members distill the traffic through their individual political prisms, looking for the signals—particularly of where other members and key interest groups stand on the issue—that will shape the final decision.

Lobbyists have to plug into this network to be effective. Hundreds of messages are competing for attention on any given issue on any given day. There is no hope for your message to be heard unless it can be used, which depends on its being understood with clarity and economy.

Lobbying materials must be concise, to the point, and persuasive on the merits. Lobbyists, and particularly those who have been off the Hill for an extended period, tend to forget this basic lesson. Corporations and interest groups thrive on paper—memorandums, concept pieces, analytical studies, and especially legal briefs filed with courts or regulatory agencies. Such papers are the subject of endless meetings with ever-larger groups of people whose views are important and needed. Often the result is the production of massive briefing books on public policy issues—tomes of information exploring in numbing detail a public policy question and its implications. Lobbyists all too often love to dump these volumes on Hill staff because it makes the lobbyist, who can report that the staff has been "briefed" and the information "delivered," feel good. But information unread is useless.

Staff has little time or inclination—and members less—to pore over dozens of pages of materials prepared by outsiders (except in the most unusual circumstances, such as when a member's initiative requires exacting study to prepare for hearings or markup, or when a legislator is trying to make his or her imprint in a particular area). Any briefing book read by a member will be compiled by the staff and drawn from many sources. The chances of inclusion of your message in such an exercise depend on the brevity and appeal of your lobbying materials.

One-page issue papers should be field-tested before delivery. Members and staff cannot be expected to understand the arcana of your issue in the abstract; they are generalists by nature and focus on the broadest range of concerns. The level of detailed knowledge by members and staff on matters outside their immediate focus is limited to that provided by the *Washington Post*, the *New York Times*, and the *Wall Street Journal*. Your arguments have to be geared to that generalist audience and framed in terms that can be readily comprehended. Field testing is simple: give your memorandum to a few reasonably intelligent persons who have no expertise on the issue. If they understand it, and agree with its conclusion, you have succeeded. If they do not, rewrite it and keep revising it until you get it right.

Lobbying materials also have to be prepared to fit into the context of legislative activity. If a deregulation bill is pending, the issue has to be posed in terms that are generally consistent, or minimally inconsistent, with the underlying bill. If a special exemption from a pending tax bill is being requested, precedents that have conferred similar treatment in the past should be cited. If your request conflicts with proposed legislation, then there is no alternative to an all-out frontal assault on its merits, with the most compelling arguments presented—reasons of policy, law, equity, and the public interest.

It is a myth that only lawyers are capable of providing the most effective lobbying materials, or that a lawyer is essential to drafting an amendment or bill. Lawyers hardly have a monopoly on the lobbying process, which is based on political and substantive expertise. In lobbying, their legal skills are secondary in importance to their persuasive and rhetorical abilities. Lobbyists have to craft arguments that win attention and support; there is nothing inherently "legal" in the exercise. If anything, lawyers tend to be verbose; on the Hill, the premium is on brevity and punch. Most congressional staff are not lawyers, and so lawyers bring with them no special rapport or entrée as professional colleagues (with the exception of work with the Judiciary committees, responsible for criminal, civil, and constitutional law, and with the Ways and Means and Finance committees, which requires expertise in the tax laws).

As with anyone else, lawyers make good lobbyists when they exhibit political skill. Expert knowledge in particular areas of law or legislation is helpful, but such knowledge also can be acquired and mastered by non-lawyers. If you as a lobbyist have an expert understanding of the body of law or statute being amended, a lawyer is not essential to drafting amendments or legislation. All staff and members have access to and rely overwhelmingly upon congressional *legislative counsel,* who draft all bills, amendments, and conference reports. Language submitted by lobbyists is invariably vetted by staff with legislative counsel, who almost always modify its construction. What lobbyists have to provide when requesting legislation are the finite specifications—a precise, detailed outline—of the bill or amendment. This gives the legislative counsel sufficient guidelines to translate into statutory language. It is a task nonlawyers are amply suited to fulfill.

But even the best one-page memorandum may be too much. A lobbyist has to be able to respond within minutes to the frantic early evening call from, for example, someone on the staff of a Finance Committee member, who says: "The senator wants to help you. The decision on your transition rule will be coming up tonight. I need a one-paragraph explanation and justification." All your arguments have to come down to five sentences. They have to be good.

Make the client part of the lobbying team.

Most lobbyists are experts on the people and processes that drive congressional decision making, but they are generalists when it comes to matters of taxation, product approval regulation, government contracting, labor law requirements, and the myriad of other concerns that define relationships between government and business. At best the individual lobbyist can become proficient in one or two of these substantive areas, but that leaves much more to be understood, folded into policy recommendations, and presented to lawmakers and their staffs. Because no one understands the client's business better than the client, the best source for this information usually resides within the client's own organization. In this sense the client should be understood not as a single entity but as a team of experts representing many disciplines. Collectively, their store of knowledge is among your most valuable lobbying resources.

Understanding this much is the easy part; getting the client to cooperate in a timely and useful manner can be more difficult. As is the case in medicine, convincing the "patient" to do what is in his or her best interest is not always a simple matter. For one thing, many businesspeople do not readily share proprietary information, even among their fellow employees. The more people who are privy to trade secrets, the greater the possibility of an unintended leak. Because many of the client's executives do not work with you on a regular basis they may view you as an outsider—one not to be trusted with sensitive product information.

Further, clients are slow to own up to their mistakes and professional insecurities; they do not want to tell you if they have attempted a regulatory shortcut or if they have committed a significant business blunder. Whatever the cause—normal protective behavior, lack of faith in you, or one group of executives hoping to keep their problems from another group within the company—the client's employees are frequently not eager to share information.

There is no fast-acting panacea for the cautious client syndrome. Even lobbyists who enjoy long-established relationships with the organizations they represent experience occasional communication lapses. Pushing too hard for too much too fast will normally exacerbate matters. In these instances your political skills must be focused inward. The client (in the collective sense) must be convinced that cooperation is in everyone's interest. Time and thoughtful discussion about what is at stake will usually bring the key executives around.

From the congressional perspective, especially at the committee and subcommittee levels, presentations by client-experts can be extraordinarily helpful. The lobbyist actually performs a service to lawmakers and staff members by making bona fide experts available to them. Whether the testimony comes from lawyers, technocrats, scientists, experts in corporate philanthropy, labor relations specialists, or any other well-trained and highly experienced professional, committee personnel usually welcome an opportunity to better understand the issues their legislation seeks to address.

As noted in this chapter, preparation is key. Your expert must understand the objectives that have been established for the meeting and the information you are interested in sharing with the committee, and be comfortable with additional issues that might arise in the course of conversation. Here there is a delicate balance to be achieved. The client should resist the normal impulse to "over lawyer" the expert presentation. The meeting is a policy discussion set in a political context; it is not a deposition. A certain amount of "rehearsal" is fine, but too much scripting can make the expert seem stilted and the presentation contrived. An opportunity to gain credibility can be lost. Worse, suspicion can be aroused.

Many firms and organizations have another important resource in addition to qualified experts—their senior executives. These people are not only knowledgeable about their business, but also usually influential within their industry and respected in the broader community. Some are national figures. These are important considerations for lawmakers who are constantly seeking to build coalitions in Congress and pluralities at home.

The general protocol is for chairs and presidents of companies to meet with representatives or senators, not with staff. (Though lobbyists who convince their CEOs to meet with staff can gain great favor for themselves and their clients. The humility is disarming and appreciated. It can be extremely effective.) Clearly this is not an everyday event. Rolling out the "heavy hitters" should be reserved for only the most important matters. Staff should be briefed on the reason for the meeting and the issues that will be raised. It is essential that you convey the message that the boss is coming to town because he deems the matter at hand to be critical and has great respect for the legislative process. The meeting must not be construed as an effort to go over the head of staff or to unduly pressure their boss. Such impressions would doom the visit to failure. Personal advocacy by a CEO with a world view will always be well received on the Hill and in the executive branch.

Go to the "outside" when required.

Occasionally it is necessary to recommend that the client supplement your efforts by retaining additional lobbying support.

Additional support may be warranted when the matter in question goes beyond the expertise of anyone the client has on staff or currently retains. What determines the need for additional lobbying counsel is not growth or contraction in federal activity, it is the specific legislative or regulatory area in which a threat or an opportunity emerges. If the area is outside of the client's and your scope of expertise, additional lobbying support should be considered.

Increased sophistication in government-business relationships has led to a more highly specialized lobbying community. There are now firms that focus on taxation, labor law, transportation, environmental protection, health care, military procurement, foreign trade, communications—the list is virtually endless. Each of these organizations tracks a policy domain within Congress and, usually, within the executive branch as well. They can counsel your client on the prevailing political landscape that exists within their particular domain. What directions do leadership and relevant committee chairs wish to pursue? In the context of current trends, what is a reasonable legislative request? At what point and in what way is a piece of legislation best amended to accomplish the client's objectives? Is report language sufficient? The resourceful specialist will know the answers to these questions and will be able to design and execute a lobbying campaign tailored to your client's needs.

Strong substantive information is often accompanied by good (if not close) working relationships with congressional committee staffs. It is not unusual for highly specialized lobbyists to be part of the "revolving door" syndrome—people who move back and forth between the private sector and government service. While some people may be critical of this process, it does afford a body of highly knowledgeable professionals who are sensitive to both public and private sector needs. The common bond, the one that frequently sustains these relationships, is a legitimate substantive interest in the relevant policy domain. Highly qualified professionals working outside of government can be as helpful to committee counsels as are their colleagues working in the public sector. Participation by these professionals is frequently beneficial to both your client and to those charged with making final policy decisions.

Anticipate the opposition.

An essential lobbying approach is to provide, concurrently with a request to a member or staff, a detailed description of the objections to your argument, the identification of those individuals or groups who will be making them, and an explanation of why they are opposed to what you are seeking. A legislator hates to be blindsided, to be moving your agenda only to suddenly discover heated opposition from another constituency or interest group that is also politically important to that member. Withholding such key information is a disfavor to the member and does the lobbyist ill. Such omissions cause a lobbyist's credibility and trustworthiness to be called into question, raising doubts about one's future relationship with that legislator.

Anticipating objections works to your advantage. It actually provides a tactical opportunity: you have the chance, first, to place a member on notice as to where trouble lies, and why; and second, you can present your counterarguments, shaping a member's response well before it is triggered by the opposition. In other words, a lobbyist should provide a measure of insurance against opposition attacks that will be directed not only at you but also, more importantly, at the legislator you have asked to publicly commit on your behalf.

Such "truth in labeling" should sweep the political horizon. A legislator needs to know—from you—whether the subcommittee or committee chair is for or against your initiative; the views of other committee members, Republican and Democrat; whether there are key individuals who are breaking with the majority of their party; and, on extremely important matters, whether members of the leadership, of either party, have an identifiable interest in the issue. All this information is crucial for a legislator to make an informed judgment—to exercise informed consent—on your request. A lobbyist must never rob a legislator of that opportunity.

More obvious is the need to anticipate your supporters and allies. Inevitably, votes are choices, and choices are made weighing political gain and harm no less than the merits and drawbacks of any issue. If anticipated opposition is outweighed by a larger coalition of allies, the choice is easier. The nature of particular allies or opponents also is crucial, because their strength depends on the extent to which they can provide real and tangible political returns or inflict real and tangible political costs. Farmer opposition has very little bearing on a member from an urban district. Consumer or public-interest support is generally irrelevant in a conservative district. Labor unions, corporations, and civic groups with roots in the district or state matter substantially. Members also care to expand their reach and influence: a promise of support from a powerful constituency that has previously been uninvolved in a member's legislative activities presents enormous opportunities to build bridges and elicit active member interest.

Lobbying and legislation are games of tactics and strategy. The common denominator to all successful strategies is anticipation—of the legislators you can approach, of the motivations that can be uncovered, of the inherent rewards to be gained by the legislator for supporting your initiative, of those who will be opposed, of the arguments they will use. In the end you want your political assets deployed in such a way that the momentum behind your effort is more powerful than the stumbling blocks in its path. Only by revealing those obstacles, sharing them in advance with the legislators whose support you need, and thereby disarming the obstacles' potency, can your lobbying strategy prevail.

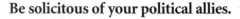

Be solicitous of your political allies.

Lobbying activities should be calibrated to provide maximum political return for a minimum expenditure of a legislator's political capital. Central to this calculation is the question of what is reasonable, and what is reasonable depends on the timing of events.

Why ask for a vote when the roll call is many days or weeks away, with intervening events potentially obviating its occurrence? Why ask for a letter to a regulatory agency before you have ascertained that a real problem exists that the agency is unable or unwilling to resolve? Why endeavor to place an issue at the top of a legislator's agenda when there is no way that issue can be considered in the foreseeable future?

Events control the timing and pace of decision making on the Hill, such as the scheduling of a bill for markup in committee, the announcement of a hearing, or the placement of a bill on the *calendar*. The moment to begin lobbying contacts is when such movement is apparent, because the issue is suddenly on the legislator's radar screen (and certainly the staff's) and not only on yours. At that moment the terms of engagement are universal, and the reasonableness of requested actions changes accordingly.

There are certain obvious guidelines. It is easier to ask a member to cosponsor a bill than to initiate one; to sign a "Dear Colleague" letter than to write one; to vote for an amendment than to offer it. At many other times lobbyists will find themselves trying to drive events. This underscores the importance of carefully selecting your leader (or "horse"), the person who will be the focal point of all activity. The general rule is that a committee or subcommittee chairman is most desirable (but note that many chairs, being the arbiters of political currents sweeping their panels, choose to place themselves above the fray, forcing a lobbyist to construct a majority on the committee that the chair can then endorse or acquiesce to). An alternative is to seek a member who is well placed and respected on the committee. The ideal champion is a member known for leadership on a given policy issue, or who has a history of building ties across party lines, or who, because of his or her stature, instantly commands respect or attention, conferring an aura of legitimacy on the issue chosen for sponsorship.

Conversely, some members are known for being ineffective or politically unhelpful because they have not mastered the issues, have alienated their colleagues, are political loners and hence unable to form effective coalitions, or are consistently cut out of decision making by the leadership in committee or caucus. (Sometimes you have no choice when your issue has direct roots in such a member's district or state, or when that member has direct committee jurisdiction over that issue.) But even these less desirable members can be helpful at crucial times. If senators are adding dozens of amendments to a bill on the floor, almost any senator can succeed in attaching another discrete provision if the amendment would cost little money, set no major legislative or regulatory precedents, and have no major adverse effect on another interest. In the House, a less effective member can be easily utilized by including him or her in a coalition of other members. A lobbyist never wants to offend a member's sensibilities—particularly when the member wants to be involved in the issue you are lobbying.

Legislators and staff never wish to be taken for granted. No lobbyist can afford to ignore a legislator whose involvement is material to the outcome. Even if such a member is not your "horse" on a given issue, he or she expects to be informed about what is occurring if the person has been involved in the past or if the issue affects a constituent interest.

More importantly, every issue is different, and the political alignments on each separate issue are never the same. It cannot be assumed that a member's position last year will remain the same this year: circumstances change. These changes have to be perceived and acted upon by continuous courting of the legislator. Members like to be asked; no lobbyist gets what he wants without asking. It is no different for staff, some of whose egos, not tempered personally by the humbling rigors of reelection, exceed those of their bosses. If they cannot be informed of events before they are a matter of public record, they expect to be briefed as soon as they are public. To assume that staff, much less a member, can keep pace with your issues without your direct and personal involvement is to take a double risk: on your issue and on your relationship.

Your ability to go to a congressional office and ask its involvement on your behalf is predicated on the relationship you have previously established or the legitimacy of your standing with that legislator (such as if you represent a constituent interest). The reasonableness of your request will be judged on those terms.

Understand the process: the rules of procedure and the rule of compromise.

The rules of parliamentary procedure dictate strategy. Understanding the rules defines the execution of the task at hand. Control over the rules is, more often than not, control over the outcome. Lobbying is the discernment and exploitation of political opportunity. Opportunity exists only when it is permitted under the rules of procedure. Mastering them takes literally years of study involving observation of the House and Senate in operation in committee and on the floor.

A lobbyist armed with an understanding of tactical parliamentary opportunity, as well as the substance of the public policy issue, is in a stronger position of authority than a lobbyist who pursues only the issue. In the overwhelming drone of legislative activity, the procedures are straightforward. In the House, for example, most bills move through hearings, subcommittee and committee markup, floor scheduling, debate and amendments on the floor, and a vote on final passage. In the Senate, following committee approval, bill scheduling is cleared by the majority leader in consultation with the minority, a *time agreement* is established (often listing the amendments to be offered and by whom), with debate and voting to final passage.

It is in the fine points of conception of procedural strategy that care must be given. A lobbyist must understand the rules sufficiently to ensure that any necessary course of action is not foreclosed for reasons within the lobbyist's control. In the House, for example, whether to move a bill under *suspension of the rules*, whether the ability to offer particular amendments is protected under the rule for the bill's consideration, or whether a desired amendment is *germane* are all crucial. In the Senate, it is critical for members to exercise, in a timely fashion, their equal rights to protect their legislative prerogatives.

As important as the rules is an appreciation of the style and mores of the committees, how they work, and what their decisions mean for the fate of your issue in subsequent stages of the process. Each committee has its own idiosyncrasies and patterns of legislative deliberation. Lobbying initiatives, to be successful, must be molded to the prevailing order. It is essential to understand, for example, that in the House and Senate Appropriations committees, subcommittee action is tantamount to final action. If a desired amendment is added in subcommittee, it is unlikely to be reversed in the full committee.

In many Senate committees, markups proceed only at the full committee level (so a potentially crucial step in the process has been removed if, for example, the political alignment on the full committee differs markedly from that of the relevant subcommittee). Before Republicans gained control of the House in 1995 it was not uncommon for bills written in subcommittees of the Energy and Commerce Committee (now the Commerce Committee) to be rewritten by the full panel. Similarly, major military and foreign policy authorization bills reported by the House National Security and International Relations committees have a history of being subject to wholesale change on the floor. During the 104th Congress Speaker Newt Gingrich and Majority Leader Dick Armey were unwilling to leave adherence to the Contract with America exclusively in the hands of Republican committee chairs. They maintained strict control over legislation produced by the panels in compliance with the Contract's most important provisions. When the Judiciary Committee reported (albeit without recommendation) a term-limits bill that the leadership found unacceptable, leaders used their control over the Rules Committee to have the bill scrapped and a "clean" measure produced in its place.

Revenue bills reported from Ways and Means are never subject to uncontrolled amendment by the full House; only those amendments cleared by the Rules Committee are made in order, and rarely are any but the most major issues put to a separate vote on the floor. Tax bills approved by the Senate Finance Committee, however, are always a magnet for dozens of amendments, as the Senate's rules permit virtually unlimited debate and amendment by members. Thus, on tax bills, a missed opportunity in the House can be recouped in the Senate.

Congress is an animate institution. It is in a constant state of flux. The rules of each chamber, and the traditions and practices of the committees, are forever evolving. What is a collegial committee today may become the uncontested domain of an authoritarian chair tomorrow. For the astute lobbyist, understanding congressional mores and work cultures provides an opportunity to be exploited. But opportunities, in and of themselves, hardly ensure victory. On Capitol Hill discretion is always the better part of valor. On some issues there can be no compromise, and contentious votes must be fought to their conclusion. But on most issues there is room to maneuver so that all sides win, or win enough, or at least emerge without a complete loss. Lobbyists have to be adaptable and creative in recognizing when compromise is necessary, and how to secure it. When you cannot carry the day on the strength of your arguments alone, and when you can no longer use the rules to delay or prevent the inevitable, it is time to deal.

For example, rather than maneuver to derail or overturn outright an unfavorable agency decision (which can be extremely difficult in the face of agency pride, administration support, and the crosscurrents between the White House and Congress), it may be preferable to obtain favorable *report language* or a commitment to hearings. A bipartisan letter to an agency head may be easier to elicit than a statutory directive. Instead of pressing for full funding of a program—at the risk of losing all funding— seeking a reduced appropriation with a presumption of continuity may be a safer alternative. The scope of an unwanted amendment, if it cannot be defeated outright, can be narrowed, transformed into a study, or given a very late effective date.

But sometimes you will be unable to cut a deal and you will lose, despite your best efforts. This will occur most frequently as legislative juggernauts emerge. In the development of reform legislation in the wake of massive industry scandal, for example, it is extremely difficult to secure favorable treatment for specific businesses or classes of interest from the new rules contained in the bill. The pressures for a "clean" bill with strong provisions designed to prevent any recurrence of abuse will often preclude adoption of language to cover extenuating circumstances, no matter how justified the request. In such cases you are left to turn to the courts or to come back next year as the new law's implementation is reviewed.

The critical judgment that must be made is to what extent pressing an issue will provoke opposition—how powerful it will be and from what source. Members of Congress seek, in almost biological compulsion, political security and safe harbor. They prefer not being placed on the spot, required to make difficult choices. They do not appreciate people, or interests, whose presence provokes the taking of sides. Words of support, therefore, are much easier to come by than votes; expressions of concern are much more forthcoming than hard legislation.

A very wise and experienced cabinet secretary once remarked, "Issues are never settled in this town." [3] In part this is due to the natural desire to compromise and to shade the difference, never wholly satisfying one side or the other, and guaranteeing that both sides will return for more. Equally important is the strength and stubbornness of competing interests and personalities themselves: they do not give up because their issues and causes are their raison d'être. But there comes a point where, for the sake of preserving one's ability to operate effectively in the political process—in other words, preserving goodwill—reasonable accommodation is required. Those unwilling to yield lose the flexibility necessary to protect their place in the future dialogue. At times, when it comes to a matter of survival, there are no options: the issue must be fought as aggressively as possible, no matter what the consequences. But this is the exception, necessary under only the most extraordinary circumstances.

---

3. Secretary of State George P. Shultz in testimony to the House Foreign Affairs Committee concerning the Iran-contra affair, December 8, 1986.

Enlist the support of your allies.

The exacting measure of success in congressional lobbying is the ability to create, join, or manage coalitions united behind a public policy proposal. Legislation affecting even a relatively discrete sector of the economy or polity—aid to Africa, support for student loans, regulation of the medical devices industry—has a collateral impact on dozens of individuals, organizations, trade associations, corporations, and their legislators.

Rarely, if ever, is only one entity in the pivotal position of solely affecting a political outcome. American society is too diverse and complex, and interest group presence and activity so centralized in Washington, to permit any item to go unnoticed. Increasingly, the array of diverse groups around a bill or amendment or policy debate will influence the course of events. By definition, a coalition is larger than any one interest. In coalition politics on the Hill, breadth is the functional equivalent of depth of support and motivation. As with other dimensions of lobbying it is critical to anticipate who might be affected by legislation and why, and how that impact can be harnessed to one's advantage—or neutralized if necessary. The lobbyist has to be able to identify and reach out to those who have a stake in an issue, to frame the issue in terms that can make a potential ally understand that your fight is also their fight, and to be able to motivate them to take effective and concerted action in coordination with your objectives and strategy.

The creation of large coalitions provides the comfort level necessary to make it easier for politicians to endorse the goal you have established. Increasingly, hard choices between competing groups are not made by Congress—owing to a combination of the dictum that it is much easier to stop something than to pass something in Congress, and the powerful aversion of legislators to making an irrevocable choice between insistent and conflicting interests. More often there is quiet but firm prodding from the leadership of a subcommittee or committee to the affected groups to get together, work out a compromise, and bring it forward to be ratified by the lawmakers. This, of course, creates the largest possible coalition for a legislative initiative, and a colossal tide of goodwill sweeps it toward the White House.

From time to time new issues emerge that require the creation of new coalitions that can capitalize on an initiative or development and confer immense political benefits on political leaders for supporting it (while meeting the self-interest of the coalition members). There was no organized constituency for tax reform or the U. S.-Canada Free Trade Agreement, for example.[4] In both instances corporate leaders and public-interest advocates, who understood the benefits of these proposals to themselves and to the nation as a whole, were able to capture the imagination of their associates and, in coordination with congressional leaders and the White House, form broad-based groups of hundreds of businesses and organizations that endorsed the legislative program.

Companies and interests targeted in the states of influential members of the Finance and Ways and Means committees (which had primary responsibility for both these issues) formed the base. These coalitions were then expanded to politically critical geographic regions throughout the country. The tactical strategy, successfully implemented, was to overwhelm disparate, isolated sources of opposition with a countervailing network of supporters. Always, the coalition delivered one message on the Hill: "This is good for us, it is good for America, and the common good must not be frustrated by the objections of a relative few." (Indeed, this is the message of every legislative coalition; only the players change.)

Grassroots mobilization is the difference between success and failure. Coalition letterheads must signify more than the names of supporting organizations. Their support must be tangible: the voices (and votes) of the individuals and industries and unions and companies must be heard from back home for their formal endorsement to carry the requisite credibility. It is the letters, telegrams, phone calls, and requests for meetings on the issue from voters in the state or district that will be decisive with Congress. If those voices are not heard, the letterhead rings hollow; a formal endorsement must be backed by real people who express real concerns if a legislator's commitment is to be sealed.

The mechanics of coalition building are its lifeblood. There are no secrets to it: lists, phone books, calls, solicitation letters, educational materials, a tracking system, a steering committee, funds, a communications network and alert system, and more lists and phone calls. The objective is to demonstrate an organic political presence on the issue from where it matters most: the constituents. Ambiguity or silence—the absence of any echo to the message delivered by lobbyists in Washington—presents an

---

4. In 1986 Congress enacted a sweeping overhaul of the tax code, eliminating numerous tax brackets and reducing overall tax rates in exchange for the elimination of dozens of exemptions, deductions, and credits. The U. S.-Canada Free Trade Agreement, enacted in 1988, implemented an orderly reduction in trade barriers between the two countries.

opportunity for a legislator to discount the need to support the initiative. The result can be a vote lost to the opposition.

Become cross-partisan eyes and ears.

Congressional offices operate with blinders. On day-to-day legislative strategy, Democratic and Republican staff generally have only limited or perfunctory contact with each other. Individual legislators and staff, from their separate offices, tend to concentrate primarily on their immediate terrain: their committees and particularly their party's colleagues on that committee. One committee is often ignorant of early activity, on the same issue, in another committee. A strategy designed by a member to get an amendment or bill through the House is often executed without regard to its fate in the Senate—and vice versa. There is so much to do in each one of the 535 separate worlds on Capitol Hill that institutional harmony is hard to achieve, often for lack of simple information.

A lobbyist, on the other hand, is in the unique position of seeing the process unfold from a distance and can take effective advantage of that knowledge. By working contacts regularly on both sides, a lobbyist has a more complete overview of the political landscape and can sense, even more quickly than a member on one side or the other, when and how an alliance—beneficial to legislator and advocate—can be forged.

A lobbyist is dead without information: a network of contacts and sources who are willing to keep the lobbyist informed of important developments. Careful attention must be paid to reporting about events elsewhere on the Hill, from the national press to specialized newsletters to the *Congressional Record*. A lobbyist has to know, instantly, who on the Hill is involved in an issue, and why, and be able to assess immediately the significance of such activity and the next events that will unfold. It is not enough solely to track the members and staff of key committees of jurisdiction over an issue (although that is always the first priority), because any legislator, from either party, at any time, can trigger the attention of those committees or a regulatory agency to a matter of the highest concern to your client.

A lobbyist's special vantage as observer over the entire field of play can be employed for both offensive and defensive purposes. Your contacts and assessments of committees and subcommittees will reveal friends and enemies, on both sides of the aisle, in both chambers.

A lobbyist can become, in effect, a cross-partisan set of eyes and ears, a messenger of timely political intelligence, a cultivator of the critical mass that suddenly makes an objective achievable. Your supporters want to know where other supporters might exist, who is opposed or on the fence, what other committees might become involved, and the reception that will be accorded an amendment or bill in the other body. Such intelligence encourages synergies that would not otherwise exist, prevents the unwelcome surprises that can make or break an important political relationship, and provides the needed measure of encouragement (or prudent forbearance from involvement) essential for an informed judgment in your best interests. Political truth is a prerequisite to political progress. A lobbyist does no favor to herself or her client by failing to comprehend the accurate state of play on a legislative matter. Your objective is to become an effective adjunct to your champions, and that means appreciating, with them, the opportunities and the obstacles. This can be achieved only if a lobbyist can face with acuity and dispassion the realities your champions will surely encounter.

Observe basic courtesies.

The primary occupational hazard of a lobbyist is to avoid becoming a pest. The temptation to be obnoxious is enormous: the insistent craving for information from clients and the desire to report back that you have just spoken to or had breakfast with or enjoyed an outing (or better yet, a trip to New York or the district) with a very important representative or senator or staff person. Your job is to be there, on the Hill, with your fingers on the pulse of the committee or the floor, to get the story first and get it accurately, and to have already set in motion a strategy that will protect your interests.

But any lobbyist is only one of thousands, and your issue at the moment is only one of dozens that legislators and staff are tracking on any given day. To be sure, it is your job to make certain that something of importance to you is automatically important to those lawmakers in whose hands your fate rests. You have to be able to put your concerns on their agenda. But too often lobbyists are blind to their own egos and shortcomings, and they overrun a healthy skepticism toward what is possible and what is not possible at any particular moment.

The worst lobbyists are those whose demands on time, particularly staff time, are so enormous that the staff members feel unable to think independently and perceive that the lobbyist is trying to massage their brains to manipulate judgment and decisions, to parse every step, every conversation, with the imprint of the lobbyist's influence.

What is important, therefore, is to place your issue in the proper perspective: yes, there is no question it is the most urgent problem in the Western world to your client, but it is probably not the same to most members of Congress.

Timing is everything in politics and, through careful planning and anticipation, the most opportune moments for an effective approach can be selected. Crises do strike, of course (such as a hostile takeover, a sudden amendment in subcommittee, an imminent decision by a regulatory agency), and you have to go to the Hill and see what support can be mustered even under the most adverse circumstances. Members will respond if the issue is important to them, because of its effect on their constituents or on principles and values they have come to care deeply about. And they will respond if you are important to them, because of past battles you have been through together or longstanding political support and friendship. But their receptiveness to your approach depends on whether you are a nuisance, demanding attention without regard to the relative importance of each separate matter, or whether, from your temperament and sensitivity to their limits and abilities, you ask for something only when it is really needed. The overriding value is basic courtesy.

A lobbyist must never wear out his or her welcome. Frequent visits on an issue should be unnecessary, unless the matter is extremely urgent and extraordinarily complex. Members and staff do not have time for the nuances and contortions of the in-house strategy sessions lobbyists always hold before going to the Hill. Those sessions should refine the issues and the tasks to be accomplished to their most basic components, so that what must be done can be easily understood and simply executed. The best meetings on the Hill are the shortest, with your message communicated and digested, with the participants understanding what will be done and by whom, and with provision for accurate reporting on those assignments. Members and staff especially appreciate efficiency and effectiveness: the greatest return for the least expenditure of effort and energy. Lobbyists should gear their visits to these objectives.

All requests from lawmakers and staff must be answered promptly. They are asking for information because they need it to act on your behalf. If you are unresponsive they will obtain it from someone else, and you will have lost the opportunity to provide the needed material with your perspective firmly etched on it. If you cannot respond, say so, and direct the inquirers to a proper source. Candor and honesty are always appreciated and will be rewarded in your future dealings.

Simple kindnesses also are essential. The pace of activity is so great, and the numbers of people involved in even the most simple legislative exercises so enormous (and increasingly unmanageable), that basic courtesies are often forgotten. Thank-you notes should be sent after every meeting. A special word to the personal secretary who got you in to see the representative or senator will help do the same the next time you need it. A steady but selective flow of information to staff who regularly follow your issues—articles, press releases, summaries of regulatory filings—accompanied by a brief personal note, will keep key players informed of developments in the least burdensome way.

Lobbyists should always be attuned to the other, myriad concerns that occupy a legislator's work. Lobbyists are valued most when they do not want anything but can provide something. You will inevitably come to care more about the activities of a selected group of legislators, usually those on the committees responsible for your issues. It is always appreciated if you see or hear something that will be of interest to them (and not necessarily of direct importance to you) and pass it along, such as an article, a study, or gossip. If you know that a lawmaker is engaged in a major hearing or bill on the floor and you have suggestions that might be helpful, let the member and the staff know. Send a short note wishing them luck in an upcoming fight, or commending them for introducing an important bill or getting an amendment adopted in conference. It is important to communicate that you care about them and want them to succeed.

Finally, smiles are not enough in this business. Lobbyists prove themselves, for better or worse, in legislative battle. It is only then that your true intentions and abilities are tested and demonstrated. When a subcommittee or committee goes through a contentious markup, or when there is a closely drawn fight on the floor, relationships and bonds are established and broken. The accuracy of your information and its ability to withstand scrutiny and assault are tested in the political marketplace. Whether you have done your work in rounding up the votes, anticipating the objections, minimizing or deflecting the opposition, winning converts, and showing how you can prevail at each step in the process are all displayed—publicly—and evaluated. It is not until a lobbyist has been bloodied in the legislative arena that the firm handshakes, the eye contact, the assuring words, and the knowing glances really become anything more than superficial gestures. It is the ultimate test of confidence in you and your abilities, and it has to be passed every time.

Chapter 4

ON POLITICAL CONTRIBUTIONS
AND FUND-RAISING

The Giving ...

There are two generally held views of Congress, its politics, and the electoral process: straight or cynical, idealistic or jaded. There is much to be said for the propositions that the House of Representatives is the most democratic institution in the world, its 435 members a political cross section of the nation as a whole, its mood a function of the country's pulse, and that no other parliamentary body can rival the Senate, which, in its greatest moments of deliberation on overriding national issues, becomes the republic's deliberative guardian and national conscience.

If Congress cannot come to grips with urgent national problems that seem to defy rational consensus and action, such as the chronic federal budget deficit or the country's dependence on foreign sources of energy, or the needs of the homeless and indigent, perhaps it is because we, as a people, are unwilling to make the hard choices that are required. Politics is the art of the possible. Alternatively, if Congress is viewed as little more than a forum for starved egos who only crave press attention, who slavishly follow the dictates of selfish special interests, and who cannot resist playing politics with anything, then expectations about what Congress can and will achieve can only be low, and one's judgments about the political process lower still. Your view of Capitol Hill will shape your thinking and policy regarding political campaign contributions.

Many lobbyists are uncomfortable with money and politics, just as they may be uncomfortable with the political process itself. Many politicians are similarly troubled with a system that virtually requires that they raise considerable amounts of campaign money from individuals and organizations with a vested stake in legislative outcomes. Too much time and effort has to be spent in raising this money, at the expense of attention to legislation and civic responsibilities. Election campaigns are too expensive. In 1994 expenditures for the average House race approached $900,000; for a Senate campaign, nearly $9 million.[1] These figures escalate every election cycle. As with the nuclear arms race during the Cold War, security has become a function of deterrence. Politicians can never have enough security, and so they raise campaign war chests that in analogy rival the state of nuclear overkill—treasuries containing hundreds of thousands of dollars, wholly unrelated to any real political threat, amassed to ward off any credible political attack.

The system is larger than any one participant in it. Politicians and lobbyists have found it easier to go along with it, and perpetuate it, than to change it. But pressure is building. Members of Congress are joining with journalists, academics, and a growing number of watchdog organizations in decrying the perception, if not the reality, of "the best Congress money can buy." Even major givers—those who allegedly benefit from the ability to raise and contribute large sums—are becoming weary of a system that seems to be insatiable. The consensus for reform is growing: that is not a question. What is a question is how fast and to what extent new rules will be enacted.

The only reform that would entirely eliminate private giving to political campaigns is full public funding. While the proposal has its advocates, it is a safe assumption that because of negative public opinion it will not become reality. Other proposals—limiting (even prohibiting) *political action committee* (PAC) contributions, capping campaign expenditures, providing free mail and television time, restricting the use of "soft" money—might reduce but would not eliminate the role of private contributions. And as long as this role exists, money raised by or coming directly from lobbyists will remain an integral part of political fund-raising.

As with lobbying itself, money in politics should be approached as a straightforward exercise. Political contributions are simply another, complementary aspect of your relations with Congress. They are a tangible means of expressing your point of view.

It is essential for those with business before Congress to support those legislators who are their allies. There is nothing wrong with it; there

---

1. These data include expenditures for candidates of both major parties in general-election campaigns.

is everything right with it. If a legislator is actively engaged on your side of an issue, that legislator deserves your support. The converse is that lawmakers are making decisions that affect the bottom line for your clients or causes or interests. Your effectiveness depends on your bottom line being taken into account by the lawmakers.

There are two obvious sources of political contributions to which legislators regularly turn: constituents (funds that can be raised locally from individuals, business, labor, and community groups) and interests affected by the lawmaker's legislative responsibilities and committee jurisdiction. To the extent that the law permits, your giving, and degree of giving, should be based primarily on those considerations.

The real meaning of political contributions is as ambiguous as any of the myriad factors that go into all political decisions. They are significant, but not controlling. Political contributions can promote your political profile with a legislator. Tangible support is noted. A contribution effectively states, "I am your ally. I want you to be reelected. We appreciate your interest in our concerns." Political contributions can promote access to legislators. Members and their political aides target and work potential contributors. Those who respond become, quite simply, friends of the campaign. And friends are listened to when they want to bring an issue to that politician's attention.

There are two routes of access to legislators for a lobbyist: contributions and expertise. Regular contributors attend dozens of fund-raisers a year and become part of the "circuit" of lobbyists around a cadre of lawmakers and their committees. Members attend each other's events. By being seen as a consistent participant, such contributors become a part of the informal interplay that is woven around day-to-day legislative activity. Contacts are made, relationships formed, and networks established. Expertise is the other avenue of access. Those known for their substantive work in any given field, and who have become respected for their insight and analysis, are solicited for testimony, issues papers, and briefings. Those who can volunteer substantive assistance—legislative proposals, speeches, floor statements, drafts of op-ed articles—are cultivated. Lobbyists whose abilities can provide both contributions and issues expertise are especially effective.

Political contributions cannot buy a vote, nor can they guarantee the outcome of legislation. Bribery is the most serious crime that can afflict the legislative process. A lobbyist must never discuss a financial contribution in the context of legislation. Telephone conversations and meetings that could reach from a bill to outside fund-raising efforts must be parsed into separate discussions, to keep these matters fully divorced. Such scrupulous care is essential for the protection of all involved and the integrity of the legislative process.

What exists between a legislator and a lobbyist is a coincidence of interests to varying degree. Of course, a lawmaker wants to support a contributor when possible, but such support also has to be consistent with his or her values and beliefs and the interests of the district or state. Often a contributor represents those interests, and the choice is easier. At other times, however, legislators do appear to be intimidated by well-financed special interests, such as the gun lobby. This is not so much because lawmakers seek their financial support, but because they wish to avoid contributions to their electoral opponents and the wrath of a motivated, grassroots, single-issue constituency.

Legislators most cherish their independence and the perception that they are independent. The ability of a lawmaker to exercise independence from outside interests is the difference between influence and control. Even the most hard-core congressional supporter of a given industry will vote against that industry's preferences if it becomes engulfed in scandal or corruption, no matter how much political or financial support has been bestowed on that legislator.

Seeking a vote, arguing for a certain position, and turning up the pressure from constituents and other supporters of the legislator are all legitimate. Demanding a vote as a price for continued or promised financial support is never legitimate and is a corruption of the process. If you view political contributions narrowly—as payments for specific results—your expectations will be self-defeating. If you view political contributions broadly—as investments in long-term political relationships—your expectations can be rewarded. Political contributions ensure a role in the dialogue—today and tomorrow, for the pending issue and for the next one—but they do not resolve the merits of the debate.

There is no legislator, however, who will not pay attention or respond positively to any constituent who faces a significant problem on which the member can be of assistance, regardless of whether there is a history of political contributions. A lawmaker may well have a hope, if not an expectation, for political financial support at a subsequent time, and the absence of such support may mean a cooler relationship in the future. But that legislator simply cannot and will not ignore a constituent or local interest confronting a bona fide governmental issue. You will be heard. A legislator can certainly calculate that support from you or your group is not essential, or that it conflicts with policy beliefs, and that therefore assistance on your behalf will not be forthcoming. A lobbyist then has to weigh whether the legislator, on balance, is worthy of any future support, through money, votes, or attempts to influence public opinion and the electorate. But that is fair political interplay.

Lobbyists also have to resolve another question: How much to give and to whom? The demands are endless; each day's mail brings several invitations to political fund-raisers, not only from lawmakers but also from ancillary organizations, such as the House and Senate party campaign committees. And always the costs go up. In the 1980s the expected donation for a standard House fund-raising event escalated from $250 to $350 to $500 and more; the minimum contribution to a Senate incumbent is effectively $1,000. A $50,000 PAC fund really does not go very far. No one has unlimited sources of money for all the contributions one should make or wants to make.

The guidelines are basic. First, support your strongest allies—those who directly represent you and those on the committees that decide your issues. Second, target the members on those committees who are most critical by placement (chairs and ranking members) and skill (those whose voice and efforts could, by virtue of their work and leadership abilities, be most helpful in important fights). Third, become involved with those political fund-raising events that bring contributors into regular contact with as many House and Senate members as possible.

... And the Getting

Giving money is only a piece of what lobbyists can do to aid the campaign fortunes of lawmakers they wish to support; in fact, it may be only a small portion of what they can do. When one considers that the average cost for a winning House campaign was well over $500,000 in 1994, and for Senate races it was in excess of $4 million, the limited amount of funding an individual or a PAC can give to a general election—$1,000 and $5,000, respectively—cannot be expected to go very far.[2] This is not to mention that relatively few individuals or PACs ever "max out" on a candidate.

---

2. Many legislative proposals for campaign funding reform would reduce the permissible PAC contribution level. The limits recommended in these proposals commonly range between $1,000 and $2,500. Other legislation would cap the overall amount of funding a candidate could accept from PACs.

So what more can lobbyists do? The answer is very simple: raise money—lots of it! While there are strict limitations on how much individuals and PACs can give to congressional races, there are no limitations on what they can raise. Lobbyists who are willing to "shake the trees" can produce thousands, even tens of thousands, of dollars by planning events and calling upon industry colleagues to support their efforts. Effectively, what they are doing is leveraging other people's money for their own interests. They understand that making a $1,000 or $2,000 contribution is a nice thing to do for a legislator, but raising several thousands of dollars is still nicer. The personal contribution will get a pleasant thank-you note in return; but raising large sums of money will earn some real gratitude.

One lobbyist had it right when he bragged: "Damn right I get in to see him [a U.S. Senator] when I want to. I raised over $160,000 for his reelection last year."

There are many ways to get involved in political fund-raising. Most lobbyists are introduced to the process when they agree to serve on a legislator's steering committee. These groups commonly range from twenty to forty people, representing a broad range of organizations. The participants usually have two things in common: (1) they are interested in the legislator, either because their client is located in the legislator's state or district, or the client is affected by the legislator's committee business; and (2) their employer or client maintains a sizable PAC.

The first thing lobbyists need to learn about steering committees is that they steer nothing—except for money in the direction of campaign treasuries. Their sole reason for existing is to raise funds. Steering committee participants are chosen with the expectation that they will make some reasonable effort to meet an established fund-raising quota—usually about $10,000 per event. That "their PAC" will contribute handsomely is considered a given.

For the lobbyist, steering committees are the classic double-edged sword. At first glance there may seem little downside in an opportunity to raise money for a member of Congress who serves on a committee with legislative jurisdiction affecting one's business.

But lobbyists who join steering committees are expected to meet, or at least approach, their quotas. Lobbyists who do not live up to this commitment could be costing the campaign in lost contributions; effectively, they may be taking the place of some other lobbyist who would be more conscientious about soliciting their industry for support.

Service on a steering committee is an opportunity to make congressional staff look good—or bad. Because most lawmakers rely heavily on their staff to select, recruit, and ride herd on steering committee participants, the committee's success or failure will reflect directly on the staff's competence. If the committee meets its objectives, the staff will receive praise from their boss; but if it falls short, they will suffer the consequences. When this occurs, lobbyists who did not "get it done" might have a few less allies to call upon the next time they need attention on Capitol Hill.

For better or worse, money and politics remain inseparable. Washington is a very sophisticated city, with politics played out at the highest levels. The stakes are great. To be a player it simply makes sense to be involved in the political process, financially no less than substantively. Political contributions—giving and getting—hedge the effectiveness of your participation. They cover your bases and highlight your presence. And you cannot be successful without a presence.

Chapter 5

LOBBYING: THE COROLLARIES

A long with the rules of the game and the fundamentals of lobbying, there are corollaries to the legislative and political process that must be taken into account. Unless these are understood and appreciated, a lobbyist, no matter how well-informed or motivated, or how compelling the issue, will be needlessly vulnerable to defeat.

It is much easier to stop something than to start something.

A modern aphorism about Capitol Hill states, "Congress does two things best: overreact and nothing." From time to time Congress is seized with paroxysms of activity, as sweeping initiatives become infused with a momentum all their own, racing from committees to the floor in an unstoppable frenzy (for example, the war on drugs and programs for the homeless, Pentagon contracting reform, the human rights amendments of the Carter years, and many of the provisions in the Contract with America during the 104th Congress). They are the exceptions that prove the general rule.

When such initiatives break out, they are uniformly characterized by commanding leadership from the president or the Speaker of the House or the Senate majority leader, or some combination of them. Once such issues become so identified and made priorities, the machinery of the Hill clicks in with hearings and markups designed to yield the requisite legislative package. Normal causes for delay—a reluctant chair or fiercely partisan divisions—are superseded. The pressure from the top (sometimes in reaction to demands from the ranks) basically ensures overall success, with the really interesting day-to-day infighting occurring at the margins (such as whether a specific industry will be rewarded or punished, or whether a particular group or income class in society will have continued access to certain benefits or programs).

But for the hundreds of bills and proposals that do not seep into the general public consciousness as national agenda items—banking deregulation, rewriting the immigration statutes, curbing Wall Street raiders, reform of the product liability laws—it is so much easier to play defense than offense.

Several factors are responsible. Time is always short, even at the start of a new Congress. It takes weeks of intensive activity to begin to educate all the relevant lawmakers on even the simplest issues. Tremendous amounts of time are necessary before members feel comfortable taking action in any given area. Major legislation (such as strengthening the nation's clean air laws) or governmental reforms (such as revision of the campaign finance laws, the balanced-budget amendment, and term limitations) are years in the making. The numerous distractions of competing issues—particularly those that are leadership priorities, and hence "going somewhere"—provide ample opportunities for delay.

Second, forward movement requires consensus. In an increasingly fractionated polity, where for almost every interest there is a competing counterinterest, rare is the issue that has no opposition and is compelling enough on the merits to warrant legislative intervention. One can almost always find a well-placed legislator who can be convinced to lodge an objection to proceeding on a given bill or amendment. In the House, a leading minority member on a subcommittee who commands the deference of his colleagues can cause a chair to hesitate to move a bill. In the Senate, any member can place a *hold* on a bill or nomination, and find at least a half-dozen colleagues willing to side with him or her. It is always easier to erect such obstacles than to galvanize the consensus that can override them. The latter, again, takes much more time and effort—commodities that are in short supply.

Third, the legislative process itself tends to defuse the impetus for action. Hearings are often the result of tension or agitation on issues. They are exercises in which concerns can be aired, witnesses from across the spectrum of opinion given a chance to express their views, and regulatory agencies (or private sector representatives) called to account or invited to share their expertise—all with no promise that legislation will necessarily follow. Members can attend a hearing, vent their anger or frustration or interest, send the proper signal to the intended target, and say, with justification, that they have "done something" and "spoken out" on the issue. It takes additional time to assess the effect of such a hearing—on an industry, an agency, the market—to see whether circumstances have changed. In the meantime, the critical mass necessary to generate legislation can easily dissipate, at least until the next outrage occurs.

Fourth, legislators want to avoid, if possible, choosing between competing interests. Political gridlock engulfs many pressing issues. Coming down on one side or another can alienate important supporters or constituencies, even as others are rewarded. Political cover is greatly valued. Thus, there is a premium on the affected groups' getting together and working out their differences, and presenting such a compromise to a committee for ratification. (Hearings also can serve this jawboning process.) Politicians therefore turn pressures to act back on those directly involved, asking them to make the hard decisions that will resolve the matter. But a recalcitrant interest group, with carefully cultivated support from members and staff, can frustrate the process (especially if the choice is simply intolerable or unworkable) and call the committee's or the chair's bluff. If skillfully executed, stonewalling can be presented as a good-faith effort to reach a compromise, but some will see through it and attack such a ploy. To be certain, such tactics invite the wrath of legislators who want a solution to be reached. But hard calculations can be made as to the risks of legislative intervention, and the costs to goodwill of procrastination. Dedicated opposition from a major interest group paralyzes and frustrates the will to act. The most incisive lobbyists, however, understand when the dynamics dictate compromise, and they unilaterally craft changes in policy or practice that respond to the political concern, without triggering legislation.

Thus, those who need to get something out of Congress—a bill, an amendment, an appropriation, a rider overturning an agency rulemaking—are in a much more difficult tactical position than those who do not want Congress to intervene. At the least, one can hope for the generation of letters from interested legislators, the introduction of legislation and the enlistment of cosponsors, and perhaps a hearing. But passing a law is another order of magnitude, fraught with the incessant hazard of derailment.

Precedent controls process.

The House and Senate are governed by their rules, which derive from precedents dating to Jefferson's time and parliamentary practices of centuries earlier. The precedents of the two chambers—how issues are decided on the floor, the prerogatives of the leadership, and the rights of the minority at any given moment in debate and voting—confer legitimacy on contemporary legislative maneuvering. The reliance on precedents also makes Congress a profoundly incremental institution. Congress is imbued with its past, so that the concept of precedent envelops all activity to the point where Congress is most comfortable in doing procedurally what has been done before. Indeed, explosions erupt on the floor when the Speaker of the House or the Senate majority leader create new precedents during legislative deliberations.

To be sure, significant procedures are established under radical circumstances. In 1981 an alliance of the Reagan administration, House Republicans, and conservative Democrats transformed an obscure technical process in the Budget Act—*reconciliation*—into a major vehicle for omnibus spending and tax policy. It had never been done before. But once it was done, every interest affected by budget decisions confronted reconciliation as the legislative opportunity on which to fight for their objectives. As "must" legislation, reconciliation was artfully used for major policy initiatives normally reserved for the standard authorization process. Tactical opportunities unthinkable in 1980 were, a year later and throughout the ensuing decade, transformed into standard operating procedure.

Reconciliation is a grand example of what a lobbyist must take into account in developing and executing strategy for accomplishing goals. The strongest arguments for or against a proposition are procedural arguments that rest on past practice. Opponents of a major bill or amendment are on firm ground if such legislation has not been the subject of hearings or reported by the committee of jurisdiction. A proposal reported by one committee can be delayed if another committee with clear jurisdiction has not been given an opportunity to consider the bill. A bill that amends one section or title of bedrock legislation generally cannot be opened up (in the House) for amendments to other sections or titles. Authorizing language on an appropriations bill is vulnerable to a *point of order* on the floor—with such points of order sustained in the House (unless specifically waived by the Rules Committee) and subject to a vote in the Senate (on an *appeal of the ruling of the chair*). If regulatory agencies disregard explicit report language issued by an authorizing or appropriating committee, the stage is set for stronger warnings or specific amendments on the matter in question.

If a fundamental and well-established public policy value is at stake (for example, limitations on foreign ownership of television stations, states' rights in regulating certain professions, regulations for airline safety) it is easier to induce attention and support for that threatened value from lawmakers. Any proposal that varies from the status quo, or disrupts a generally accepted consensus for no immediately apparent reason, is subject to substantial challenge.

So change, fundamental change, does not—and many would argue, should not—come easily in Congress. The Republican leadership of the 104th Congress learned this when they attempted to pass term-limitations and constitutional amendments to provide for a balanced budget and a line-item veto for the president. While other provisions in the Contract with America were controversial, if not revolutionary, these measures struck closest to established norms of governing in a separated system. In these instances, precedent and procedure were in fact the substance of governance, and Congress balked at passage even though a fair body of public support for the proposals had been generated.[1]

But even failure has its benefits. A measure that clears one chamber but not the other, or one committee but not the floor, has generally earned priority treatment for expedited action in the next Congress. What has been done before can be done more easily again.

Issues also have to be placed in the context of prevailing ideological trends. The 1986 Tax Reform Act was governed by the principle of revenue neutrality. The burden on lobbyists was to demonstrate how their proposals would not lose money, or how they could be paid for by other revenues. Similarly, the 1995 Republican reform agenda was predicated on "downsizing" the federal government, reducing costs, and returning responsibilities to the states. In order to be taken seriously, lobbyists had to prove that their proposals would save money for the federal government or, alternatively, make it function more efficiently. Chronic budget deficits rewarded initiatives that could be shown to require little or no additional federal funding. When Congress becomes gripped by the mantra of "infrastructure" or "competitiveness" or "getting government out of the people's business," proposals have a greater chance of success if they can be successfully packaged to show that they will further such goals—even if the linkage is tenuous at best. Legislative initiatives are successful when they are crafted to fit the mold of politically popular themes.

Inattention to the role of precedent on procedure can be extremely costly. Proposals presented as "technical" changes to law, but that are in reality substantive, can backfire when revealed. Proposals not cleared by at

1. The House of Representatives rejected the term-limits proposal, and the Senate failed to approve the House versions of the constitutional amendments.

least the leadership of the authorizing committee—attempts to amend law within that committee's jurisdiction—can cause future enmity for yourself and your clients in dealing with that committee. The potential that an amendment might be tagged as a "special interest giveaway" on the front page of the *Washington Post* or any widely read newspaper must be appreciated by both the lobbyist and the legislator, because the lawmaker especially will have to withstand the scrutiny that will follow. All such "end-arounds" test the precedents and traditions of the legislative process, and the comity between legislators—issues of accountability and justification that cannot be avoided.

Precedents and procedures are, in the end, the province of the legislators themselves. Each member's temperament must be assessed in discerning tactical opportunities and openings to affirm existing precedents or to establish new ones. Whether a chair permits the relatively open and "hands on" involvement of lobbyists in committee decision making; whether an appropriations subcommittee chair tolerates funding for an unauthorized program; whether a chair is willing to be creative in grafting a proposal onto a reconciliation bill or a *continuing resolution*; whether a member of the Rules Committee is willing to fight to waive a point of order against a provision of a bill or conference report; whether a senator is inclined to appeal a ruling of the chair; whether a senator is willing to include a narrowly tailored provision in a "technical amendments" package to a tax bill—all are questions that will determine if you have a chance to succeed. Without that commitment the normal, regular, and more time-consuming procedures will govern congressional consideration and the outcome.

Defer to your leaders.

Ultimately you the lobbyist have to trust, and defer to, the judgment and ability of the legislators who are sponsoring and advancing your objectives. They hold the election certificates, they are sitting on the dais and in the closed meetings of conferees, they are facing the glares of their panel leader and the rhetorical attacks from legislators on the other side. At the moment of decision, they have to make the choice whether to proceed, how much to compromise, what to trade, whether to press for a vote, or whether to retire from the field and try again another day.

A good lobbyist spends hours in preparation before visiting the Hill (perhaps ten hours of study, discussion, and strategizing for every hour on the Hill), developing a proposal, conducting legislative research, framing the arguments, writing the materials: getting ready, in short, to do battle. The most important tactical decision is determining who should be your leader, and how you will convince him or her to become your leader.

Several cross-checks guide the decision. Every issue—without exception, domestic or international, no matter how esoteric—is under the jurisdiction of one or more committees and subcommittees in each chamber. Jurisdiction will determine the first tier of legislators who will have a say on any given matter. Once the committees have been defined, their rosters have to be studied for prospective leaders, with two factors being decisive: constituent interest and issues interest. If a member represents a district or state that harbors your client (headquarters, facilities, employees), he or she is a primary target. If a member has a history of involvement in the issue—health policy, immigration, banking, transportation—he or she may be responsive to your concern. Often, a lobbyist is out of luck: there is no obvious connection on the committee. You should then turn to those legislators off the committee who have supported you, those who represent you or your client directly, and ask them to intervene on your behalf with their colleagues on the committee of jurisdiction.

Whether your potential leader is in the majority or minority will also influence your decision to ask that person to sponsor your initiative. (A House minority member, generally, has less ability to shape legislation than does a minority member of the Senate.) If the objective is to try to influence a federal agency, and the minority party in Congress controls the White House, you may want to target only members of the minority to send letters to that agency.

All lobbyists want to enlist the support of the chair and *ranking member* of the key subcommittee, and the full committee, but the style of the lawmaker has to be taken into account. Some do take the lead and constantly develop bills and amendments for their panel's agenda; still others reserve their political ammunition, entering the fray at a decisive moment to resolve the issues. But each chair or ranking member will break out of his or her distinctive pattern as an issue might warrant. Often the urgency of a situation—a hostile takeover that threatens layoffs in the state or district; a sudden, unfavorable action in another committee of shared jurisdiction; a response to a breaking scandal or public policy crisis—can spur a normally complacent legislator into action.

When deciding whether to approach a legislator to be a potential leader on your behalf, you must consider the legislator's personal strengths and deficiencies. Aside from political placement—chair or junior member; majority or minority; liberal, moderate, or conservative—the legislator's temperament and effectiveness are critical to your ultimate success. By becoming a student of Congress, a lobbyist can apprehend the political and personal relationships between members: who leads and who follows; who breaks with the leadership, and on which issues and why; which members regularly consult with each other and which act alone; who takes the initiative, and on which issues; who generally prevails on amendments and who regularly fails; who takes the time to study and master an issue, and who grandstands for the cameras and is substantively shallow.

Sometimes you are stuck: the potential leader is a junior member, an ideologue who loves rhetoric, or a legislator who represents your client but has no inroads to the committee. Then you are reduced to pleading your case, hoping someone will listen. In those instances there is no choice but to go after the best legislators and staff who can be found, present the most compelling arguments, and ask for their help on the basis that it is the right thing to do. And you keep working until either they listen or you lose. (They will listen if the issue you care about is in the headlines. They will listen if your client is prominent, even if it does not have tremendous constituent or grassroots clout—the motion picture industry, investment banking houses, a meritorious cultural or educational institution.)

Lobbyists also spend hours "gaming" the play of events: who will say precisely what to whom, and when; what message will be conveyed; how will that message be echoed by other sources; what will be the sequence of such reinforcement. Entire scripts can be developed (sometimes literally, as in the development of *colloquies* for floor debate) and sold in discussions with staff and lawmakers. Members and staff appreciate and welcome a well-thought-out plan: introduction of a bill or sponsorship of the requisite amendment; identifying the bill to which the amendment should be offered; enlistment of cosponsors; development of other endorsements from outside groups; contact with key members of the leadership; anticipation of objections from other members, a regulatory agency, or the White House; a strategy to neutralize such objections; a parallel plan for the other chamber; a discussion of potential fallback positions, if any.

Members also appreciate and value the path of least resistance, such as report language instead of an amendment, a colloquy on the floor instead of a change to the bill, a letter from the Hill to an agency instead of legislative action, or a hearing instead of a markup.

After the hours of preparation and execution, after all the visits and letters and distribution of materials, after all the arguments have been made, it is the judgment of your leaders on how to proceed that will be decisive. You may know the best bill to amend, but they will have to agree. You may want a *record vote*, but they will have to consider the mood of the committee at any given moment (and their future role on that committee) in asking for a vote. You may not want to make any concessions, but they may reach a different conclusion as to what is acceptable. Ultimately, your leaders define what is possible, and you have to live with it. You have chosen them to represent you as best they can.

Don't burn votes—you may need them tomorrow.

Political relationships are never over. They always return to be engaged anew, for better or worse. They are never over because issues are never over. Public policy is considered in cycles as expiring authorizations are renewed, as annual appropriations are revisited, as events or scandal demand attention to ongoing programs, as committees exercise their oversight responsibilities. Even the sacrosanct, "untouchable" issues, such as Social Security, are always on the table under the pressure of federal budget deficits. The members involved with issues stay involved with them, even if they change committees (they can still lobby their colleagues from their former committee) and even if they retire (and become lobbyists themselves). No fight is over, no issue resolved forever, no controversy ever finally laid to rest. If you win, you have to defend your gains against those you defeated; if you lose, you want to live again to fight another day.

Your relations with members and staff, even your most bitter opponents, must always remain civil. There is always the temptation, when you have been skewered, to write off that legislator forever, to exact retribution, to make the offender pay a penalty. Two cautionary notes. As Ralph Waldo Emerson wrote, "When you strike at a king, you must kill him." If you only nick him or wound him, he will be back with a vengeance, and you will be worse off than before. Your enemy also has friends, who do not appreciate attacks on their friend. Second, you never know when you might need the legislator who opposed you in the past. Even the most singular or discrete issue has many aspects as it evolves. A legislator may oppose you on a policy matter—how your client might be regulated—but could have great sympathy for your concern on tax legislation. A legislator who opposed you on an important issue last year may want to "make up" or compensate by being helpful on a different matter this year. A politician may suddenly face a tough reelection campaign and need all the friends he or she can get.

A lobbyist has to have the patience and fortitude to take the hit, understand the inherent value of long-term relations, and devise approaches that can enlist that legislator's support the next time. You never know when you might need that politician's vote in the future, and you never know what issue might command that vote. Aside from lying or misleading, burning a vote is the single worst mistake a lobbyist can make.

Differences must be professional, not personal. If you cannot stomach a legislator, ignore the person—no overtures, entreaties, solicitations, stroking, communications. But you must always know where such persons are and what they are doing: political intelligence must be maintained. You also must shore up support from your allies to isolate your opponent.

A lobbyist lives for and through his or her political priorities and objectives. Inevitably, these concerns are shared only to a partial degree by your legislative champions. They cannot be expected to internalize your personal antipathy toward another politician. The urge to defame must be kept in check at the risk of your integrity. If you talk about others in scathing terms, your political associates may believe you are capable of talking about them in the same way. There are no secrets in the Capitol. Everyone, in the end, knows where everyone stands, and why. Words return to haunt—along with the issues, the legislators, and the votes.

The best ideas are worthless without the votes.

As any proviso, statute, or administrative decree is deemed constitutional whenever five justices of the Supreme Court rule it constitutional, so a bill or amendment has value only if it can command 218 votes in the House and 51 in the Senate. It does not matter if you have developed the answer to rising health-care costs, the federal budget deficit, the trade imbalance, the Third World debt conundrum, unemployment, or depression in the farmland: ideas have force or power in Washington only to the extent they win the votes. Everyone—politicians, academicians, lobbyists, public-interest groups, scientists, foreign dignitaries, editorial opinion writers—comes up with interesting and provocative analyses and remedies, and they are injected into the dialogue on the issues of the day. (Members read the newspaper in the morning and are on the floor that afternoon with amendments inspired by the reports.) But unless and until these advocates get the attention of those who will vote on their prescriptions, and until a majority of the Congress coalesces around them, they remain merely good ideas or debating points, and decidedly not the law of the land.

If your client is getting crushed by a regulatory agency, or run out of business by a predatory competitor, or languishing for want of a line-item appropriation or "technical fix" to a pending bill, the injustice faced by your client is irrelevant unless and until there is intervention on your behalf. Depending on the circumstances, a stream of letters and phone calls to the Hill and the introduction or threatened initiation of legislation may provide relief. But in the face of an obstinate bureaucracy or a determined corporate raider, nothing short of legislation, ratified by a majority of the legislators involved, will suffice. Those who are self-righteous, committed, and zealous have to temper their passion to this dose of reality, lest their advocacy degenerate into frustration and recrimination.

Patience and staying power are essential for remaining in the game. A powerful chair's advocacy of a consumption or value-added tax more than a decade ago was said to have cost his reelection; lawmakers may yet adopt such a tax in the 1990s to reduce the deficit and promote savings and investment. The social and economic agenda of the conservative movement languished for twenty years before Ronald Reagan assumed the presidency, and it was reignited with a vengeance when Republicans took full control of Congress in 1995. The difference is not the ideas, of course, but the votes, and the votes are everything. Without them, you come away with nothing.

What cannot be achieved from the ground up, because of apathy or lack of time or the press of other priorities, can win a chance for consideration through pressure from the top down in committee or on the floor. Majorities are best finessed through the support of key leaders. Legislators regularly defer to those with more seniority or power. If a subcommittee chair makes clear she wants something, prospects for success are immeasurably improved. It is likely she will get most of the votes from her party colleagues, if not all of them—a majority of the panel. If there is a pattern of cooperation and trading between the chair and ranking member, near-unanimous approval should be expected. The chair of the Rules Committee can generally control the drafting of rules for bills headed to the floor, but the majority leader and especially the Speaker can sharply influence the panel. Similarly, senators will defer to the wishes of the majority leader in scheduling bills and protecting amendments crucial to him. The minority leader can also play an influential, though less decisive, role. But these are the exceptions. Chairs and members of the leadership use their power judiciously, particularly if it is directed at overturning the opposition of another committee or subcommittee and its leadership.

Majorities also can be created through trades. Differing pluralities on discrete issues can be joined in coalitions of convenience, with each side accepting—and then protecting—the other's agenda. In such circumstances the whole package becomes greater than the sum of its parts. The precedent of such approval by a panel's majority is important if the bill ultimately fails and the process has to begin again. This technique also can be used to roll—or threaten to roll—an intransigent chair, who then faces the choice of joining the new coalition (letting the committee "work its will") or bargaining for a better agreement. Trades also can demonstrate to a chair that a majority is ready to act, making it easier for the chair to act.

Real majorities, however, those that have enduring support, are retailed: office by office, staff by staff, member by member. There are no shortcuts. But even a majority in hand can be illusory. (A simple majority in the Senate is insufficient to break a filibuster of a determined minority of opponents.) Two hundred and eighteen cosponsors in the House can still be insufficient to move a bill if the chair with jurisdiction or the Speaker is unalterably opposed to the measure. In the House, only extraordinary procedures in committee or a *discharge petition* on the floor—both politically unappealing routes for a lobbyist—can dislodge the bill. And then the votes must be there to sustain the test of wills between the majority and the leadership.

If you don't ask, you don't get.

Politicians like to be asked; they are in the business of being asked. If possible they want to respond; it makes them popular. Legislators do things out of both the goodness of their hearts and opportunism: to capitalize on a morning headline, a brewing scandal, a foreign policy controversy, an injustice that needs to be righted. They have come to public office with a working ideology and a world view, with personal and professional aspirations, and with an intention to do good for their constituents and the country. They also come to public office with ambition.

A lobbyist never knows what is possible until you ask a legislator for something. You cannot expect a legislator to act spontaneously on your behalf. You have to judge your relationship with that lawmaker carefully. If you have known or worked with each other for a long time, if you have been a political supporter, if you are friends, you can be relatively candid. Your ties should be strong enough to withstand an ill-timed or very difficult request. The context of events also defines what types of requests are acceptable. If your opposition is engineering letters from the Hill to an agency, it is perfectly appropriate to generate your own letters and ask legislators not to sign the competing correspondence. If a bill has been introduced that is against your interests, it is timely to fight broad cosponsorship, seek the introduction of alternative legislation, and turn up the decibel level of debate.

No matter what the nature of your relationship with any given representative or senator, the operative dynamic is the same: you need him, you are coming to him because you need him, he knows you need him, and you really have no other choice. And he may well need you in the future on legislation of importance to him, for support in an election campaign, or for advice on a difficult issue.

Lobbyists must not ask that which is improper or, if not formally improper, could create a questionable appearance. As a general rule, the most a member can be expected to ask of a regulatory agency is full and fair consideration of a constituent or policy perspective—no more, and no less. Regulatory agencies have *ex parte rules*; members of Congress should not be asked to ignore them, no matter how imminent or urgent an agency ruling. Legislators are little inclined, and should not be asked, to intervene in legal enforcement actions. Congress regularly defers to the civil and criminal process (except in its investigation and oversight functions), and should not be put in the position of second-guessing the proper exercise of legal authority. There will be sufficient opportunity for appeal.

Your ability to ask is premised on access. Staff will never turn down a request to meet on a legitimate issue on which you are both working. A member's time is of course more guarded. Whether in fact you need access to the member depends on the staff and the urgency of the request. Only through experience can you determine whether the staff has that member's ear and can be said to speak for that member. If you cannot get the answer you need from the staff, and have to see the member personally, let the staff know what you are doing. You may or may not succeed, the staff may or may not help you see the boss, but the necessary base will have been covered.

A representative or senator will ultimately be responsive based on what you represent and who you are: a voice from the state or district; a respected professional whose advice has been helpful in the past; a political supporter, fund-raiser, or contributor; a person who demonstrates an interest in that legislator's activities outside of your issue areas alone; a person who has been referred by a colleague of that legislator, who has asked the legislator to listen to you and help if possible.

But if you cannot ask your friends in power for something, and if they in turn cannot come to you for support, who can you ask, and to whom will they turn?

In the end, politics is based on trust, on personal ties between individuals, on the credibility and veracity of the exchanges between them. These things are built over time: they are the fruit of experience. They cannot be hurried.

Chapter 6

LOBBYING THE EXECUTIVE

I f read literally, the Constitution gives virtually all direct policy-making authority to Congress. As a practical matter, however, Congress does not enjoy an absolute monopoly in lawmaking; the president and his administration are constant and key players in the legislative process. From the constitutionally provided authority to veto legislation to acts as simple as communicating the administration position in telephone calls and hallway conversations, the executive branch is a force in determining legislative outcomes. And while this may change by matters of degree during periods of divided government (the Congress controlled by one party and the White House controlled by the other), it remains a relative constant in the policy-making mix.

Despite this considerable influence, many veteran lobbyists rarely, if ever, set foot in an executive agency. Whether because they see themselves as "creatures of Capitol Hill" and disdain the "bureaucracy," or because it is an unfamiliar political venue with its own sets of rules and mores, these lobbyists virtually ignore the existence of the executive branch. They do this at their client's peril.

Most executive branch employees—subcabinet officials and members of the career service—are not among the high-profile Washington "stars" whose names, faces, and words dominate the national media. They work in the nooks and crannies of the federal government, attracting little attention, infrequent praise, and cheap insults from election-minded politicians. The first challenge outsiders confront in working with them is finding out who they are, what they do, and where they do it. Directories, organization charts, and titles can help, but they do not tell the whole story. In fact, they can sometimes be misleading.

The general rule is that the subcabinet, which includes assistant and deputy assistant secretaries, is a part of the administration's policy-making apparatus and that members of the career service are responsible for running government programs on a day-to-day basis. But this may be a bit too simplistic to rely upon. There is no clear dichotomy of function that is universal, none that holds from administration to administration or, for that matter, from department to department within a single administration.

Knowing a person's title (even job description) is not enough to understand where he or she fits into the legislative power equation. Some members of the career service have earned respect for both their program knowledge and political savvy; they have become trusted advisers to cabinet officers and invaluable resources to Congress. They exert influence well beyond what one might expect from their position on an organization chart. Conversely, political appointees with impressive titles may be beneficiaries of spoils-system politics and enjoy little or no real influence with those who count. Their reputations never rise beyond the designation of political hack.

So figuring out whom to approach in government is not an easy matter. But once the right official is located and access is gained (also not easily done), the payoff for the lobbyist can be substantial. The executive branch is a treasure of information, and given the right circumstances executive officials can prove valuable allies when attempting to influence congressional committees.

Executive influence in legislative affairs occurs through both *official* and *unofficial* contact networks. As one might expect, the *unofficial* is more subtle and more intriguing. By some definitions, it is how influence is really exerted in Washington. But each network has its role to play, and each offers important mechanisms for influencing the lawmaking process. Conscientious lobbyists will not overlook opportunities to gain executive branch support from whatever source possible. If successful, they enlist a prestigious and powerful ally to their client's cause. It is well worth the effort to understand where and how executive power is exerted on congressional decision making.

Official Contact Networks

Vetoes and legislative messages. The authority to veto legislation is the executive's ultimate check on the legislature. When Congress is in session the veto has the practical effect of raising the requirement for passing legislation from a simple majority in both chambers to a two-thirds vote in each body. When Congress has adjourned and left legislation on the president's desk, his veto is absolute.

It is clear, then, that the veto—if it does not actually kill legislation—ups the ante for its supporters. Override efforts are expensive in legislative management and political terms; they take time from busy floor schedules and often require a significant investment of scarce political capital in order to achieve the necessary votes. And they are rare.[1] So even the threat of a veto can cause Congress to seriously reexamine the product it is about to send "downtown."

Presidential vetoes and legislative messages present important opportunities for aggressive lobbyists and their clients. Admittedly, these are at the high-stakes end of the lobbying spectrum: it takes a fair amount of clout to convince a president to veto a bill or to include a policy position in his State of the Union address. Because it is the rare lobbyist who is granted audience in the Oval Office, these objectives must ordinarily be pursued at the White House staff, cabinet, and subcabinet levels. And even here access is not easily gained.

Lobbying in these rarified atmospheres usually requires that the interests of more than one client or company be involved. Broad questions of policy and the potential for widespread impact—economic, quality of life, or political—must be at issue. This defines the classic situation in which active participation by an association or ad hoc coalition will be needed in order to achieve the desired attention. Just as the Congress looks for indications of popular support before moving on major issues, so too do employees of the executive branch gain political confidence when an entire industry or other well-defined constituency within the broader community endorses a policy position. In a sense this reinforcement is even more important for executive officials than it is for members of Congress; the administration is accountable to the entire nation, not to a single congressional district or state. For them it is as much a duty to know that a broad national constituency supports a position as it is a matter of political security.

Administration testimony. Short of threatening a veto or offering its own bill, an administration has other ways in which to play a formal role in the legislative process. Perhaps most significant among these is through testimony delivered by department or agency officials at congressional hearings. The political and substantive ramifications of an administration position presented to a committee or subcommittee can be appreciable. These presentations are always taken seriously, if only for

---

1. From 1989 to 1995 only two presidential vetoes were overriden by Congress.

their political significance—though the content is usually at least as compelling on its merits.

The machinations that occur during the development of administration testimony are complex, convoluted, and frequently confounding. What is important here is that the content of these statements is not necessarily beyond the influence of diligent lobbyists. To the extent that the administration's comments are taken seriously by lawmakers, it can only be helpful if the client's views are reflected and supported in the department's official testimony. Lobbyists can help themselves immeasurably by convincing administration officials that their cause is of sufficient weight to merit articulation during committee hearings. Further, even if the administration is already inclined toward the client's position, the lobbyist may be able to contribute to a more powerful statement by supplying additional arguments and supporting data.[2]

At a minimum, lobbyists must make it their business to know what the administration intends to say. If the position accords with their client's point of view, they can take prudent steps to facilitate broad and strategic exposure for the testimony. This might include encouraging members and their staffs to attend the hearing; or it might entail hand-delivering written copies of the statement to key congressional offices or alerting the general and trade media.

If the message is not going to be favorable, advance notice will provide an opportunity to warn allies and prepare appropriate responses for the press. Frequently, the effect of negative testimony can be blunted by well-constructed follow-up questions designed to poke holes in the administration's position. These can be prepared by the lobbyist and placed in the hands of friendly lawmakers for use during the hearing. This is an effective tactic, but it is also a dicey business. The member must know enough about the subject and be sufficiently quick-witted to engage in a give-and-take with an administration witness who is apt to be both smart and well informed. Planting a question is one thing; anticipating the response and controlling the subsequent dialogue is quite another. Unless the lobbyist has total confidence in the allied member, it may be wiser to simply absorb the hit delivered in the statement than to magnify the point by additional public debate.

---

2. A caveat is in order here: Only a select number of issues will rise to a level of importance sufficient to merit inclusion in an administration's congressional testimony. The lobbyist who pushes too hard to include unimportant or irrelevant material in the testimony makes a fool of himself and does harm to his client.

Unofficial Contact Networks

End runners and whistle-blowers.   In any decision-making environment there is always a place for knowledge, competence, and good faith. Nowhere is this more evident than in relationships that form between members of Congress, their staffs, and executive branch personnel. They may have fundamental disagreements about political philosophy and approaches to public administration, but beneath it all, there is more often than not a genuine respect born of a mutual desire to write good law. This places a premium on good information; and for this there is no better source than the federal executive branch, especially the career service.

Political appointees have the final say on administration policy—and to that extent they are important players in influencing legislative outcomes—but often it is the career civil servant who has the raw information lawmakers need to define and evaluate policy options. While civil servants have their own vested interests—a natural inclination to protect jobs and professional reputations—they are best positioned to know precisely which parts of their programs have worked well and which parts have failed. They also are well suited to recommend improvements.

Further, given the relatively rapid turnover that occurs among congressional staff and among cabinet and subcabinet officials, the career service provides the best—maybe the only—source of institutional memory in the federal government. Long-term employees are able to provide useful background information on the political dynamics and policy rationales that affected earlier committee decisions. This intelligence allows lawmakers to anticipate, and perhaps avoid, mistakes previously made.

So the back and forth between the legislative and executive branches is constant, especially at the staff level. Some administrations have attempted to control the frequency and the content of these exchanges by issuing edicts preventing "unauthorized" personnel (usually the career service) from talking to congressional staff unless in the company of an "authorized" official.

These efforts to censor the flow of information have never worked. Instead, they have encouraged the now well-established, almost customary practice of the "end run" or, in its most extreme form, "whistle blowing." Employees of the executive branch may be sitting at hearings in the morning supporting the administration's "line," and in the afternoon they may be cloistered with congressional staff telling them that what they heard in the morning was a bunch of bunk. Insubordination? Probably. But in the minds of the end runners and committee counsels they are performing an important public service.

Policy triangles.   Together, congressional staffers and executive branch personnel make up two-thirds of the classic policy triangles that heavily influence lawmaking in Washington. The final third includes sources from outside of the federal government—affected industries, academics, think tanks, state and local government officials, and virtually any other source that can make a meaningful contribution to resolving the issues at hand. These triangles are usually nonpartisan, substantive in character, and focused on a particular policy domain. The currency for obtaining "membership" is counted not in terms of financial resources but, rather, in terms of how much good information and how many worthy ideas a participant can bring to the table. These are quality, not quantity, operations.

Membership is not easy to come by, especially for commercial lobbyists. But once earned, it provides an ideal position from which to represent clients' interests. As long as the client's needs are legitimate, arguments credible, and information accurate, the lobbyist can represent the client and, at the same time, play a constructive role in moving legislation forward. It is only when a participant gives reason to doubt good faith and integrity that the risk of being disinvited becomes a problem.

Policy triangles are not, by any definition, formal membership organizations. They have no names, logos, bylaws, or established membership criteria; they may never come together as a group, and many participants have no idea who else is involved. They are ad hoc collections of people whom lawmakers have learned to depend upon for reliable information and good ideas. Other than candor, honesty, and—when required—protecting confidentiality, there are few ground rules that must be observed. What rules there are exist more as a function of political sensitivity and common sense than as a result of intentional design.

The ideal is to become part of this inner sanctum. But whether personally included or not, lobbyists should know who is in the best position to influence the course of legislative events. Gaining the ear of those whom members of Congress seek for counsel can have nearly as much value as direct communications with senators and representatives. It can even add to the power of an argument by demonstrating support from well-respected and objective authorities. Executive branch employees are able to provide such credibility.

But how does this get accomplished? Accessing and influencing executive branch employees is its own expertise. The lobbyist who attempts to conduct business "downtown" in the same way she would on Capitol Hill makes a serious mistake. While there are clear similarities, there are also important distinctions. These are evident in attitudes toward lobbying; expectations for the content of meetings; and even in the logistical difficulties that must be overcome in attempting to meet with executive agency employees.

Lobbying the Executive Branch versus Lobbying Congress

Culture. Whether by well-paid lobbyists, members of public-interest groups, administration officials, or individual constituents, congressional offices expect to be lobbied. This is not the case in the executive branch. With the possible exception of some regulatory agency officials and political appointees, most government officials are not accustomed to being lobbied and are uncomfortable with it. It is not a part of their work culture, and, in their view, it is intrusive and potentially compromising of agency integrity. Their client is the president first, and all other interests are second.

As a consequence, meetings with executive branch personnel are often difficult to arrange. The person with the requisite information and reputation among lawmakers may be buried in the bureaucracy and reluctant to meet with representatives of private interests.

So, while such meetings do occur, lobbyists should be aware of the attitudes and professional sensitivities of those who sit on the other side of the table. When in doubt about these, it is a good idea to adopt a no-nonsense, no-frills approach. Anticipating and responding to the concerns of those who are not in the habit of being lobbied—especially as their concerns relate to meeting tone and content—can relax tensions, establish some level of trust, and, hopefully, help create a working environment conducive to achieving positive results.

Content. It is common for meetings on Capitol Hill to have a political cast to them. Participants are well aware of whom the lobbyist represents, whether or not this is openly acknowledged. The fact that the client is a major constituent, a significant contributor, or an active fundraiser will almost always color the meeting. If nothing more, it will guarantee a respectful, even cordial, audience. And while the client's political clout may not be determinative of legislative outcomes, there is little doubt that it will be considered when final decisions are made.

A different set of circumstances pertains to meetings with executive branch officials, especially members of the career service. These meetings tend to have fewer political overtones and are more consistently substantive in character. The client's esteemed political position is irrelevant, and it may even be regarded negatively. Not that these officials are unaware or unused to legislative politics—they are often among its most skilled practitioners—but their political interests are usually confined to the future of the programs they manage: Are they going to be adequately funded? Will the legislative mandate change? Will they have sufficient authority to accomplish their mission?

Here, knowing and focusing on policy rationales (discussed in the context of congressional lobbying in Chapter 3) is especially important. In Congress, the existence of a member-constituent relationship may provide some degree of justification for producing legislation that skirts the merits and favors a specific local interest. This we have come to expect of legislators.

But executive branch officials see the nation in bigger chunks. Because their charge is broader in scope, they are most favorably influenced by policy recommendations that define legitimate national policy objectives. This calls for satisfying a higher standard than the "red-face test" that sometimes suffices on Capitol Hill; it means plausible positions backed up by well-documented facts and, if appropriate to the argument, carefully constructed data.

It is certainly possible for private sector lobbyists to develop productive working relationships with members of the career service. When this occurs, it is almost always because the lobbyists have been able to rationalize their clients' needs in the context of bona fide national interests. Effectively, they have merged their interests with broader policy objectives. In so doing they have gone a long way toward gaining the confidence of federal employees who may enjoy quiet but considerable influence on Capitol Hill.

Proceed with Caution

Lobbying is always a business of choices: Which amendment to move forward? When to move it? Who should speak to whom? It is in making these kinds of calls that professional lobbyists earn their keep. This is true for legislative and executive branch lobbying, but it is especially true when lobbying the executive.

For all of its wheeling and dealing, Congress is, in many ways, a straightforward and reinforcing place to do business. It is possible to learn where staff and members stand on most issues and to know which political options are best pursued. And, while there may be hundreds of variations on dozens of procedural themes, the process is generally open. Those who take the time to understand it can make well-informed judgments on which strategies they wish to employ. What is more, there is seldom a shortage of knowledgeable allies willing to share their wisdom and offer advice on how to achieve sought-after objectives.

The rules are different in executive agencies. With the exception of certain regulatory proceedings, there is no general requirement that meetings in the executive branch be open to the public.[3] Executive agencies—unlike the House and Senate—do not readily reveal the secrets that underpin their internal power structures and shape their influence networks. It is not a simple matter to identify the officials who have strong subject knowledge and the ear of congressional staff. There are no hearings or markups during which they routinely display their expertise and savvy. And, as already discussed, they are not always available or willing to meet with those who seek to win their support.

So, when attempting to work with the executive branch, lobbyists are most often left to their own devices. Counsel is not as readily offered as it is on the Hill. Moreover, danger points may be obscured, and the motives that compel people to act or not to act may be difficult to discern. Political appointees and members of the career service have their own, sometimes conflicting, agendas; departments and agencies vie for turf; and, even in the best of circumstances, policy clearance procedures can be interminable. This is no environment for the novice, the naive, or the timid.

But lobbyists who do decide to venture into the executive branch can be well rewarded for their efforts. The right testimony delivered at a pivotal hearing, the persuasive argument presented by a respected agency official during a clandestine meeting with congressional staff—these can be among the strongest elements of a lobbyist's legislative campaign.

Yet, as is so often the case, the opportunity to succeed is the opportunity to fail. In attempting to engineer support for their clients' causes, lobbyists run the risk of offending powerful interests within the adminis-

---

3. Under the Freedom of Information Act, members of the public must (with notable exceptions) be granted access to written communications between federal agencies and parties attempting to influence agency decisions. The act is important because it compels public disclosure, and thus broad evaluation, of data and other material used to support sensitive regulatory actions and other policy determinations.

tration. Differences of opinion expressed in public are a part of what legislatures are about; they are not a part of what the executive is about. Legislators thrive on open disputes with their colleagues; presidents and cabinet officers go to great lengths to conceal conflicts within their ranks. These are essential differences between the two branches: one thrives on diversity and openness, the other on unanimity and secretiveness.

It is not possible for outsiders to know where the political booby traps are hidden within any administration. An argument made in the best of faith to one office may be viewed as subversive to another; a conscientious effort to invite all relevant officials to a meeting may result in inadvertently omitting a key player; and efforts to placate fears can create suspicion and provoke hostility.

So, while venturing into the executive branch may offer the promise of much-needed support, for legislative lobbyists the sign at the agency's door might well read, "Proceed with Caution!"

Chapter 7

LOBBYING FOR THE SMALL BUSINESS

W hen members of the popular press write about lobbyists, they often convey the impression that all lobbying is done by slick Washington insiders working for wealthy corporations or huge trade associations. Without question, powerful special interests do exist, and they certainly exercise considerable influence. But lobbying Congress is not the exclusive domain of the rich, powerful, and well-connected. While corporate interests and full-time lobbyists enjoy many advantages, there is ample opportunity for less experienced and less well-financed players to make an impact on public policy. The challenges may be greater for small business owners, but the job is doable given realistic objectives, careful planning, the right help, and—perhaps most important—the courage to try.

Big versus Small

If large corporations do have lobbying advantages over smaller businesses, their ability to maintain a sustained presence in Washington may be most important among them. Well-financed organizations can have skilled professionals, whether on payroll or retainer, "bird dog" their issues through every step of the legislative process. Most small business owners cannot afford this; they are manufacturers, engineers, builders, retailers—and so on. They do not employ professional lobbyists and, unless they are extraordinarily profitable, they are not likely to retain high-powered Washington consulting firms for months, or years, at a time.

To compound matters, owners find it difficult to be away from their businesses frequently and for long periods; thus, their ability to personally stay on top of an issue is limited. Congressional schedules are erratic and notification times short: you are needed when you are needed, but seldom can one know exactly when that is going to be. Without a full-time

Washington presence it is difficult to guarantee that you can be available when and where required. Under these circumstances it is virtually impossible to sustain an effective lobbying campaign.

So having full-time representation in Washington is a major advantage for those who can afford to pay for the service—namely, big businesses. Another financial advantage for large corporations is the ability to establish and operate political action committees (PACs). The impact of campaign contributions was discussed in Chapter 4; suffice it to say here that most small businesses have either no PAC or a very small one. To the extent that these organizations are involved in making political contributions at all, the money generally comes from the private checkbooks of owners and, maybe, a few senior managers. Their efforts are dwarfed by what larger organizations can afford to do.

The small business executive who thinks that his or her $250, or even $500, contribution will swing doors, hearts, and minds wide open faces an unpleasant surprise. This does not mean that contributions are a bad idea—they are not—it just means that the small and infrequent contributor should not expect them to produce more than a modest amount of good will.

It is clear, then, that the "big fellas" do enjoy distinct lobbying advantages. But it would be a mistake to think big versus small is always a one-sided proposition. In fact, there are definite pluses for small business operators who lobby Congress on their own behalf.

Small—as in small business—can, and does, have its own appeal in Washington. No image is more fundamental to opportunity in the United States, and more politically popular, than that of the entrepreneur risking everything to establish and build a business. If from time to time corporate America is portrayed as a collective villain, "Mom and Pop" remain everyone's heroes. The political stigma that frequently attaches to "business" is almost always reserved for big business; small business is a different matter.

But respect for the entrepreneur helps only to create a positive political environment; it cannot guarantee favorable results. More is needed if the entrepreneur is to convert potential goodwill into legislative support. A well-planned, carefully prepared lobbying campaign is essential.

While thorough preparation is a must for all lobbying efforts (see Chapter 3), it is especially important for small businesses—if for no other reason than to prove that they should be taken seriously. Beginner status has its charm, but with it comes an underlying and unspoken suspicion that inexperienced and modestly funded lobbyists will not be able to uphold their end of the legislative bargain. The surest way to reinforce this view is to make telltale mistakes early in the lobbying process. Unreasonable requests, presentation of poor data, and naive strategies are all obvious signs that one is a novice.

What this means is that there is a delicate balance to be maintained by small business people who represent their own interests with Congress. They benefit from the sense that they are entrepreneurs and not professional lobbyists representing multibillion dollar interests; at the same time, they must be careful to avoid the kinds of mistakes that convey faulty political judgment or total ignorance of the system.

Careful preparation can help to avoid the amateur stereotype. But this is not to suggest that first-time or occasional lobbyists can reasonably aspire to become what they are not: Capitol Hill experts. It means only that by attention to the basics—integrity and good judgment—especially early in the process, small business people can establish the credibility necessary to be viewed as serious petitioners.

Because smaller organizations usually do not own or retain full-time government relations services, the first order of business in preparing a lobbying campaign is to seek help from those who understand legislative procedures and substance. While selecting the right combination of advisers and supporters will be a function of the petitioner's knowledge, experience, and level of commitment to the lobbying objective, there are a few resources that are worth consideration by virtually all entrepreneurs seeking to represent their own causes. These are: the local member of Congress, associations and coalitions, and professional consultants.

Seeking Help

The local member of Congress. Washington may be where legislative issues are ultimately decided, but long before arguments are presented on Capitol Hill one should be cultivating a relationship with the local member of Congress.[1] The process is easier than most people anticipate. Every representative maintains at least one office in his or her district. (Most members maintain two or more.) These offices are legislators'

---

1. This segment will focus on members of the House of Representatives, as opposed to U.S. senators. While senators generally have more opportunity to influence legislation than do representatives, senators and their staffs usually have broader jurisdictions to cover and more demands on their time. It is the representative who has the most direct interest in responding to small business constituents.

primary vehicles for servicing and reaching out to constituents; local business leaders are always among their most important "clients." And this is for a good reason; voters expect that their representatives will be sensitive to the district's economic needs.

Relationships between legislators and businesspeople need not be based on a sense of political affinity. As long as each has something to gain from the other—a voice in Congress on the one hand and influence in the community on the other—a basis for cooperation exists. These are relationships founded on mutuality of interests, not on compatibility of thought. And no interest is more consistently compelling to public and private sector people than economic vitality. The "clubhouse" politicians had it right: "Politics is about three things: jobs, jobs, and jobs."

It makes sense, then, for the business owner to begin an association with the local member of Congress by stressing the contribution his or her company makes to the district's economy. No mechanism is better suited to this task than a "site visit"—a tour of the company's offices or manufacturing facilities. These visits offer an opportunity to educate the legislator about the business, how it is affected by federal programs, and the number of people who depend upon it for their livelihoods. Equally important, everybody gets to know everybody during such a visit. By spending time with the owner and employees in their place of business, the legislator is more apt to remember and, hopefully, be responsive to their concerns when issues affecting the business arise in Congress.

Of course nothing is ever certain, especially in legislative politics. Not even the most informative and cordial visit can assure a positive lobbying result. Members are subject to many pressures, some from within their districts, some from external sources. In spite of the small business owner's best efforts to establish an early relationship with the local member, he or she may find support lacking when needed. Members are skilled politicians and are extremely adept at making people, especially constituents, feel as though each one is the center of the political universe. It is no wonder that many businesspeople, small and big, feel they have been misled when, after an ostensibly successful visit or meeting, the member does little or nothing to further their interests in Washington.

Members also are skilled at giving the impression that they have more influence among decision makers than they really do (the "As I was saying to the president last week" syndrome). It is fascinating how much "closer" to national leaders many members are when they are in their districts than when they are in Washington.

The reality is that some legislators are better at what they do than others. Some are well-respected leaders, others are followers, and, worse yet, still others are considered incompetent by their peers. Some members will take chances; others will consistently cave in to the strongest political interests.

What all of this means is that, as in the case of campaign contributions, the business owner must make a realistic assessment about how much benefit the local member is likely to produce. False expectations based on an overestimate of the member's ability or willingness to perform can throw lobbying efforts off track before they even begin. The opening wedge, the entrée that had been counted on to get into the right offices and to see the right people, may simply not exist. The owner is forced back to square one and valuable time, the irreplaceable ingredient of all lobbying campaigns, is lost.

The member's staff. Regardless of how much (or how little) personal effort your local member of Congress is willing to give to your case, there is almost always value in working with the member's staff. Though district offices are not usually involved in legislative work, they can provide a valuable starting point for the inexperienced lobbyist. If nothing else they will act as a liaison between the lobbyist and the member's Washington office.

This link is important; it is in the Washington office that the member's legislative staff works. The administrative assistant and the legislative assistants deal with bills and amendments on a daily basis. They know the shape and form of legislative language and have a feel for what kinds of provisions members will take seriously and which they will dismiss immediately. They know which committees have jurisdiction over which issues, and they may know some of the committee staff who have expertise in the constituent's issue. In short, they are a window into the legislative scene. At the very least, they can provide good advice on how to avoid some of the obvious mistakes discussed earlier in this chapter.

Trade and business associations and coalitions. It is alleged that there is an association for every type, size, and category of occupation. This is probably not an exaggeration; but that in no way diminishes their value, especially for smaller organizations. From the U.S. Chamber of Commerce to the National Federation of Independent Businesses to individual industry associations, there is no shortage of organizations for the entrepreneur to join. Each has its own mission, and the business owner must decide which is right for his or her needs. Whatever the choice, it is probably wise to select at least one. Membership in the right association will provide the business owner with valuable information on federal regulatory and legislative action. It also will facilitate opportunities to protect your business interests by participating in industrywide lobbying campaigns.

Perhaps most important, it will give the small business person a friend in Washington, someone to consult for advice—and not have to pay an outrageous fee for the pleasure. Even if the matter is of no consequence to the broader association membership, a professional staff person will usually take the time to share some gratuitous wisdom, and maybe even initiate a contact or two. The association also may hold annual meetings or conventions that can bring members together with the legislators of greatest importance to the industry.

So the synergies and resources that derive from association membership can be especially helpful to small businesses. It enables them to expand their political reach well beyond the few members of Congress who might have an interest in serving their needs. It gives them a toehold for their lobbying efforts on Capitol Hill. Along with the local member's office, it is a place to begin.

Contract services. The small business owner-lobbyist must avoid trying to be the quintessential do-it-yourselfer. There can come a point at which conservation becomes costly. When lobbyists begin to lose credibility for themselves and their organizations, that point has been reached, maybe even surpassed. Prudent business owners will not let this occur; they will recognize their limits and the limits of those whose services they can have for free, that is, their local representative's office. At this point, if budgets permit, they must seek help from outside sources. In Washington, plenty of help is available, but the price can be steep.

Lobbying consultants, whether in the form of law firms, public affairs specialists, or free-standing contract lobbyists, never come cheap. Competent professionals charge hefty fees; $300 per hour is not unusual. This puts them beyond the financial reach of most small businesses.

Even though Mom and Pop cannot hope to surround themselves with a large corps of high-priced consultants, they can make careful decisions that balance their lobbying needs with their ability to pay—not much different from any other business decision. While circumstances vary, there is a useful rule of thumb for purchasing outside government relations services in limited quantity: Technical services will usually prove to be more cost-efficient than political services.

For instance, skilled attorneys or other experts who understand the legislative process can advise on what the immediate objective should be: Do you need an amendment to an existing law or bill? At what point in the text should the amendment be inserted? Would committee report language suffice?

Once this is decided, the experts can draft the language in appropriate form. This, then, becomes the "product." Without it, the lobbyist has nothing to sell; with it, he or she can begin to seek allies and formulate strategies directed specifically to the identified needs. There also is the benefit of conserving committee staff time in drafting a reasonable starting point. The professional touch will be noticed and appreciated.

Another area in which technical services can be purchased is in research and data collection. It is not likely that most small businesses will have the means to generate their own studies, but literature searches and other forms of information can be obtained for reasonable amounts of money. Congress likes—often requires—this sort of background material. Providing it at an appropriate time and in a useful form will enhance professional stature with legislators and staff and will help stave off opposition if it arises.

What these services have in common is that they can be delivered within a relatively predictable period of time; they are closed-ended. Political, or hands-on, lobbying services are very different. Consultants in these fields may provide wonderful insights and access to key players, but their services are open-ended, as legislative struggles can span the course of several congresses. Circumstances and participants will change, and periodic reminders and other forms of attention will be necessary on a continuing basis. This all requires time, and time translates into money for the client. For organizations on a limited government relations budget, the costs are usually more than is affordable.

Taking Inventory and Establishing Reasonable Goals

For all lobbyists—big or small, first-timers or veterans—it is important to take an accurate inventory of political stock: What legislative resources do you control? How much are you willing to spend in order to buy assets you do not have? How much of your own time are you willing to commit to the project? How appealing is the policy position you are advancing? Many lobby campaigns fail because people overestimate the value of their political stock and thus their ability to influence decisions. As a result, they set unrealistic goals.

Businesspeople, more than others, should understand that to be successful they must have a useful service or attractive product to sell; no business can long endure if what it offers is of inferior quality. It is the same for lobbyists; what they ask of members (the product) must make sense when measured by substantive and political standards. This means that the original request—the lobbyist's "going in" position—must be credible. It does not have to be a finished product, nor does it have to be acceptable to most members. It must, however, demonstrate that the petitioner understands, and has regard for, the substance of the issue at hand and is aware that there are political and ethical limits on what members can be expected to pursue. As federal budgets have become tighter and subject to more public scrutiny, the leeway for including self-serving provisions that unduly favor specific interests has become commensurately more narrow.

With this understood, a small business lobbyist may be able to carve out a niche in a larger legislative effort or in an existing program. If the position is credible—reasonable and not overreaching—a modest provision might prove easier to move forward than anticipated. The key is reasonableness, and reasonableness must be defined in the context of all other relevant interests: economic, competitive, environmental, consumer protection, and the purely political.

It is important to understand that the concept of lobbying for passage of a small, or niche, provision should not be equated with attempting to slip an amendment through. If one can demonstrate that a provision will harm no legitimate interests and, at the same time, create a more equitable circumstance for his or her business, the owner has defined a reasonable policy position more digestible to lawmakers.

It is not necessarily the case that smaller businesses have smaller legislative problems. What is the case, however, is that small businesses have less opportunity and fewer of the resources necessary to build the large coalitions required to carry most broad provisions. This places a premium on the ability to think small, to chart a course designed to minimize political resistance. The narrower the scope of the solution sought, the less likely it will be to offend other interests.

The specific vehicle (bill, amendment, report language) selected for achieving the objective also can have a bearing on how much opposition is attracted. Some matters do not need to be addressed by full-blown legislative language. Frequently, report language will prove especially suitable for small business lobbyists. Such language can put just enough spin on the provisions of a bill to assure an interpretation favorable to the petitioner. This may be all that is needed. Again, the strategy is not unique to small businesses, but the economy of legislative resources that flows from a minimalist approach can have special value to lobbyists with limited means.

Playing with the Big Guys

Lobbying does not come naturally to most businesspeople, whether corporate CEOs or entrepreneurs. They are used to being "somebody" within their communities. They chair the local hospital boards, serve on fund-raising committees, and preside at service club meetings. At their places of business they are the boss, and, to a greater or lesser extent, what they say goes. They are used to having some degree of control over their professional lives and to being important within their most proximate spheres of business activity—their own companies.

For such people, Capitol Hill can be a demoralizing and ego-shattering place. They find themselves sitting in dingy anterooms, one of several pleaders, waiting to see a congressional staff person not yet five years out of college. To compound matters, the priorities of interest to the lawmaker that day may be far removed from the bread-and-butter concerns of the entrepreneur.

Businesspeople have virtually no control over this environment; they do not fully understand its rules, and it affords them no special privileges. On contested issues, virtually everything they say is challenged by forces equal to or superior to the ones at their command. Worst of all, the process of legislating seems to go on forever. Instead of making things happen, they wait for answers that never come. Instead of being "somebody," they feel like "nobody."

The CEO of a large corporation has the option of never coming to Washington in the first place, or, once having come, not returning; there will always be an army of skilled lobbyists eager to represent his company's interests. The small business executive has less flexibility. If he or she does not sit in the waiting room, does not meet with the young staffer, no one will be there to argue the case. The choices, then, are not many and are not difficult to grasp: subdue the ego, learn the system, make the case.

Perhaps the biggest lobbying mistake most entrepreneurs make is that they do not even try. For them Congress and the Washington decision-making environment seem remote and unfathomable. They see little percentage in placing hard-won assets against a function that, in their minds, is the province of highly paid, well-connected political professionals, or that is seen as impervious to pressure from "real" people. It is difficult to fault such logic; certainly nothing in this chapter has argued that small business owners are an advantaged class when lobbying Congress. But neither are they so disadvantaged that they should concede policy issues without a contest.

Mom and Pop, working alone, may never qualify as a lobbying force on Capitol Hill; but if they are realistic about their objectives, seek the right help, and prepare well, they may be surprised by how seriously their message will be taken.

Chapter 8

GRASSROOTS LOBBYING

To paraphrase an old saying: "The best way to a legislator's vote is through his constituency." While members of Congress vote as they do for a variety of reasons—pressure from party leadership, logrolling and deal making with other members, the quest for higher office, and a genuine desire to make effective public policy—no factor is more determinative of their voting behavior than the expressed will of the people back home.

This makes sense. Issues of courage and political philosophy aside, legislators work very hard to win and retain their seats in Congress. Whether the motivation is public service, economic enhancement, or ego gratification, being a U.S. senator or member of the House of Representatives may be the most important thing in their lives. It is understandable, then, that they would not place their seats in jeopardy by neglecting the interests of those who determine whether they will continue in office or be forced to find another source of employment.

Sticking close to the electoral constituency is a basic strategic interest common to all legislators; as such, it is a prime factor for lobbyists to understand and, when necessary, convert to their own advantage. If the objective of lobbying is to convince the legislator that supporting a recommended position is in his or her best interest, and if the member associates "best interest" with votes on election day, it follows that enlisting key constituents in support of the client's cause can pay significant legislative dividends.

None of this is new—grassroots political power is, after all, inherent in the notion of republican democracy. The civil rights movement and organized labor have long understood this; each has an impressive history of organizing for political action at the grassroots level. Other groups—most notably consumers, environmentalists, and gun owners—also have been successful in going directly to "the people" as a means of influencing decisions in Congress and the state legislatures.

What is new is the power, intensity, frequency, and variety of grass-roots campaigns that have developed during the past decade. The "high tech" campaigns of the 1970s and early 1980s are the dinosaurs of today. And while the good old-fashioned "letter to your congressman" remains an important (maybe the most important) staple of the genre, it is now supplemented by faxes, E-mail, systems for 800-number telephone patch-es directly into congressional offices, and the Internet.

How does all of this affect lawmaking? What does it mean for leg-islative offices that receive the communications and for lobbyists who engineer them? Are "everyday citizens" being empowered, used, or both?

Just as there are basics for hands-on, or direct, lobbying, so too there are fundamental rules for grassroots communicating.

Five Rules for Grassroots Lobbying

The message must be real. Genuine spontaneity is not a require-ment for successful grassroots campaigns. Everyone in Congress knows when communications are being engineered by a centralized source. They may even know that a wealthy interest group has contracted with an out-side organization to design and implement the campaign. An attempt to hide this from members and their staffs would have about as much chance of succeeding as efforts to hide the proverbial elephant. What is worse, the ruse would make the lobby organization look deceitful and foolish—not desirable traits for people trying to influence sophisticated politicians.

While communications, regardless of form, need not be sponta-neous, they must reflect legitimate concerns and opinions. Congressional offices should have a sense that the writers and callers would have deliv-ered the same or a similar message on their own had they known the facts and had they been aware of how to contact their member of Congress. Letters discussing some arcane point of product liability law that are writ-ten by production workers in a chemical plant are not likely to ring true. At the same time, notes from senior citizens deploring increases in the cost of health care can, and do, convey a sense of genuine concern. Each set of communications may have been generated as part of a transparent grassroots campaign, but the latter has the benefit of high credibility and thus will be taken more seriously by congressional offices.

Communications should require some degree of effort on the part of communicators. This is a logical extension of the previous rule. The more effort a person puts into a communication with a member of Congress, the more impact that communication is likely to have when it reaches the Hill. Clearly, a member will impute a greater degree of awareness and concern if a constituent has taken the time to personally frame her own letter, as opposed to merely signing a preprinted postcard.

The message of concern works on a legislator at two levels. First, because the legislator may see added legitimacy in the issue, he or she may decide to take a more aggressive role in supporting, opposing, or modifying relevant legislation; thus, a useful ally would be recruited for the legislative cause. Second, the member has every reason to assume that a correlation exists between the amount of effort one is willing to put into a personal communication and how likely that person is to remember the legislator's response at election time. For the majority of constituents, their vote is the most powerful "chit" they have to play in attempting to influence policy making in Congress.

Grassroots, not astroturf. Without question, grassroots tools have become much more sophisticated over the past decade. And, while these tools may permit more people to be heard on more issues, they also have increased opportunities for deceiving congressional offices. The line between playing hardball—doing everything that is possible and proper for the client—and outright fraud can be thin. Occasionally grassroots campaign operators step over that line.

Lawmakers and their staffs are aware of the possibilities that exist for deceit. They know that grassroots campaigns can generate counterfeit cards and letters and use assumed names when making telephone calls. And they have become increasingly aggressive in defending themselves against these and other ploys. Many offices now spot-check communications by calling people whose names and addresses appear on letters or were given during the course of phone conversations. The first objective is to verify authenticity; the second is to gain an understanding of how much the constituent really knows and cares about the issue. One office reported, "It's amazing how many callers say things like 'I don't really know much about it. The boss just asked that we make the call. He even let us use his office phone.' " Such gratuitous information obviously undermines the credibility of the campaign.

Most legislators and senior staff have a good handle on the political "personality" of their district. From instinct or experience, or a combination of the two, they begin to sense when they are receiving bogus communications. So grassroots campaigners are best advised to resist temptations to pad their numbers with phony letters, cards, or calls. Misleading legislators about what is important to their constituents is no different, and in some ways may be worse, than misrepresenting the facts of a policy issue. It signifies lack of respect for the institution and for the legislator. If exposed, the lobby organization could suffer permanent and widespread damage to its reputation. The first "commandment" of lobbying, "Tell the truth," applies to the conduct of grassroots campaigns as much as it does to any other element in the lobbying process.

Another risk for grassroots lobbyists is in excessive use of new technology. Here, too, there can be a thin line between looking professional and up-to-date, and seeming slick. An example is video productions; for a short time these were all the rage in grassroots communications. They enabled lobby organizations to combine a visual presentation of their best arguments with a graphic display of constituent support for these positions. But, like so many things that gain great favor inside the Beltway, the vehicle became overused. What was clever became a gimmick. What was effective became annoying. Similarly, computer-generated postcard campaigns require increasing numbers of cards received to make any impact at all on a congressional office.

Grassroots appeal is based on a plausible (though often just barely) argument that an issue is important enough for a broad segment of voters to spontaneously, or with only limited encouragement, express their views to a member of Congress. At its core, grassroots is a populist expression. Big money and slick production are not part of this ethic; in fact, they are inconsistent with it.

Lobby organizations can use the most sophisticated tools available to locate and energize potential communicators, but the most effective communications programs are those that are kept simple. Letters and phone calls, while they may be the obvious product of an organized campaign, are still the most effective means of communicating with Congress on a mass basis. These should be the mainstays of most grassroots campaigns.

Control is important. Giving communicators latitude to construct their own messages does not mean that anything goes. Minimum standards of civility and consideration pertain even in the rough-and-tumble environment of legislative politics. In this sense, doing business with Congress is no different than doing business in any other setting: you are more likely to receive a full airing of your views if you are courteous and respectful of other people's needs and feelings.

Abrasive and threatening messages will scare no one and possibly anger everyone. It is fine to be firm and to let legislative offices know how deeply you care about an issue; it is not acceptable to suggest retribution if the legislator does not act in accord with your position. Organizers of grassroots campaigns should never take for granted that all people understand this. Their organizational efforts should include instructions that encourage, if not actually spell out, a basic standard of civil conduct they demand of their recruits.

It also is wise to guard against overheating the system. Once people learn how easy and inexpensive it is to contact their senators' and representatives' offices, they may decide that more is better. This can be especially true during call-in campaigns. Congressional offices are busy places; they are particularly frantic during hotly contested legislative battles that have spawned a number of grassroots communications. In these circumstances, the caller is more likely than usual to get a harried staffer on the other end of the telephone line. Here again, campaign organizers should instruct their recruits that being thoughtful is more than good manners, it is a wise political tactic. More plus points can be gained by keeping the call brief and to the point than by subjecting the staffer to a long-winded diatribe.

Even written communications can increase workloads and add to stress levels for overworked congressional offices. No matter what its form—regular letter, E-mail, fax, or telegram—each communication must be processed and answered. Add to these written contacts all of the oral communications an office receives, and the potential for oversaturation is very real. Under such circumstances legislators and their staffs often feel that they are living under siege with their options cut off. It is no wonder that they frequently resent, and want to lash out against, those who mastermind and finance these onslaughts.

Intelligent control mechanisms built into the campaign from its inception will give communicators the flexibility they need to be credible while at the same time protecting the client against potentially disastrous errors by the too well-intentioned.

Target the right legislators. Targeting, as in any campaign, is a critical component of grassroots success. It does little good to direct hundreds of calls to legislators who will have no or very little interest in, or say about, an issue. To do this is to waste resources, unduly burden congressional staffs, and portray the lobbyist and the client as unknowledgeable, inconsiderate, or both.

For the vast majority of grassroots campaigns the best strategy is to focus communications on those members who are working on, or soon will be working on, the targeted issue—particularly those members who have not yet decided what position they will take. So if a bill is nearing consideration in committee, that is where attention should be concentrated. Winning a point in committee can save money and conserve valuable political capital. Why lobby 535 representatives and senators if lobbying a few dozen will get the same, and maybe even a better, result?

Some members will never be persuaded by certain arguments. They are dead set against the client's position, and no amount of pressure will change their minds. Here again it makes no sense to keep these members on the target list. In fact, there are good reasons to avoid them. First, pressure on these legislators will become a source of irritation and will damage future relations with them. Only the most zealous single-issue interest group can be indifferent to this. Other groups must be sensitive to members' limitations; this will preserve the possibility of working with them in the future. Grassroots campaigns should focus on "gettable" members, and try to avoid lost causes.

Second, there is always the chance that someone will give false information to a legislative office or will be abusive. Nothing could better play into the hands of the opposition. They will be delighted to share these indiscretions with the media and other members of Congress. The more hotly contested an issue is, the greater the chance that someone will become overzealous or too emotional. This is when mistakes are most likely to occur; it also is when adversaries have the greatest incentive to prey on these mistakes. Careful targeting promotes political and economic efficiency by focusing resources on strategically placed swing members. It also helps to reduce political costs by narrowing the margins for error.

The Grassroots Components: Quality and Quantity

When we think of grassroots lobbying, we think of numbers: How many letters can be generated? How many postcards delivered? How many phone calls and visits made? Ideas may be the cerebral component of lobbying, but numbers, when they are available, are its sinew. Some campaigns rely on messages from well-regarded community leaders living and working within states and congressional districts; others emphasize sheer volume—the more cards and calls the better. Still other campaigns employ both high-quality and high-volume strategies. In fact, the best campaigns frequently make use of this combination.

Quality. Not all grassroots campaigns are designed to unleash a torrent of cards and calls to Capitol Hill. Some issues simply do not have the appeal necessary to stimulate a high-volume response. In other cases the sponsors of a campaign may make strategic or economic decisions to forego a mass effort—perhaps because they were involved in a major campaign within the last few months and do not feel they can "go to the well" again. In still other cases, a thoughtful presentation delivered by a highly regarded constituent may reasonably be considered the most effective way of gaining a legislator's attention. It is in these circumstances that a quality-based grassroots strategy may be the best path to follow.

In each state and congressional district there are opinion leaders. Some leaders play important roles in molding and reflecting general public opinion, some are more persuasive in labor and industry or in academe, and still others are forces among a variety of public-interest groups. To members of Congress, opinion leaders are important political players. "One person, one vote" may apply to the ballot box, but it does not apply to influence within the community or to relations with public officials. In these matters some people are clearly more equal than others. A phone call from the dean of the state university, a note from the plant manager for a major employer or the president of a union local, will mean more to a legislator than a call from Joe or Jane Average from Main Street.

Messages from opinion leaders often express broadly held views, and this is why legislators are eager, or at least willing, to cultivate relationships with these people. Good leaders know what people in their spheres of influence are saying and, more importantly, thinking. They can provide the lawmaker with insight into what a segment of the community understands about an issue, what needs to be better explained, what constituents favor, and what they worry about. Even after accounting for biases, information gleaned from opinion leaders can help a legislator understand where he or she stands with a portion of the electoral constituency. In the final analysis, then, this is very much an election day matter for the member of Congress.

But effective legislating is more than pressing yea and nay voting buttons in response to constituent demands; it also is the art of persuasion. No member, regardless of how powerful, can get much done on his or her say-so alone. Consistently effective legislators are able to combine an understanding of what they need for their constituencies with an equally astute grasp of what other members need to accomplish and what is essential for sound policy. In short, they are able to balance a variety of political interests with substantive requirements. This is where quality grassroots communications can play an important role.

Legislators need to hear about the potential effects of legislation from knowledgeable people within their constituencies. Certainly lawmakers are interested in the number of votes leaders may represent. If a company has hundreds of people on payroll, and if it can be assumed that these people support their boss's position, there is an obvious political imperative for listening to the company's argument, especially if it is presented by a local manager. Beyond this, however, a discussion with the manager offers an opportunity to learn the details of *how* and *why* a legislative provision might affect a plant (and the employment opportunities it provides) in the legislator's state or district. Trade association lobbyists may be able to discuss general themes, Washington counsel for large corporations can be more specific, but the best and most relevant information for a member will come from the person running the facility back home.

Armed with this information the lawmaker can weigh the views of other constituents and other members of Congress and, hopefully, craft a position that will come as close as possible to accommodating all legitimate interests. Without the information, the legislator is "flying blind" and has little opportunity to form rational compromises and effective coalitions.

Providing quality grassroots communications can be anybody's game; it does not require sophisticated systems for identifying messengers and communicating opinions. This is something the individual company or association can do for itself. All it takes is a little assertiveness, a good command of the issues, a reasonably thoughtful and articulate spokesperson, and some common sense. Congressional offices will always make time for responsible opinion leaders—it is in their interest to listen to them.

Quantity. What was political sci-fi ten or fifteen years ago is now routine, or very close to it. The ability to reach out to millions of people to learn what they are thinking and then spur them to action has created a whole new dynamic for lobbying and lawmaking in Washington. No longer are companies, trade associations, public-interest groups, and other organizations solely dependent upon their employees, managers, and memberships to supply grassroots muscle; whole new universes of potential allies now may be identified and enlisted for their causes.

The ability to reach beyond immediate stakeholders is what the grassroots revolution that began in the late 1980s is largely about. Technology is the tool, but it is not the revolution in the political sense. What matters in political terms is that more people can participate in the legislative process. More constituents are communicating with their senators and representatives on more issues than ever before.

In the vanguard of the revolution is an elite corps of outside contractors, or consultants. These specialists now are available to design and implement grassroots campaigns of any dimension, for virtually any type of client. Costs for their services can range from $20,000 for a modest in-house effort to several millions of dollars for a broad-based, public campaign.

It is this new industry that has taught clients, especially in the business community, that there is a nation of potential allies out there to be recruited and pressed into service. Contractors provide the expertise, the manpower, and a variety of mechanisms—including direct mail, telephone interviews, and group meetings—necessary to identify, contact, and educate people who are most inclined to support their clients' causes. Those who accept the argument are then recruited to become foot soldiers in the grassroots wars.

For the recruits there are any number of ways to make contact with congressional offices: "individual" letters can be preproduced (by the contractor) on "personalized" stationery and then mailed in preaddressed and prestamped envelopes; key-point outlines can be provided for communicators who want to compose their own fax or E-mail letters; 800-numbers can be used to patch callers directly through to a member's office. These require only a reasonable amount of effort to use, and they incur no expense for the sender or caller. Some campaigns use all of these tools; most focus on one or two of them.

Regardless of how potential communicators are identified—whether they are employees of a company sponsoring a grassroots campaign or are members of some newly defined but not yet organized interest group—computer technology has enabled consultants, associations, and companies to know precisely what political resources they have at their disposal. Interest groups can press a few buttons to learn which allies have how many supporters in any given state or congressional district. In most instances, an "action alert" can be transmitted to the network and communications generated within hours.

Equally sophisticated systems are used to keep callers and writers up-to-date on all relevant public affairs information. Newsletters, the well-established staple of most education programs, are supplemented by

E-mail letters and "fax-o-grams" to provide full and constant coverage of pertinent events. When the time comes to activate the network, communicators are well informed and usually more than willing to do their part for the cause, whatever that might be.

The result is that grassroots programs have been elevated from a secondary—frequently last ditch—status to a primary weapon in many lobby campaigns. Organizations now build grassroots plans into their campaign designs and integrate them with more conservative and more traditional forms of lobbying—direct argument and political action committee contributions. While not yet the rule, they are no longer the exception.

At their best, grassroots campaigns educate citizens and help to amplify their role in the legislative process. At their worst, they are vehicles for deceit orchestrated by purveyors of self-interest. In either case, they do not just happen. They are almost always the product of careful planning and energetic implementation.

Members of Congress are well aware of this. The reputations of those who sponsor and those who manage campaigns rest with the tone, content, and veracity of the communications that they generate. And with reputation rests the lobbyist's ability to continue as an effective player on Capitol Hill. Once again, to paraphrase an old saying: "In Washington, reputation is not everything. It is the only thing!"

Part II

Case Studies in Lobbying

Introduction

CASE STUDIES IN LOBBYING

I n the first part of this book Bruce C. Wolpe and Bertram J. Levine set forth the elements of lobbying Congress, explaining how the system works and listing the "do's" and "don'ts" that practitioners must observe to be effective. The case studies that follow, adapted from the *Congressional Quarterly Weekly Report*, are intended to show how these techniques have been applied—or misapplied—in recent heavy lobbying on major issues before Congress.

One of the fundamentals—"prepare materials"—did not go unheeded during the health-care reform debate. The task force headed by Hillary Rodham Clinton was inundated with information from a wide range of sources, each seeking to influence the final recommendations. Orchestrated grassroots efforts also were employed during the health-care debate. For example, House Ways and Means and Senate Finance committee members were targeted with a letter-writing campaign. The failure of the Clinton health-care reform plan reflected, in part, the notion that "it is much easier to stop something than to start something." A number of factors contributed to the demise of the proposal, including its tremendous scope, which made it vulnerable to the tactics of special interests that opposed a change. The issue also made for strange political bedfellows. For example, a business group, seemingly uncharacteristically, sided with proponents of a single-payer plan. The reason was that they shared the same goal: defeating the Clinton proposal. Health-related interest groups also substantially increased their contributions to congressional campaigns, particularly those of members who served on committees with jurisdiction over health policy.

Because they "understood the process," three environmental and consumer groups were able to seize the opportunity to stall action on the North American Free Trade Agreement (NAFTA) implementation legislation by filing a lawsuit. Resolution of the issue took months. Meanwhile, the Clinton White House pushed strongly for enactment. It had the disadvantage of not being able to rely on the normal Democratic support system in the House, because two members of the leadership were opposed to the agreement. As a result, members with constituencies with interests at stake were able to make demands on the administration in exchange for their support. The implementing legislation passed amid a flurry of old-fashioned political horse trading.

Lawmakers were spurred into action in 1994 in response to rising public clamor that something be done about crime. The result was an omnibus anticrime package, which included provisions sought by interests ranging from one end of the political spectrum to the other. Citizens' concerns about crime were enough, too, for members to oppose the politically potent National Rifle Association (NRA). The NRA could not beat back a ban on certain semiautomatic assault weapons.

The struggle over cable television reregulation brought out three powerful groups with deep pockets—the cable industry, broadcasters, and Hollywood. Significant sums were funneled into congressional campaigns. Among those receiving the most money were members of the House Energy and Commerce and Senate Commerce, Science and Transportation committees, which were responsible for telecommunications policy. In addition, the cable industry used television advertisements, direct mail, and telephone calls in its attempt to sway public opinion.

One particularly intense lobbying episode—for and against the Supreme Court nomination of Robert H. Bork—included the widespread use of "Dear Colleague" letters by senators trying to confirm or defeat the nomination. Preparation of materials on the nominee's views also figured prominently in the Bork lobbying, as did employment of lobbyists who knew the players in the Senate and on the Senate Judiciary Committee. In a vain effort to save the nomination, the Reagan White House brought in a veteran Senate specialist, Tom C. Korologos.

"Tell the truth" is the first of "the five commandments" for lobbyists and lobby groups. Two such groups, both claiming to speak for the elderly, were accused of not telling the truth to Congress on catastrophic health cost insurance. One group allegedly misled Medicare recipients to believe that all of them would have to pay an $800 surtax for the insurance. The other group, a supporter of the program, lost credibility when an outcry from its members helped to pressure Congress into repealing the law a year after enactment.

Also falling under the rubric "it is much easier to stop something than to start something" was the failed effort to increase federal grazing fees. Many, if not most, members acknowledged the unfairness underlying grazing fee policy: federal rangelands were leased at a fraction of what private landowners charged. However, western and Northern Plains states members had the votes to block action and used them.

Family and medical leave had the support of a majority of members of Congress; legislation on the subject cleared three times between 1990 and 1993. However, two of those efforts were doomed by presidential vetoes that could not be overridden. The fate of family leave changed only when the occupant of the White House changed—from George Bush to Bill Clinton. That is, leave proponents could not succeed until they had touched all the political bases pertinent to the outcome of the issue. In this case, the linchpin was the president.

Case Study 1

HEALTH-CARE REFORM

B ill Clinton assumed the presidency with ambitious plans to retool the nation's health-care system. Attempting to influence the administration's plan became a cottage industry for members of Congress and interest groups. For various reasons, including the persuasiveness of wide-ranging lobbying efforts, the president failed to see his top legislative priority enacted.

Background

On January 25, 1993, five days after his inauguration, President Clinton announced that his wife, Hillary Rodham Clinton, would oversee the newly formed Task Force on National Health-Care Reform. Others appointed to the task force included six cabinet members and a key player on the White House domestic policy staff, Ira Magaziner. In addition, the White House set up fifteen working groups on different health-care topics. Members included more than one hundred congressional staffers, health-care experts from federal agencies, and experts from across the country with both public and private sector backgrounds. The task force was to fashion a system that met two seemingly contradictory goals: expanding health-care coverage to the thirty-eight million Americans who were uninsured and reducing the rising rate of health-care spending. The money spent on health care reached $832 billion in 1992—one-seventh of the U.S. economy—and was projected to rise to $1.6 trillion by 2000.

Clinton's health-care bill was formally introduced November 20 (HR 3600, S 1757). It offered guaranteed coverage from birth to death for all Americans. Employers would pay 80 percent of their employees' health insurance costs; employees would pay the rest. To provide subsidies to small businesses and the poor, the plan called for cuts in Medicare, the federal health insurance program for the elderly, and Medicaid, the federal-state program for the poor. It also included a seventy-five-cents-a-pack increase in the cigarette tax and a tax on large employers that did not join health alliances.

To make this system work, the bill outlined a new framework for the purchase and regulation of health insurance and the delivery of health care. The federal government would determine a basic package of health benefits to be offered under all plans, set the standards of care, and reorganize the market. Once the system was in place, the government would be its watchdog and enforcer.

Consumers would be organized into large purchasing blocs, or health alliances, to bargain for lower prices from medical providers. Health-care providers would be organized into health plans—groups of doctors, hospitals, and other caregivers—who would offer the guaranteed package of benefits to consumers. The alliances would help members choose among plans by supplying them with consumer information. Consumers would pay insurance premiums to the alliance, which would funnel the money to the providers. To control costs, the plan provided for a cap on insurance premiums. Key to Clinton's proposal were checks and balances designed to protect consumers' rights and ensure that all players fulfilled their responsibilities.

In February 1994 the Congressional Budget Office (CBO) issued an analysis of the Clinton plan, spelling out its potential economic consequences for the nation and the federal Treasury. CBO estimated that the plan would increase the federal deficit by $74 billion between 1995 and 2000 and by $126 billion between 1995 and 2004, at which point its effect on the deficit would be less than $500 million. After that, the plan would help reduce the deficit.

Several alternative proposals were introduced in Congress. From liberal Democrats came a plan for a Canadian-style single-payer system, under which the government would replace private insurance companies, collecting premiums and paying health-care providers. The plan promised to cover everyone, control prices, impose massive new taxes, and sharply cut health-care profits. From the other end of the political spectrum came Republican plans, including one by Sen. Phil Gramm of Texas, to minimize government involvement in health care and instead encourage consumers to put aside savings for their own health-care expenses. The two leading alternatives emerging from the center were sponsored by Rep. Jim Cooper, D-Tenn., and Sen. John H. Chafee, R-R.I. Neither proposal included an employer mandate; both aimed to reorganize the health-care market, instead of controlling it through government regulation.

All indications were that the effort to restructure the health-care system was dead by late August 1994, when lawmakers took an abbreviated summer recess without either chamber having passed a health-care reform bill. House and Senate leaders maintained that they could complete work when they returned, but by then too little time remained and virtually no momentum was left. Democrats were divided over Clinton's approach, notably his proposals that employers pay for most of their workers' health costs and that the government be given a hands-on role in the health-care system. Republicans, for the most part, were united in opposition to the whole effort, which they regarded as relying too heavily on taxes and regulation. Although big business initially pushed for reform, many of its leaders became convinced that Clinton's proposal would mean new taxes and more detailed prescriptions from the federal government about what kind of health-care insurance they could provide. Small business groups worried that the costs would mean job losses.

Three basic reasons were evident for why the process went awry. First, Clinton's health-care proposal, which sought to remake the entire system, suffered from being too sweeping and too difficult to explain to the public and to lawmakers. The very size of the plan made it vulnerable to criticism by special interests. Second, the congressional committee process broke down, particularly in the House, with multiple committees given jurisdiction and no committee achieving a bipartisan consensus that could serve as a basis for floor action. Third, no visible effort was made by the Clinton administration and the Senate leadership to produce a bipartisan measure until the final weeks of the session, when it was too late. Democratic leaders, unwilling to break with Clinton's goal of providing affordable health coverage to all Americans, never made a meaningful compromise offer to Republicans. GOP leaders, for their part, had the luxury of being in the minority and, therefore, without any ultimate responsibility for the legislation. That freed them to criticize Clinton and the Democrats instead of attempting to craft visible alternatives.

Administration Efforts

President Clinton opened the health-care debate with a nationally televised speech before a joint session of Congress on September 22, 1993. For lawmakers the address culminated a week of activities carefully cultivated by the White House to create an atmosphere of bipartisanship and to guarantee media attention. For two days a majority of members—House and Senate, Democrat and Republican—came together for an unprecedented series of briefings from the president and first lady. While members listened to technical details, the White House put on a public relations blitz. The day before the speech Clinton brought 250 talk-show hosts to the White House to discuss the plan, and the Clintons hosted a lunch for selected journalists. The day after the speech the Clintons and members of the cabinet went on the road to sell the plan to the country.

Hillary Clinton testified the week of September 27 before five key congressional committees that would share jurisdiction over health-care reform legislation. Most members expressed unalloyed praise for the first lady's performance. She seemed as at home with complicated theories and contradictory statistics as she did talking about childhood immunizations or the dangers of cigarette smoke. Furthermore, her familiarity with members' views and personal histories reflected her assiduous effort to gain the trust of Congress.

The first lady garnered considerable media attention November 1 when she used the bully pulpit to speak out in a pointed attack on the Health Insurance Association of America (HIAA), a well-funded consortium of 270 insurers opposed to key aspects of the Clinton proposal. The HIAA had been running ads featuring a couple called Harry and Louise sitting at a kitchen table contemplating life under Clinton's system and expressing fear that the plan would limit doctor choice and health spending. "One of the great lies that is currently afoot in the country is that the president's plan will limit choice," Hillary Clinton said. "It is time for you and for every American to stand up and say to the insurance industry: 'Enough is enough.' " Her comments sparked a heated response from HIAA, which promptly unveiled a new commercial. The first lady and the president subsequently characterized the insurers as special interests that benefited from the status quo.

As time went on and while Congress considered health policy reform, key cabinet members continued to publicly campaign for the Clinton overhaul plan. For example, during the 1994 congressional spring recess, agency executives fanned across the country to discuss the administration's proposal. They appeared at nutrition centers, nursing homes, and business luncheons. Health and Human Services Secretary Donna E. Shalala alone visited fourteen congressional districts. Meanwhile, however, the president largely pulled back from the public debate.

Clinton on May 25, 1994, made a private speech to inspire House Democrats to fight special interests and Republicans who opposed his health reform plan. The president's visit to Capitol Hill included the House rally and a private strategy meeting with Democratic leaders and key committee chairmen from both chambers. At the strategy meeting Clinton obliquely underscored his willingness to compromise. Clinton did not discuss these specifics with rank-and-file House Democrats, who were treated instead to a rousing fighter speech. He took this tack in part to help members face an onslaught of lobbying at home by special interests opposed to his plan. Lobbying—especially by small businesses—had been particularly intense during the spring recess.

In mid-June 1994, with time running out, Clinton began talking with Democrats and Republicans on the Senate Finance Committee; his direct involvement in the negotiations marked a change in his tactics. Clinton's talks with the committee members came after months in which he had taken a hands-off approach to the congressional health-care debate. The meetings helped create a feeling of good will between the White House and moderate members of the committee. Under discussion was a possible compromise on how to pay for affordable coverage for all Americans, designed to give lawmakers a politically acceptable way to delay the Clinton proposal to require employers to pay most of their workers' health-care costs. Under a time-sensitive trigger, an employer mandate would not take effect unless market competition failed to achieve universal coverage. The presence of Treasury Secretary Lloyd Bentsen, former chairman of the Senate Finance Committee, as a key administration player on health policy was seen as a particularly potent symbol of Clinton's commitment to bipartisanship and his willingness to work toward a compromise.

In late July the president and Mrs. Clinton again took their message on the road. They embarked on a bus trip modeled after the splashy Clinton-Gore campaign caravan. Designated stops included Dallas, New Orleans, and Boston.

The Lobbying Flood

From the point of view of lobbyists, the administration's proposals to overhaul the health-care system created a demand unlike any other in recent memory. Because so much was at stake—financially, politically, and the kind of health care every American would receive—everyone from consumers to gastroenterologists to risk-management companies tried to get the attention of the White House and key members of Congress. "It's not just something that affects one subsidy or one regulation," said Frank Mankiewicz, who had served as a regional Peace Corps director under President John F. Kennedy and was a partner at Hill and Knowlton, a leading public relations firm. "With health care, we're dealing with the reform of a whole aspect of American life."

Interest groups adopted approaches that played to Clinton's political persona: a mix of deference to expert public policy analysts and a sensitivity to grassroots sentiments. For example, the Medical Rehabilitation Education Foundation hired Hill and Knowlton and sent out a press packet featuring an eighteen-page article with footnotes titled "Medical Rehabilitation and Public Policy." The article, written by a former analyst in the Office of Technology Assessment, the now-defunct scientific research arm of Congress, aimed to convince lawmakers that rehabilitation should be covered in the standard package of health benefits available to all consumers. The foundation was funded by the three hundred rehabilitation hospitals, hospital units, and professional organizations that provided rehabilitation services. If medical rehabilitation was not covered, rehabilitation employees might be out of work.

The National Association of Psychiatric Health Systems presented Clinton's task force with a "Comprehensive Mental Healthcare Reform Proposal." It suggested controlling costs by adopting a heath maintenance organization (HMO)-type arrangement for mental health care. Psychiatric hospitals would become the entry point to this new system, and networks of psychological service providers—psychiatrists, psychologists, substance abuse specialists, and social workers—would deliver care. This framework would allow the association's three hundred private psychiatric hospitals to flourish, and many independent psychiatrists and therapists would likely have to either join a network—a controversial way to practice psychology—or risk losing insurance coverage for their services.

Several of the nation's largest insurance companies—Prudential, Aetna, and Cigna—sought to influence the debate through their involvement in the Jackson Hole Group, made up of academics, business people, and physicians who had been meeting in Jackson Hole, Wyoming, to brainstorm on how to revise the health-care system. The group pioneered the concept of managed competition.

The other approach that steadily gained ground was grassroots pressure. Lobbying campaigns enlisted professional groups and consumers to lobby Congress and the administration on behalf of a client, which could be a company, a public-interest group, or a coalition. For example, members of the House Ways and Means Committee and the Senate Finance Committee received letters along the lines of the following: "I am very concerned about any proposal that would place government-imposed price controls on prescription medicine. Centralized price control schemes have not worked in the past and I see no reason why they would work now. Removing incentives … that result in new wonder drugs is not the way to go." These letters were part of a grassroots campaign run by the Pharmaceutical Manufacturers Association (PMA) to fight the administration's proposal to put price controls on drugs. The campaign was designed by the Sawyer Miller Group, a Washington lobbying firm, according to Jeffrey Warren, PMA vice president for communications. About thirty of the association's member companies sent letters to their employees describing the dire consequences that price controls would have on the industry and urging them—as well as retirees, stockholders, and vendors—to write to Congress. Shortly after letters went out, volunteer operators at company phone banks called to make sure they arrived.

Grassroots sentiments also were conveyed to the White House through polls. Consumers Union, which supported a health-care system in which the government was the main insurer, commissioned the Gallup organization to run a poll asking Americans whether, among other things, they wanted a choice of doctors. The poll found that 43 percent of Americans would pay more to have the privilege of choosing their own doctor; 91 percent said it was important to choose their own specialist. These questions were designed to underscore to the Clinton administration the lack of popular support for a system that pushed people into HMOs that severely limited choice of doctors. Citizen Action, another group that favored a Canadian plan, got one million people to convey their sentiments on postcards to Hillary Clinton.

Numerous other means were used to get messages to the White House. The broad-based Coalition to Preserve Health Benefits held a news conference to describe its opposition to one of the fundamental concepts of Clinton's plan: putting most consumers into large pools of insurance purchasers. The coalition represented hundreds of small and large employers, pension and health benefits administrators, and self-insured companies. Members of Physicians for a National Health Program wrote to medical journals arguing against Clinton's managed competition approach and in favor of a system in which the government would pay for everyone's care through taxes. They touted this single-payer approach to their patients and politicians. "Our doctors are very active talking to citizens groups, labor unions, church organizations, elderly organizations," said Robert Dreyfuss, spokesman for the group. "Our contact with members happens where it counts: back at home." The Christian Coalition sent out a list of pointed questions for people to ask at town meetings. The conservative Citizens for a Sound Economy ran a sixty-second TV ad in which a group of doctors warned that Clinton's plan would result in rationing, long lines, and an invasion of privacy. The National Federation of Independent Business (NFIB) dispatched its members to make personal visits while lawmakers were home.

Because of the complexity and broad reach of the health-care overhaul proposal, the coalitions that emerged often ran counter to the traditional liberal-conservative fault lines of previous employer mandate debates. The NFIB, for example, aligned itself temporarily with proponents of the single-payer government-financed system. Although the business group had no intention of backing the Canadian-style approach in the long run, it nevertheless expected to find allies in the camp who shared the single goal of defeating the administration plan. Similarly, the NFIB lobbied members of the Congressional Black Caucus, a group historically in favor of stricter labor laws, arguing that minority businesses faced great financial risk under the Clinton plan. But if the NFIB saw friends in unusual places, it also found foes close to home. The NFIB could not entirely rely on groups such as the U.S. Chamber of Commerce or large employers such as Ford Motor Company. "Today, businesses providing health-care coverage are subsidizing those who do not," said Ford's executive vice president for corporate affairs, Peter J. Pestillo. The numbers explained why Ford and many other large employers embraced the Clinton approach. According to Pestillo, the huge automaker spent about 20 percent of its payroll on health care for its workers and retirees. The Clinton plan would provide relief in two major areas: all corporate contributions would be capped at 7.9 percent of payroll, and the federal government would take over much of the responsibility for retiree health benefits. Ford's savings could reach $1 billion over ten years, Pestillo said.

The High Cost of Lobbying

The lobbying effort spurred by the health-care reform debate was unmatched in scope as well as cost. A survey by the Center for Public Integrity, released July 21, 1994, concluded that at least $100 million had been spent by interest groups. The report identified $25 million in health-related campaign contributions, 97 firms hired to lobby on the issue, and 181 congressional trips sponsored by health companies.

According to industry experts, hiring a public relations firm could cost from $5,000 to $30,000 a month. Running a quarter-page ad in the *Wall Street Journal* cost nearly $29,000 (with a 25 percent discount for nonprofit organizations). The HIAA spent $14 million to make its Harry and Louise commercials. Most of the nation saw little of the homespun pair. Instead, HIAA aimed its ads at policymakers in Washington, D.C., and key congressional leaders in a handful of states.

The overwhelming interest in health care from lawmakers had much to do with the power that accrued to committees that controlled such vast legislation. Besides having pride of authorship, the committees that worked on the legislation were in the spotlight. They got attention from the White House, the leadership, the media, and the hundreds of lobbyists. Members working on the legislation would see a boost in contributions to their reelection campaigns. "Money follows power," said Ed Rothschild, press and energy policy director of Citizen Action, who tracked campaign contributions by the health-care industry to members of Congress. "To the degree that members of Congress are going to have influence over the final health-care reform package, then the special interests are going to have an interest in giving to them," he said. According to the Center for Responsive Politics, a nonprofit, nonpartisan group that studied the role of money in politics, the health and insurance industries gave $10.6 million to congressional candidates in 1991 and the first half of 1992. They also contributed $6.8 million to the Democratic and Republican parties.

Despite the costs, groups with high stakes in health care spared no expense. For example, the Health Industry Manufacturers Association, which represented the three hundred firms that produced medical equipment, pursued "a several-tiered strategy," according to G. Thomas Long, vice president for payment and policy. Besides staff lobbyists, the association hired Stuart E. Eizenstat and his law firm to represent the group's concerns. It was hoped that Eizenstat, a prominent Democrat who served as a domestic policy adviser to President Jimmy Carter, would help the organization get its points across. The association also created a grassroots program using computers to put manufacturers in touch with their members of Congress.

On a slightly different track was HIAA, which represented commercial health insurers. In addition to using lobbyists, it enlisted former representative Bill Gradison, R-Ohio, to head the association. Gradison was widely viewed as one of the most thoughtful, well-informed, and influential players on health issues. HIAA also took out a full-page ad in the *New York Times* on behalf of the "Coalition for Health Insurance Choices." The ad offered to send readers a copy of the coalition's plan to overhaul the system. The Coalition for Health Insurance Choices was made up of independent insurers and the businesses that relied on them, as well as independent health insurance agents. These were the companies and individuals almost guaranteed to lose out if Clinton adopted a managed competition arrangement in which only a handful of insurance companies survived.

The Democratic National Committee

The Democratic National Committee (DNC) took a ground-up approach in its strategy to win congressional votes for Clinton's health reform plan. The DNC envisioned its effort working as follows: DNC members would talk in their communities about health care with friends, neighbors, classmates, shopkeepers, and so on. Those people, in turn, would do the same. Subsequently, this ever-growing circle would write letters and place calls to lawmakers. Then, either because they felt compelled to reflect the sentiments of their constituents or because the groundswell had provided them with the necessary political cover, members of Congress would vote for the administration's bill. The DNC strategy paralleled a traditional political campaign. This type of grassroots strategy had factored more and more prominently in recent elections and local referendums. Rarely, if ever, however, had an administration relied so heavily on average voters to sway Congress on a single piece of legislation.

The DNC also hired former Ohio governor Richard F. Celeste as its point man on health care, a decision widely praised by party members and health-care activists. "In terms of anyone whose last name is not Clinton, he is just about the best spokesperson on reform," said Arnold Bennett, a spokesman for Families USA, a nonprofit group that promoted health-care revisions similar to Clinton's. Furthermore, the media team that produced Clinton's campaign spots and landed him appearances on MTV signed on to produce the DNC-sponsored ads on health-care reform.

On the night that the president presented his health-care reform proposal in a televised speech before a joint session of Congress, the DNC helped organize more than five hundred house parties across the country.

113

In Jefferson City, Missouri, a group of supporters watched the speech in the governor's mansion. The evening was a giant party complete with a country-western theme and local news coverage. Other parties took place in hospitals and restaurants.

Each morning the DNC shipped out a memo, via fax machines, to its health-care coordinators, state party officers, and other allies. The briefing included status reports on the Clinton proposal, warnings of any rumored attacks, and tips on how to counteract criticism. "We've taken the daily briefings and extended them through our office to hundreds of other political activists," said Gary Corbin, chairman of the Michigan Democratic party. There also were bumper stickers, bright yellow buttons, and an 800-number.

DNC organizers did get a false start in their effort to form a bipartisan health-care team, separate from the political party. With about $100,000 in seed money from the DNC, the National Health Care Campaign opened its own office in Washington with twenty-seven people, who began searching for partners and money. The plan was ambitious. Organizers hoped to raise as much money for the health-care campaign as for a presidential race. A lobbyist involved in the early discussions remembered talk of raising between $25 million and $35 million; the *Washington Post* put the figure between $7 million and $37 million.

But interest groups were not eager to sign on, fearing that the campaign would always be viewed as an arm of the Democratic party. "When they started coming around to organizations, there were not a lot of us that gave them positive feedback," said Richard H. Wade, a spokesman for the American Hospital Association. "It would always be clear who the parents were—a couple of donkeys." Groups such as the AFL-CIO and the American Association of Retired Persons also rejected DNC entreaties. "We were listening to the DNC initially because they were talking bipartisan, but it never materialized," said Charles G. Huntington, Washington director for the American Academy of Family Physicians.

With lackluster response from potential partners, skepticism from health-care veterans on Capitol Hill, and some negative media coverage, the operation shut down and the campaign became a special project of the party. "The judgment was made that even if it was a bipartisan effort nobody would ever have believed it," said Kent Markus, DNC chief of staff. The revised DNC effort was considerably scaled down. Spending was set at $3 million in 1993 and an undetermined amount in 1994. About fifteen staff members at the DNC's Washington headquarters worked full time on health care, although the party said virtually all 150 employees contributed to the effort. A list of "National Health Care Campaign contacts" distributed by the DNC named people in all fifty states. But about twenty contacts also served as executive directors or chairs of their state party; some coordinators were responsible for more than one state, and others were simply volunteers with other full-time jobs. The DNC had twenty-six paid field organizers on the health-care campaign.

Case Study 2

NAFTA

President Bill Clinton placed his prestige and political bargaining clout on the line in 1993—his first year in office—by forcefully lobbying Congress to approve the North American Free Trade Agreement (NAFTA). Pleading, pushing, and bargaining his way, Clinton overcame strenuous objections from within his own party, forged a centrist coalition, and achieved a historic, bipartisan victory. As a result he was able to bolster his claim to be restoring direction to the nation's economic policy in a time of turmoil and uncertainty.

Background

President George Bush and the leaders of Canada and Mexico signed the trade pact in December 1992, leaving to the incoming Clinton administration the task of negotiating with Congress the details of legislation to approve and implement the agreement. NAFTA made some changes to the U.S.-Canada Free Trade Agreement, which was approved by Congress in 1988. It also extended the barrier-free trade principles embodied in that accord to the entire North American continent. Tariffs on goods shipped across the U.S.-Mexico border were to be eliminated—most on January 1, 1994, and the remainder over fifteen years. To qualify for duty-free export within the three-nation trade zone, goods were to be substantially made within one of the three countries. Restraints on U.S. investors operating in Mexico were to be eliminated, and Mexico was to adopt new rules granting broad protections to patents, copyrights, and other intellectual property. Never before had the United States been part of a trade agreement based on removing all economic walls that guarded the nation from a country as poor and as different as Mexico. Bringing Mexico into the alliance with the United States and Canada was projected to create a huge, tariff-free, $6.5 trillion market with 358 million consumers.

Although Clinton endorsed NAFTA during the 1992 presidential campaign, he said that the agreement lacked adequate provisions to protect the environment and clean up pollution in the region along the U.S.-Mexican border. Upon taking office, Clinton reopened negotiations on supplemental accords to improve protections for the environment and for workers. The supplemental agreements would not affect the basic NAFTA text agreed to by the Bush administration. The negotiations to strengthen the pact were intended, in part, to mollify Democrats in Congress, many of whom campaigned against NAFTA in 1992, arguing that it would cost jobs and induce companies to relocate to Mexico and take advantage of looser enforcement of environmental laws. The talks also were intended to head off multibillionaire businessman and 1992 independent presidential candidate Ross Perot, who fought hard against NAFTA.

Clinton on November 3 transmitted to Congress the NAFTA implementing bill, on which Congress would vote; a statement laying out the actions the administration would take on its own to put the agreement into effect; and several separate agreements on environmental, labor, and other subjects. The legislation (HR 3450, S 1627) had been the subject of mock markups in both the House and Senate for several weeks. Congress would consider NAFTA under so-called fast-track procedures, which prevented amendments and required a vote in both chambers within ninety days after the agreement was formally submitted for approval.

Court Action

In an effort to stall and possibly derail NAFTA, three environmental and consumer groups—the Sierra Club, Friends of the Earth, and Public Citizen—filed a lawsuit contending that the 1970 National Environmental Policy Act requiring environmental impact studies of major federal actions should apply to trade agreements. Siding with the plaintiffs, U.S. District Judge Charles R. Richey of Washington, D.C., ruled June 30 that a "reasonable risk" existed that NAFTA "may cause environmental injury" and that the administration therefore was obligated to conduct a comprehensive review of the environmental impact of NAFTA. The Clinton administration, like the Bush administration before it, had argued that the law did not apply to trade agreements. Completion of environmental impact studies often take years, because the law requires highly detailed analysis and gives outside groups the opportunity to challenge government findings.

In addition to citing grave pollution problems along the U.S.-Mexico border, Richey raised the question of whether NAFTA could flood the U.S. market with lower-priced agriculture commodities, spurring U.S. farmers and ranchers to increase production in ways that would damage the environment. Richey also acknowledged concerns that NAFTA would create "pollution havens" in Mexico, enticing U.S. companies to relocate. He rejected the administration's argument that requiring an environmental impact study would impede the president's power to conduct foreign policy. "The NAFTA is a completed document," Richey said. "The only remaining step to be taken regarding the NAFTA is a domestic one, specifically, the submission of the NAFTA for approval by the Congress."

Immediately following the ruling U.S. Trade Representative Mickey Kantor announced that the administration would seek a reversal on an expedited appeal. In a victory for the White House and a blow to environmental groups and others opposing NAFTA, a three-judge panel of the U.S. Court of Appeals for the District of Columbia Circuit unanimously ruled September 24 that the Clinton administration would not have to prepare an analysis of the environmental effects of the trade agreement. The appeals court did not rule on the specific issue of whether the failure to complete an environmental review of NAFTA violated the National Environmental Policy Act. Instead, the ruling dealt with whether the courts have authority to review the president's actions under the Administrative Procedure Act, which allowed relief through the courts to people who were harmed by the action of a federal agency, once the agency's action was deemed final. "The president is not obligated to submit any agreement to Congress, and until he does there is no final action," wrote Judge Abner Mikva, adding that "the president's actions are not 'agency action' and thus cannot be reviewed."

The federal appeals court action cleared the way for a decisive up-or-down vote in Congress on NAFTA.

Rift within the Democratic Party

NAFTA created a large rift within the Democratic party, with Clinton and other supporters of free trade with Mexico on one side, and the party's more protectionist wing, composed mostly of Rust Belt lawmakers, opposed to NAFTA on the other. Among those in Congress who spearheaded the fight against NAFTA were two members of the House Democratic leadership—Majority Leader Richard A. Gephardt, Mo., and Majority Whip David E. Bonior, Mich. Speaker Thomas S. Foley, D-Wash., aligned himself with the administration, albeit not enthusiastically. With the leadership and the party so split, Foley said that it would be impossible to employ the normally effective Democratic whip organization or to appeal to Democrats with the argument that they should vote for NAFTA out of loyalty.

Gephardt had pressured Clinton not to seek congressional approval of the NAFTA text negotiated by the Bush administration. In his view the agreement was flawed, because it did not contain adequate protections to enforce workers' rights in Mexico, such as collective bargaining and right-to-strike laws. Nor did it provide mechanisms to ensure that Mexico would keep wages rising with productivity, which was crucial, he believed, to prevent U.S. companies from moving to Mexico to take advantage of cheap labor. Gephardt, however, did not openly declare that he would vote against the accord until after the Clinton administration had negotiated the side agreements, which Gephardt said did not go far enough. Declaring that the trade pact would create downward pressure on U.S. wages and living standards, Gephardt said he had reached the decision to oppose NAFTA after determining that its passage would "ratify and even worsen the status quo." He said that meant enshrining a system in which Mexican wages were kept artificially low to attract U.S. companies, pollution problems along the border remained unaddressed, and U.S. workers who lost their jobs when companies moved across the border received little retraining assistance from the government.

Since the failure of his presidential campaign in 1988, Gephardt had struggled to define a trade position that was somewhere between the tough, retaliatory stance he took as a candidate and the free trade position of Republican presidents Ronald Reagan and George Bush. Gephardt had successfully refashioned himself as a beacon of the political middle ground within the Democratic party. His defection on NAFTA was important because he was one of the party's most respected voices on trade. NAFTA supporters contended that they had been anticipating Gephardt's opposition all along and that his opposition did not mean he intended to line up votes to defeat NAFTA in the House. Gephardt played down suggestions that his stature on trade issues and his leadership position would exert decisive influence on other members of Congress. "I bring to this one vote," he said.

Closer to organized labor than Gephardt, Bonior opposed NAFTA from the start. Bonior echoed the arguments that the AFL-CIO made against NAFTA: It was premature to consider a free trade agreement with a country where workers made a fraction of what their U.S. counterparts earned. "With or without the side agreement, NAFTA rolls out the red carpet for more multinationals to close their plants in the U.S. and open them up in Mexico instead, leaving hundreds of thousands of American workers without jobs," he said. Furthermore, Bonior maintained, NAFTA would do nothing to improve environmental conditions in Mexico.

Bonior said that he would lobby his colleagues as hard as possible and employ all the resources at his disposal as whip to defeat NAFTA. Among other assets, those included his leadership staff and a computer database with detailed information on all the House Democrats' positions on NAFTA. NAFTA supporters said that whatever advantages Bonior possessed by virtue of being the whip, they were far outweighed by his personal skills at vote gathering and the relationships he had formed over the years with members. Supporters of the agreement contended that Bonior was the natural leader of a bloc of pro-labor Democrats and, to a lesser extent, environmentally minded lawmakers who saw NAFTA as irreparably flawed and never had any intention of giving their support.

Regarding the split in the Democratic party, Bonior said, "Nobody likes this situation." But Clinton should realize, he said, "that there are large numbers of the president's own party" who opposed NAFTA because "it's a survival issue" in many communities that were hard hit during the 1980s.

White House Lobbying, Deal Making

The Clinton administration took an aggressive and multipronged approach to gaining approval for NAFTA from a deeply divided Congress. Its mission was to persuade members that the pact would strengthen the U.S. economy, not cost jobs and drive down wages. Like a retailer with a product that is difficult to unload, the administration faced intensifying pressure to cut deals with members of Congress, many of whom were withholding their support in hopes of wringing substantial concessions from the White House. Administration officials had to seriously consider every complaint and demand in an effort to win votes, because they did not have enough to pass NAFTA. The vote deficit was most critical in the House, where the opposition was large and well organized.

Instead of depending on the whip operation normally headed by Bonior, the administration worked with NAFTA supporters to establish an ad hoc arrangement that relied on House Ways and Means Committee Chairman Dan Rostenkowski, D-Ill.; Rep. Robert T. Matsui, D-Calif., head of the special House task force on NAFTA; and Bill Richardson, D-N.M., a deputy whip. The administration also had to depend on Republican backing to help get the pact through. To that end, Clinton named former representative Bill Frenzel, R-Minn., as special adviser on NAFTA. Furthermore, the selection of William Daley, a Chicago lawyer who had strong ties to organized labor, as chief lobbyist on NAFTA reflected the administration's determination not to alienate pro-labor Democrats, such as Gephardt, and perhaps even to win over some who remained on the fence.

When NAFTA opponent Ross Perot began to prepare an attack against the agreement in a series of television and radio appearances that coincided with the release of his anti-NAFTA book, *Save Your Job, Save Our Country,* Daley and U.S. Trade Representative Kantor released a seventy-four-page rebuttal of the Perot book. The White House also recruited retired Chrysler Corporation chairman Lee A. Iacocca, a supporter of the pact, to make advertisements intended to counter Perot. The administration hoped that Iacocca could help debunk Perot's contention that the pact would cost more than five million U.S. jobs and endanger the domestic auto industry. And Vice President Al Gore put in a good showing, according to commentators, in a debate against Perot on the nationally televised Cable News Network program *Larry King Live.*

Clinton, meanwhile, upped the stakes with various public statements. He warned, for example, that failure to approve NAFTA would damage his ability to press for further trade liberalization around the world, discrediting the United States as a beacon for free trade. Clinton was slated to attend a summit meeting in Seattle in November 1993 with Asian leaders, and the administration was continuing to press for a worldwide trade deal in Geneva. If Congress voted down NAFTA, "it would limit my ability to argue that the Asians should open their markets more," Clinton said. "More importantly, my ability to argue that the Asians and the Europeans should join with me and push hard to get a world trade agreement through ... will be more limited." Clinton also issued dire warnings about the consequences of rejecting free trade with Mexico: illegal immigration from Mexico would rise, he said, adding that Japan and Germany were poised to infiltrate the Mexican market if the United States declined. "I'm telling you, everything people worried about in the 1980s will get worse if this thing is voted down, and will get better if it's voted up," he said. Clinton went on to publicly attack organized labor in an interview on the NBC program *Meet the Press* for what he called "roughshod, muscle-bound" tactics in opposing NAFTA. He was referring to the AFL-CIO's tactic of warning Democrats that, if they voted for NAFTA, they would be denied campaign cash and other support from labor in the 1994 elections. In response, Thomas Donahue, secretary-treasurer of the AFL-CIO, said, "We are not threatening anybody." But, he added, "if you vote to ship jobs of our members out of this country, we're not going to support you anymore."

Behind the scenes the president was having face-to-face meetings with undecided members and making phone calls at all hours, while administration officials worked feverishly to win votes for the agreement by cutting deals on issues of specific concern to lawmakers. To attract support from those whose states—such as Louisiana—produced sugar, the administration extracted a commitment designed to prevent Mexico from exporting sugar to the United States in the indefinite future. U.S. producers were worried that Mexico would substitute corn sweeteners in domestic products and export their surplus sugar to the United States. To attract Florida lawmakers, the administration worked out a system under which the price of orange juice concentrate would be tracked on the New York Commodity Exchange, and if it fell below a certain level, tariffs could be reimposed on imports from Mexico. Similarly, the administration agreed to reinstate tariffs on Mexican vegetables, including tomatoes, in an expedited procedure designed specifically for perishable products in case of a flood of imports. Mexico also agreed to begin negotiations, soon after NAFTA took effect, on more quickly phasing out its remaining tariffs on such products as flat glass, wine, appliances, and bedding. U.S. producers of those products complained that the agreement retained Mexican tariffs on them for as long as ten years. Furthermore, the administration negotiated with Rep. Esteban E. Torres, D-Calif., who wanted loans and loan guarantees to be made available for public works projects in communities that lost jobs to Mexico. This provision was sought by members of the Congressional Hispanic Caucus who wavered on NAFTA. Many of their Hispanic constituents were industrial or farm workers who feared NAFTA would spur an outflow of working-class U.S. jobs to Mexico. Treasury Secretary Lloyd Bentsen subsequently proposed the creation of a North American Development Bank and a Border Environment Cooperation Commission to carry out environmental improvement and economic adjustment efforts spurred by NAFTA.

Members received other rewards for their support. After announcing that he would vote for NAFTA, Rep. Floyd H. Flake, D-N.Y., got a call from Clinton, who told him that a Small Business Administration pilot program would be located in his Queens district. NAFTA supporter Peter T. King, R-N.Y., was dismayed to discover the week before the scheduled House vote that the Army Corps of Engineers was blocking a dredging project at Jones Beach in his Long Island district. He later explained that he called the White House and said: "I asked for nothing for my vote. Now you're taking something away from me. You're making me look like a schmuck." The White House quickly responded with a letter informing him that the project would go forward. Also, when Tennessee Democrat Bart Gordon decided to switch from opposing to supporting NAFTA, the White House sent Gore to join him in a live news conference beamed back home to defend his change of heart.

Legislative Action

For more than thirty years presidents generally enjoyed broad support for lowering U.S. tariff barriers in return for comparable concessions from trading partners. But that equation did not work with NAFTA, especially when political alliances were scrambled in ways rarely seen. Perot joined with conservative Republican Pat Buchanan and liberal crusader Ralph Nader in opposing the agreement. Organized labor and some environmental groups, which rarely agree on anything, opposed it as well. Farmers in the Midwest were avidly for it, but growers in Florida, California, and North Dakota were against it. The complexities of the issues surrounding NAFTA were demonstrated by the fact that Clinton owed his victory more to opposition Republicans than members of his own party.

In the dramatic House showdown November 17, HR 3450 (H Rept 103-361, Parts I-III) passed 234-200. Democrats supplied only 102 votes for NAFTA, while 156 Democrats and one independent voted against it. Republicans voted 132-43 in favor. As a Democrat in conflict with labor, Clinton could have easily let the trade agreement die instead of pushing for congressional approval. But Clinton did not back down. When it became clear that labor and its supporters in Congress were not going to be swayed, he turned to Republicans to get the necessary votes. It was a bipartisan streak Clinton had not evinced since taking office. While most Republicans were philosophically inclined to support NAFTA all along, it was an open question until days before the House vote how many GOP members would do so.

House Republican leaders were in a quandary. Both Minority Leader Robert H. Michel, Ill., and Minority Whip Newt Gingrich, Ga., supported

NAFTA. But they were concerned that Clinton would rely too heavily on Republican votes to pass the agreement and would not push Democrats from marginal districts to vote "yea" and jeopardize their reelections. To signal the White House that Clinton would have to engage himself personally, Gingrich insisted that Republicans could supply only half the votes to pass NAFTA. Democrats would have to provide the rest. Slowly, however, Clinton convinced Republicans that he did not intend to play politics with the agreement. At Gingrich's request, Clinton even took the unusual step of sending a letter to Capitol Hill reiterating his pledge to defend NAFTA supporters—whether Republican or Democrat—from attack for voting for NAFTA. "I hope to discourage NAFTA opponents from using this issue against pro-NAFTA members, regardless of party, in the [1994] election," Clinton wrote. In the end, Gingrich supplied far more GOP votes than advertised. Clinton's assurance gave "members a little comfort level," Michel said.

Labor groups were bitterly disappointed in Clinton's decision to push NAFTA to a vote. Relations between the White House and the AFL-CIO, which endorsed Clinton during the 1992 presidential election campaign, became acrimonious as the vote neared, and Clinton denounced labor for threatening to defeat members who voted for the trade pact. When Clinton triumphed, it provoked an angry outpouring. "We won't forget what happened here," Teamsters President Ron Carey told the Associated Press. "We're the folks who went out there and worked for a president who talked repeatedly about jobs, and here what we've done is export jobs."

Clinton's ability to put together a centrist coalition, even at the expense of alienating major constituency groups within his own party, earned him plaudits from pro-NAFTA forces. Gingrich said the turning point in the effort to round up GOP votes came when Clinton denounced labor for its "muscle-bound" tactics. "It said to a lot of our guys that, if he's going to take that kind of risk in taking on labor unions, how can I turn my back on him?" he said.

The Senate November 20 passed HR 3450 on a 61-38 vote. The Senate companion measure, S 1627 (S Rept 103-189), had been reported November 18. The margin of victory in the Senate was larger than in the House partly because senators represent an entire state and were therefore less susceptible to the pressures from within smaller congressional districts that caused many House members to vote no. Most states would derive some benefit from free trade with Mexico; not every House district would. The pact had enjoyed consistently stronger support in the Senate than in the sharply divided House. And, although the comfortable Senate margin was expected, the vote reflected the same divisions that made NAFTA such a tough sell in the House—particularly strong opposition from organized labor. Clinton once again owed the victory more to opposition Republicans than to members of his own party. Thirty-four of forty-four GOP senators voted for the agreement, as did twenty-seven of the fifty-five Democrats casting ballots.

President Clinton signed HR 3450 (PL 103-182) into law December 8.

Case Study 3

CRIME PACKAGE

W ith intense public concern over crime prompting them into action, lawmakers in 1994 cleared a $30.2 billion legislative package (HR 3355—PL 103-322) aimed at reducing violence in the United States. Also encouraging action was an energetic and high-profile lobbying campaign by President Bill Clinton and his cabinet.

One of the most controversial provisions of HR 3355 was a ban on certain semiautomatic assault weapons. Gun control proponents had long enjoyed strong public support in opinion polls but uncertain political support in Congress because of the intense political pressure generated by gun rights advocates. Inclusion of the weapons provision reflected a chink in the armor of the National Rifle Association (NRA), one of the capital's most influential lobbying groups.

Background

Americans owned more than two hundred million guns, and congressional researchers estimated that more than four million handguns, shotguns, and rifles entered the domestic market each year. Gun ownership typically was the political given; control advocates were left to make the case for restrictions. The Second Amendment states: "A well-regulated Militia, being necessary to the security of a free State, the right of the people to keep and bear Arms, shall not be infringed." That right is legally ambiguous, and the courts upheld significant gun control restrictions as constitutional. In 1939, for example, the Supreme Court upheld the conviction of a man arrested for transporting an unregistered sawed-off shotgun—in violation of the 1934 National Firearms Act. The Court said possession of such a gun had no bearing on the preservation of a "well-regulated Militia." Nevertheless, gun rights advocates generally relied on the Second Amendment as the legal and moral foundation for preserving access to firearms. It took the gangster violence of the 1930s to prompt federal legislation to curb gun trafficking.

Congress passed its last major gun control legislation in 1968, prodded by urban riots and the assassinations of the Reverend Dr. Martin Luther King, Jr., and Sen. Robert F. Kennedy, D-N.Y. That law blocked the interstate sale or shipment of firearms and ammunition and required dealers to keep transaction records. The NRA and its political allies threw their energies into rolling back those regulations. They partially succeeded in 1986 with legislation to lift the ban on interstate rifle and shotgun sales. For their part, gun control advocates were occupied first with fighting to preserve the 1968 law, then with efforts to enact handgun restrictions. Many polls, including some dating to the late 1960s, suggested that they had the public on their side.

Many members of Congress, particularly those from southern states and rural areas, were sympathetic toward sportsmen's desire for guns and wary of laying federal restrictions on top of state laws. Channeling, and some would say funneling, such sentiment was the NRA. Some lobbying groups had money to spread around; others, an energized grassroots constituency. The NRA had both. During the 1992 election the rifle association distributed $1.7 million to congressional candidates and spent another $870,000 in independent expenditures for congressional races. But some lawmakers said that more intimidating still was the human clout the rifle association could muster against a wayward lawmaker. Members who voted against the lobby could return home to find their town meetings and phone lines dominated by irate gun rights advocates. As of 1994 the NRA had an estimated 3.4 million members.

1993 Action

Clinton unveiled an omnibus anticrime proposal in August 1993. It included money to help hire 100,000 new police officers, new federal death penalties, and an overhaul of the federal appeals process for death-row inmates. Clinton also endorsed a ban on assault weapons and supported the so-called Brady bill, which called for a waiting period and background checks for handgun purchases. Congress cleared the Brady bill, HR 1025 (PL 103-159), separately in 1993.

The House in 1993 was unable to galvanize support around one wide-ranging bill and instead passed a series of smaller bills: HR 3355, providing for 50,000 new police officers; HR 3350, mandating drug treatment in federal prisons; HR 3353, authorizing funds to help states fight youth gangs and drug trafficking; HR 3354, authorizing funds to state drug treatment programs for inmates; HR 3351, authorizing state grants to develop alternative sentencing for offenders who were age twenty-two or younger; HR 3098, banning minors from possessing handguns; HR 1133, encouraging states to toughen laws against domestic violence, providing grants to law enforcement to prosecute and prevent crimes such as rape, and making interstate stalking and domestic violence a federal crime; HR 324, requiring those convicted of a crime, such as sexual assault, against a minor to notify the police of their addresses for ten years after their release from prison or their parole; HR 3378, making it a federal crime for parents to kidnap their children and take them out of the United States; and HR 1237, establishing a national system for conducting background checks on people applying for jobs as child-care providers.

The Senate passed HR 3355 on November 19, after substituting the text of S 1607. The Senate version was a $22.3 billion bill that embraced police hiring, prison construction, a ban on specific assault weapons, programs to prevent and prosecute violence against women, and tough new sentencing measures, including requiring life imprisonment for a third felony—the "three strikes and you're out" provision—and mandating minimum sentences for gang violence and gun-related crime. It also created a novel payment scheme for the programs by dedicating anticipated savings from planned federal workforce reductions to a special Violent Crime Reduction Trust Fund.

The Senate on November 17 had adopted the Dianne Feinstein, D-Calif., amendment to ban the sale, manufacture, or possession of nineteen powerful assault weapons as well as yet-to-be-built "copy-cats" that had features such as a pistol grip to facilitate rapid fire from the hip. The 56-43 vote for the amendment came a week after a motion to table it had failed, 49-51. The ban, which was to sunset in ten years, also covered large-capacity ammunition clips. More than 650 models of semiautomatic weapons were exempted, and gun owners would be allowed to keep any guns they already legally owned. Gun control advocates in the Senate considered filibustering the entire bill over the weapons ban language. They dropped their plans, however, apparently in hopes of gutting or narrowing the provision in conference with the House, which had rejected an assault gun ban in 1991. Senate Judiciary Committee Chairman Joseph R. Biden, Jr., D-Del., a supporter of the ban, said it faced "an uphill fight." Sen. Dennis DeConcini, D-Ariz., also a supporter, said he would not be surprised if the conference committee killed the provision, given the strong influence of the NRA in the House. The NRA considered outright gun bans a greater threat than the Brady bill, according to NRA lobbyist Tom C. Korologos.

Over the winter recess lawmakers watched the crime issue climb in importance in public opinion polls and heard an earful from constituents about their fear of crime. Republicans and Democrats alike returned to Washington in 1994 determined to pass omnibus crime legislation.

1994 House Action

House Judiciary Committee Chairman Jack Brooks, D-Texas, created a new anticrime package (HR 4092) for House floor consideration by combining the various crime-related bills passed by the House in 1993 with thirteen pieces of legislation reported from House Judiciary in 1994. The thirteen bills were: HR 3968, providing grants to states to help build new prisons or expand existing ones; HR 4035, establishing guidelines for determining whether a defendant should receive the death penalty, applicable to defendants eighteen and older; HR 4018, overhauling the rules for death-row inmates who exhausted the state appeals process to make federal appeals contesting their sentences; HR 4017, permitting prisoners to use sentencing data to contest a death sentence as racially discriminatory; HR 665, making defrauding an insurance company a federal crime; HR 1120, strengthening federal penalties against people convicted of assaulting children sixteen and younger; HR 3993, strengthening laws against individuals who sexually abuse children; HR 4033, providing for ten prevention programs in a $6.9 billion package; HR 4030, permitting victims of crimes and sexual abuse to present information or make a statement at the defendant's sentencing; HR 3981, mandating life in prison for anyone convicted of a third violent felony; HR 3979, allowing judges to drop mandatory penalties for first-time, nonviolent drug offenders; HR 4032, establishing dozens of new federal crimes subject to the death penalty, including first-degree murder, kidnapping, taking hostages, drive-by shootings, and carjackings resulting in death; and HR 4031, allowing individuals thirteen and older to be tried as adults in federal court for crimes such as murder, assault, robbery, and rape.

Action on HR 4092 came amid a flurry of political activity on the issue. President Clinton and Attorney General Janet Reno had been stumping for crime legislation around the country, and their lobbying intensified the week of April 11. Clinton began the week with a campaign-style pep rally at the Justice Department, urging speedy congressional action. On April 14 he hosted mayors and law enforcement officials at a

White House rally to press the same point. Republican lawmakers and conservative anticrime activists held their own Capitol Hill news conference the same day to highlight their complaints about the bill and to urge stiffening amendments. Most House members needed little encouragement to get moving. During town meetings and district tours over the spring break, lawmakers heard from many constituents who were worried about crime.

The House passed the $28 billion HR 4092 on a 285-141 vote April 21. Unlike the Senate-passed HR 3355, the new House measure did not include an assault weapons ban or the crime trust fund. HR 4092 was generally more liberal than the Senate-passed HR 3355, being less punitive and more generous toward prevention programs. Conservatives attacked its approach, urging more prison construction. Some liberals, however, also disliked the measure, objecting to the new death penalty offenses and to rigid sentencing provisions.

Brooks opposed the weapons ban but agreed to take up the issue in separate legislation. The House Judiciary Committee on April 28 voted 20-15 in favor of an assault weapons ban (HR 4296). The vote came amid intense lobbying by groups for and against the ban, as well as by the Clinton administration. The president urged the House to support the legislation. "Assault weapons were not designed for sport," Clinton said at an April 25 White House event. "They were specifically designed for war and have no place on the streets of America." Attorney General Reno and Treasury Secretary Lloyd Bentsen made public appearances, and supporters showcased the views of people whose relatives had been killed by assault weapons and who supported a ban. Rep. F. James Sensenbrenner, Jr., R-Wis., a ban opponent, argued that "more people are killed by fists and feet than are being killed by assault rifles." He said assault weapons accounted for less than 1 percent of the nation's murders, compared with 5 percent for fists and feet. HR 4296 was formally reported (H Rept 103-489) on May 2.

As HR 4296 moved to the House floor, the lobbying campaigns surrounding the legislation reached a fever pitch. Clinton stepped up his calls for the ban, saying the issue was "a lay-down no-brainer." Clinton telephoned dozens of members on the issue, as did Reno and Bentsen. Bentsen also went to the Hill, holding last-minute meetings with undecideds in a room off the House floor. Administration calls reportedly had less influence on wavering Republicans—who may have been more susceptible to a May 3 letter endorsing the bill from former presidents Ronald

Reagan, Jimmy Carter, and Gerald R. Ford. (George Bush did not sign it.)

Handgun Control, the leading gun control lobby, worked to mobilize support for the ban in pivotal congressional districts. But most members said the pressure at home was fiercest from gun rights advocates, including voters who were confused about whether the ban would affect their guns. It also came in telephone campaigns and radio ads that lawmakers attributed to the NRA. Gun rights advocates said no difference existed between assault weapons and other semiautomatic guns. They opposed the ban as ineffectual and as the first step toward more sweeping prohibitions on gun ownership. But supporters said these guns had features that made them more efficient for killing humans, yet of little use for sportsmen. Federal records indicated that, while assault weapons accounted for a small percentage of the nation's guns, they showed up in a disproportionate number of crimes, lending some credence to claims that they were the preferred weapons of criminals.

In the final days of the House debate, lawmakers and lobbyists said the overall movement was toward supporters. On May 5 the House passed the bill by a close 216-214 vote. Like the Senate-passed measure, HR 4296 banned nineteen weapons. Members who supplied the swing votes for passage of the ban did so not because they thought it would do much to stop crime, but because doing even a little something suddenly seemed so important. Only two and one-half years earlier, the House defeated a similar bill by a seventy-vote margin. This time, the framework of the debate had changed, and a vote to ban assault weapons was seen as a vote to fight crime. "At a time when there is a very real and palpable fear of violent crime in this country, when law enforcement officials are outgunned by the offenders ... we must do something significant to protect our families," said Michael A. Andrews, D-Texas, who switched from his 1991 vote and supported the ban.

After the vote, Wayne R. LaPierre, Jr., NRA executive vice president, called the bill "make believe" crime control and warned of voter backlash. But Rep. Charles E. Schumer, D-N.Y., and other supporters held a jubilant news conference on the Capitol lawn. Schumer cast the victory as a slap at the NRA. "The special interests can be beaten," he said.

Brooks unsuccessfully fought to weaken the assault weapons ban in closed-door negotiations leading up to the formal conference on HR 3355. But he was able to score a small victory for gun rights advocates when he attached provisions limiting the Brady law: pawnshops were granted a total waiver allowing them to forgo background checks on customers trying to reclaim their own guns. Handgun Control, the lead lobby for the Brady bill, complained that gun control advocates should not have been forced to soften the Brady law to obtain an assault weapons ban approved by both chambers.

Conference Action

House and Senate negotiators agreed on a final version of HR 3355, which totaled $33 billion, on July 28. The measure included a ban on certain semiautomatic assault weapons but left out an explosive provision in the House bill, known as the Racial Justice Act, that would let defendants use sentencing statistics to challenge a death penalty as racially discriminatory. President Clinton and Democratic leaders hailed the result as a promising blend of crime-fighting strategies and a likely political breakthrough after years of partisan gridlock on the issue. "After nearly six years, congressional leaders and people in both parties have agreed on what will be the toughest, largest, and smartest federal attack on crime in the history of the United States," Clinton said at a Justice Department rally for the bill held minutes after the conference finished. Republicans did not share the enthusiasm. They attacked Democrats for weighing down the bill with billions of dollars for social programs that they said had little to do with crime fighting.

House Speaker Thomas S. Foley, D-Wash., put off a vote on the conference report on HR 3355 after acknowledging that Democrats did not have the votes needed to bring it to the floor. Democrats who opposed the assault weapons ban vowed to oppose the rule governing debate on the measure, as did some African-American members who objected to its death penalty provisions. Clinton on August 5 lashed out at the NRA and others for seeking to keep the bill from ever reaching a vote in the House. "Do not let us pull another Washington, D.C., game here and let this crime bill go down on some procedural hide-and-seek," he said. "If we're going to have a shootout, let's do it at high noon, broad daylight."

A brigade of lobbyists worked furiously to make their case to lawmakers. The NRA labeled the assault weapons ban an unconstitutional attack on gun rights and a useless tool in the war on crime. "We cannot accept a bill which will have its biggest impact on the rights of law-abiding firearms owners," Tanya Metaska, one of the group's lead lobbyists, wrote in a letter urging member to oppose the rule and the bill itself. NAACP Executive Director Benjamin Chavis urged the same votes for different reasons; his organization objected to expanding the federal death penalty without measures to counter perceived racial bias in sentencing. The administration countered with fact sheets detailing how much crime-fighting money each state could expect to receive under the legislation, as well as the array of law enforcement and civic groups backing the bill. Clinton and Reno also called lawmakers, urging support.

The conference report on HR 3355 (H Rept 103-694) was filed in the House on August 10. In a stunning move the next day, the House rejected, 210-255, the rule (H Res 517) providing for floor consideration of the bill. It was an act of protest by Republicans and fifty-eight Democrats, who opposed the assault weapons ban or the death penalty provisions. Before the vote, White House Chief of Staff Leon E. Panetta and other administration officials arrived on the Hill to lobby undecided lawmakers. The Democratic whips set up a command post in a room off the chamber with an open telephone line for Clinton to speak to wavering lawmakers.

On August 12 Schumer and Handgun Control held a press conference vowing to resist attempts to drop the assault weapons ban. They were counting on a public outcry against the rule vote to save both the gun ban and the crime bill. Police organizations and the U.S. Conference of Mayors were among the biggest supporters of the bill and immediately launched rescue missions as well. To promote the Democratic crime proposal being held hostage in the House, Clinton took his message straight to the people, seeking strength in Congress with appeals outside its marble halls. It was a model perfected by the most popular recent president, Ronald Reagan. On the evening of August 12, at a rally at the National Association of Police Organizations meeting in Minneapolis, Clinton stood surrounded by uniformed officers and American flags as he blamed special interests for the House vote defeating the rule for floor consideration of HR 3355, as he attacked Republicans for playing politics with Americans' safety, and as he tapped widespread public support for a ban on assault weapons. The evening news pictures were vintage Reagan. Within a week, a *USA Today* poll showed that confidence in Clinton's handling of crime had bounced up to 42 percent from 29 percent just a month earlier.

Conferees subsequently shaped a $30.2 billion bill that was fundamentally similar to the one that was blocked in the House. The modifications centered on provisions regarding prevention programs, sex offenders, and the sentencing safety valve. But Clinton stood firm on keeping the assault weapons ban, and only minor changes were made in the related provisions. The House adopted the second conference report

(H Rept 103-711) 235-195 on August 21. Senate Republicans skirmished the week of August 22 to amend HR 3355 further, purportedly to cut spending and add tougher sentencing provisions. However, many Democrats felt that the GOP, at the behest of the NRA, was trying to hold up the bill to remove the assault weapons ban. "The real reason that many senators are opposing this bill can be summarized in three letters: NRA," said Tom Harkin, D-Iowa. The Senate, on a 61-38 vote August 25, subsequently agreed to the conference report as approved by the House, clearing HR 3355.

Case Study 4

CABLE TV REREGULATION

C ongress in 1992 overrode a presidential veto to enact legislation (S 12—PL 102-385) intended to lower cable television rates and increase competition in the industry. The congressional victory marked the first major reregulation of an industry since the outset of the Reagan and Bush administrations in 1981. The legislation provoked intense lobbying by a number of interest groups, which also made generous campaign contributions to members of Congress. (See Campaign Contributions box, p. 138)

Background

The Cable Telecommunications Act (PL 98-549), enacted in 1984, eliminated the authority of state and local governments to regulate the rates that cable operators charged to subscribers as of December 29, 1986, with some exceptions. The act also capped the franchise fee a local government could charge a cable operator at 5 percent of the system's gross revenue.

Cable operators and their trade association, the National Cable Television Association (NCTA), argued that rate regulation, high franchise fees, and other restrictions imposed in the franchising process limited cable's ability to finance investments needed to reach more subscribers and to increase program offerings. However, a Federal Communications Commission (FCC) report issued in July 1990 contended that deregulation had contributed to a growth in cable service. Investment in new and expanded capability, spending on cable programming, and the percentage of households with cable service available all increased between 1984 and 1989. At the same time, rates for cable service increased faster than the rate of inflation.

Members of Congress, citing individual instances of rates doubling or tripling, charged that cable operators had engaged in monopolistic price gouging. As a result, pressure mounted for legislation to restore some government regulation of cable rates. In addition, some lawmakers wanted to deal with the concerns of broadcasters, wireless cable providers, and satellite dish makers that the increasingly integrated cable industry was choking off competitors by keeping cable programming from other multichannel services, shutting out other program suppliers, and disadvantaging broadcasters in their placement on cable systems.

In 1990 cable television reregulation legislation, promoted as consumer protection, was approved by the House but was blocked in the Senate by intense opposition from the cable industry and the Bush administration. Supporters learned that consumer groups alone could not win a battle against the cable industry. The appeal of the measure had to be broadened. The answer was to recruit the lobbying clout of the broadcast industry.

Though cable operators had to pay heavy capital costs to get a signal into a home, they got a triple revenue stream from advertising, subscriptions, and pay-per-view channels. Broadcasters made money only on advertising. Distressing to broadcasters was that cable operators retransmitted broadcasters' signals—which accounted for about three-quarters of what viewers watched on cable—at no cost, even though operators had to pay for other cable-only programs.

The cable industry saw the reregulation legislation as a thinly veiled attempt to rescue the failing and outdated over-the-air broadcast industry. "Broadcasters are trying to use [the legislation] as a device to put cable back in its box," said James P. Mooney, NCTA president. "Broadcasters have lost about thirty prime-time [market share percentage] points in the last ten years, much of it to cable, and they don't like it." Broadcasters could not agree more that their industry was taking a beating from cable. To networks and local affiliates the legislation could mean the difference between renewed prosperity and a future as second-string video distributors. Unless Congress made their business more lucrative, broadcasters threatened, viewers would be left with no choice but to pay for television.

Congress's inclination to help broadcasters was strong, deeply rooted in a communications policy that promised broadcasting to anyone who could afford a TV set. The 1927 Radio Act and the 1934 Communications Act gave radio, and later TV, broadcasters free rights to the radio spectrum in exchange for a duty to play a "public trustee" role. Because airwaves were available only to those who held a license, broadcasters agreed to act in the community interest. Cable's challenge was to persuade lawmakers that the explosion of new, diverse outlets for communications meant broadcasters no longer were exalted trustees of the public interest but just another group of video channels.

House and Senate Action

The Senate on January 31, 1992, passed S 12 (S Rept 102-92), 73-18, to allow government and the FCC to regulate rates for basic cable service in areas where cable operators lacked effective competition. Such competition would exist only if another multichannel provider, such as satellite or wireless cable, were available. The bill also would dissuade cable operators from shifting popular programs away from the regulated low-priced basic package. Perhaps most vexing to the cable industry were provisions aimed at curbing the consolidation of cable operators and programmers and those that would ban cable programmers affiliated with operators from unreasonably refusing to deal with competitors. The FCC would limit the number of subscribers that a cable company could reach nationwide, and programmers would be prevented from discriminating in the price and terms of their programs to impede competition. In addition, broadcasters would be allowed to negotiate with cable operators for the rights to retransmit their broadcast signal for a fee, at the risk of being dropped by cable operators reluctant to pay, or they could forfeit that option and simply force cable operators to carry their signal free of charge.

As Senate deliberations began, cable lobbyists got off to a rocky start and never quite caught their stride. A memo revealing the cable industry's lobbying strategy, written by NCTA president Mooney, was leaked to the media. The memo indicated that the trade group would try to steer votes toward a substitute measure in an effort to defeat the main cable bill by drawing support away from it. The disclosure allowed the substitute to be attacked as a lobbying ploy. The Senate on January 31 rejected the alternative, 35-54. The substitute attempted to weaken the regulatory provisions of S 12, by eliminating language aimed at giving cable competitors better access to cable programs and by containing no limits on cable system ownership. A January 27 White House statement opposing the cable bill further weakened prospects for the substitute. It warned of a veto of the main cable bill but did not explicitly favor the substitute.

The House passed its version of the cable reregulation legislation (HR 4850—H Rept 102-628) on July 23, by a 340-73 vote. The House then

Campaign Contributions

Affected parties in the cable reregulation debate—the cable industry, broadcasters, and Hollywood—poured significant sums into the coffers of key 1992 congressional campaigns.

Political action committees (PACs) identified by Congressional Quarterly as representing cable interests gave $1,033,459 to congressional campaigns from January 1, 1991, through June 30, 1992, in the 1992 election cycle. In the same time period broadcasting concerns—primarily the National Association of Broadcasters, which controlled the broadcasting industry's only major PAC—gave $372,287. Hollywood groups contributed $342,550. The top recipients were members of panels with jurisdiction over telecommunications policy: the House Energy and Commerce and the Senate Commerce, Science and Transportation committees.

Hundreds of industry executives also gave directly to campaigns. For example, the chairman of MCA, Lew Wasserman, donated $126,730 to congressional candidates and party committees as of June 30, 1992. Executives of Walt Disney, the highest grossing studio in 1992, gave at least $251,350. And those with the nation's largest cable concern, Time Warner, and its affiliates in New Jersey, New York, and Ohio gave a minimum of $167,950. Those sums did not include donations from other studios and cable company executives or from spouses, friends, and employees who failed to list their place of business on contribution forms—nearly 15 percent of all contributions to campaign committees, according to the Center for Responsive Politics, a campaign finance watchdog group.

passed S 12, after substituting the language of HR 4850, by voice vote. The bill would require the FCC to set a nationwide rate for the basic offerings of the country's eleven thousand cable operators that did not face competition. The basic package would include all local and distant broadcast signals carried by a cable operator, as well as public and government channels. The average price for such basic cable service was around $17 a month. Sponsors said rates were on average 34 percent lower in the sixty-five communities where cable faced competition. If the FCC used those figures as guideposts, the bill could bring average basic rates down to around $11 a month.

The biggest fight on the bill was over competitors' access to cable programming. While some members argued that government should not interfere in the marketplace, satellite companies that packaged programming for dish users complained that the cable industry charged as much as 500 percent more than cable operators paid for the same programs and offered terms that effectively kept many cable programs out of dish owners' reach. Much of the cable industry was vertically integrated, meaning most of the nation's largest cable operators also owned the bulk of cable programming. W. J. "Billy" Tauzin, D-La., argued that just as the cable industry relied on free network broadcasts when it was in its infancy, cable's competitors now needed government help to purchase cable programs at fairer prices. Tauzin offered an amendment providing that programmers affiliated with the cable industry would be barred from discriminating in the price, terms, and conditions of programs they sold to cable's competitors. Programs could be sold at different prices under certain conditions, such as volume discounts. Detractors said the Tauzin amendment would set a government-mandated price for programming and cause program creators to lose control over their product. They also noted that cable's competitors already had access to programming.

The House adopted the Tauzin amendment July 23 with a surprisingly strong show of support—338-68. Tauzin had faced formidable opposition from House leaders, and he was saddled with the task of selling a complex provision. Furthermore, at one point, Tauzin had to caution Democratic Caucus Vice Chairman Vic Fazio, D-Calif., not to write a "Dear Colleague" letter opposing the amendment: the Senate sponsor of a similar provision was the party's vice presidential nominee, Al Gore, D-Tenn.

Conference Action

Upon completion of the House-Senate negotiations on S 12, Jack Valenti, president of the Motion Picture Association of America, vowed to join cable industry efforts to stop the legislation. Hollywood opposed a provision that would give broadcasters the right to charge cable operators for use of over-the-air signals. Broadcasters would not be required to give any of those new revenues to the film industry that created the programs. "The industry cannot allow its valuable copyrights to be so casually treated and will fight side by side with opponents of the bill," Valenti said.

Hollywood's help was welcomed by the cable industry, which tried to rebound from its legislative defeats by launching a massive last-minute advertising blitz. The effort included full-page newspaper ads and targeted mailings claiming that the regulation bill would boost, not lower, cable rates. The industry argued that any fees paid to broadcasters would have to be passed on to consumers in the form of cable price hikes. "There should be no doubt that this bill is anticonsumer," said NCTA president Mooney. "Its passage would create major new costs for cable companies, which will have to be paid for by cable subscribers."

Conferees accepted the House bill's process for requiring the FCC to set a price for basic cable television service. The commission would have to set its price based on several factors, including the price of basic cable service in the few areas that did have competing cable or satellite systems. That could result in basic cable fees dropping by as much as 30 percent. The Senate formula for determining whether cable operators faced competition—and thus were exempt from basic rate regulation—was cut, in favor of a tougher House provision that would allow the FCC to regulate more cable systems. However, the House definition of "basic" cable was narrowed. Instead of including long-distance broadcast superstations in the basic package, conferees included only local broadcast signals and government access channels.

The final bill would allow both subscribers and local cable franchising authorities to file complaints with the FCC alleging that rates for other nonbasic cable services were unreasonable (excluding premium movie channels or pay-per-view events). A House provision that would allow the FCC to grant refunds to overcharged customers was retained. And within ten years, as opposed to five in the House bill, all cable operators would have to upgrade their systems with addressable converter boxes that enabled subscribers to order a premium movie channel without being forced to subscribe to an entire higher-priced tier of programming. The cable industry had protested that a five-year conversion was not technically feasible.

The home-dish satellite and wireless cable industries would get a leg up in their efforts to gain cheaper access to cable programming. The conferees accepted House language, similar to a provision in the Senate bill, that would bar cable operators who owned a financial interest in programming from improperly influencing decisions regarding the price, terms, and conditions of program sales to noncable competitors.

Conferees sparred over whether to forestall the ongoing flight of sports programming from free television to the pay-per-view arena. Many professional and collegiate sporting events, including hockey, baseball, and basketball games, were increasingly available only on a pay-per-view basis. Rep. Edward J. Markey, D-Mass., said the public should not be forced to pay to watch pro sports on television, particularly because the teams enjoy public benefits such as exemption from antitrust laws and taxpayer-financed stadiums. A House provision that would have allowed local governments to set the price for pay-per-view championship professional sporting events was rejected, but negotiators agreed to allow the FCC to study the issue.

Conferees also agreed to allow the FCC to determine after nine months whether cable operators should be forced to carry home-shopping broadcast stations on their systems. In the meantime, cable operators would not be forced to carry the channels.

Senate negotiators, along with House Republican conferees, opposed a House provision that would have restricted the foreign ownership or control of any cable system in the United States on grounds that the language would hinder efforts to lower trade barriers worldwide. Markey argued that the cable industry had an increasingly vital hold on the nation's "telecommunications nervous system" and that the restrictions should be extended to cable for national security reasons. Senate negotiators won their bid to remove the ownership restrictions but accepted a related Markey "antitrafficking" provision that would require investors to wait three years after purchasing a cable system before selling the system.

The House adopted the conference report on S 12 (H Rept 102-862) on September 17, 280-128. Before the vote, Bush renewed his threat to veto the legislation. "My vision for the future of the communications industry is based on the principles of greater competition, entrepreneurship and less economic regulation," Bush said in a September 17 letter to Republican leaders. "This legislation fails each of these tests and is illustrative of the congressional mandates and excessive regulations that drag our economy down."

Hollywood's active opposition to the bill put Democrats in an uncomfortable position. The House Democratic leadership did not work to rally floor votes for the conference report, and Democratic sponsors stressed the bipartisan nature of the final bill. But the tough choice for Democrats was evident in the vote. Almost all of the lawmakers who did not cast a vote on the measure were Democrats. Among them were three California Democrats, including Barbara Boxer, who would have had to choose between consumer interests and Hollywood. Howard L. Berman, D-Calif., switched his "yea" vote on the bill's passage to oppose the conference report. "My motivation?" he asked. "I'm from Los Angeles."

Lawmakers on both sides of the aisle faced hometown pressures. Of the five members who switched their original July 23 "nay" vote on the bill to a "yea" on the conference report, four were rural Republicans whose constituents relied most heavily on cable service to improve their television reception. Lawmakers also showed allegiance to their committee interests. Nine lawmakers who served on the Judiciary Committee switched their votes to "nay" following the lead of Judiciary Chairman Jack Brooks, D-Texas, who defended Hollywood's copyright interests and opposed the bill. The power of media conglomerates based in California and the New York-New Jersey area, such as Walt Disney and Time-Warner, had at least as much influence on vote switchers as any fealty to Democrats, Bush, or hometown constituents. "Basically," said bill advocate Dennis E. Eckart, D-Ohio, most vote switching was "out of respect for the Judiciary Committee chairman and out of fear of Hollywood."

The lobbying war intensified in the days leading up to the House vote. Cable's ad campaign, which included two television spots aired by more than a dozen cable channels nationwide, was combined with a direct-mail effort that included fliers mailed in the monthly cable bills of thirty-five million subscribers. The direct-mail campaign also pushed the claim that cable rates would rise dramatically if the bill were to become law. Local cable operators also set up telephone conference calls, which cable officials monitored, for consumers to complain about the bill to lawmakers' aides, and formed what their opponents called "consumer front groups" to espouse their position.

A group called "Pennsylvania Consumers Opposed to S 12," along with a similar group in Georgia, sent mailings to voters urging them to sign telegrams to lawmakers. The Pennsylvania group's membership roster was made up of people affiliated with the cable industry, including an official from a regional sports channel owned by Tele-Communications, the Denver-based owner of the largest group of cable systems; a local university coach who appeared on the sports channel's talk shows; and the publisher of a local newspaper that owned part of the local cable system. The Georgia group had similar cable affiliations.

A September 3 memo by senior National Association of Broadcasters (NAB) board members urged the news departments of member stations across the country to "tell it like it is" on the cable issue and "generate the news stories." Tim Wirth, D-Colo., the cable industry's leading Senate Democratic advocate, cried foul. "The NAB wants broadcasters to manipulate the content of their news programs, which viewers presume is fair, objective and impartial, to influence legislation that advances their own economic interest," he said. "The public trust has been replaced instead by the desire to advance their own narrow economic interests."

The Senate September 22 adopted the conference report on S 12, on a 74-25 vote, completing congressional action. Judging from the vote, the cable industry got the least amount of bang for its lobbying buck. Opponents were able to persuade just four Republicans and one Democrat, Wyche Fowler, Jr., of Georgia, to vote "nay," switching their original January 31 vote on the bill's passage. Fowler was a friend of Ted Turner, president of Atlanta-based Turner Broadcasting Service, a cable conglomerate that owns the TBS superstation and CNN, TNT, and Headline News channels. And Atlanta-based Cox Cable Communications was one of the nation's largest cable system operators. Fowler also was one of the top recipients of campaign contributions from the cable industry and from Hollywood. Bill Bradley, D-N.J., who as a top recipient of film industry campaign contributions also was under pressure by Hollywood to vote "nay," instead supported the measure. Two other Democrats, Alan Cranston of California and David L. Boren of Oklahoma, were not present for the earlier vote and voted against the final bill.

Veto and Override

President George Bush, despite his repeated threats to veto legislation to reregulate the cable television industry, came under stiff pressure from Senate Republicans and some of his longtime allies in the Christian Right movement to reconsider that vow. Throughout the week of September 28 the White House conducted an intense lobbying campaign, with strong appeals made to GOP loyalty. But as of early evening October 2 it remained doubtful that Bush could sway enough votes his way. At afternoon meetings in the Capitol, Chief of Staff James A. Baker III had offered a compromise to nine Republican swing votes: If they switched to the president's side, Bush would sign an executive order requiring the FCC to write new rules achieving much of what the bill would do, including regulating basic cable rates and setting uniform customer services standards. The order also would go further toward allowing telephone companies into the video programming business, a move the Bush administration has long advocated as a way to enhance competition to cable.

Complicating Bush's task was an unexpected announcement from religious broadcasters, his longtime allies. They came out strongly in favor of the bill because of a key provision giving broadcasters the right to force cable operators to carry their signals or even to charge cable for signals. "Carriage of local Christian stations by cable is essential if many stations are to survive," said an October 1 letter from the National Religious Broadcasters to Bush. The group included Moral Majority founder Jerry Falwell, a Sunday morning TV preacher and conservative activist. The letter said, "We will support an override if it is necessary."

The president's lobbying drive appeared to be faltering amid reports on October 1 that White House officials were exploring ways to avert an embarrassing legislative defeat by having the president sign the bill. A White House official contacted Louise Gardner, the Republican mayor of Jefferson City, Missouri, to discuss the possibility of holding a weekend signing ceremony in her city. Missouri was the home state of Republican John C. Danforth, the sponsor of S 12. Jefferson City was confronted with some of the most highly publicized cable troubles, including stiff rate increases and service complaints. Christopher S. Bond, Missouri's other Republican senator, who faced a tough reelection race, also voted for the cable measure. Missouri was considered crucial to a Bush 1992 reelection victory. Administration officials ultimately issued a statement saying the veto threat was still in effect.

Bush vetoed S 12 on October 3, saying the burdens of new regulation would cause cable television rates to rise, not fall. Bush, Baker, and Senate Minority Leader Bob Dole of Kansas worked hard to persuade enough senators to abandon their support for the legislation. When it became apparent that the votes could not be mustered, senators who promised to switch were released from their commitments. As a result the Senate October 5 voted 74-25 to override, with no senators switching positions from when the Senate adopted the bill's conference report on September 22. Hours later the House followed suit, voting to override by 308-114. No House lawmakers switched their votes to support Bush, while fourteen switched from "nay" to support the bill.

For bill backers the override vindicated a risky strategy in which consumer groups courted the broadcasting industry to help peddle the bill. By granting broadcasters a provision allowing them to reap new revenue from cable operators, sponsors fell prey to accusations that the bill was nothing more than special interest legislation. Bush wasted little time in making that very point after the override succeeded. "It was a battle between the networks against cable, and the networks did a very good job of convincing people that their approach would keep costs down," Bush said on ABC-TV's *Good Morning America*. "We were overwhelmed by a very good sales job on the part of the networks." Ultimately, however, lawmakers sided with the argument that a vote for the cable bill was a vote to lower the rates of cable television viewers—and voters.

Case Study 5

BORK NOMINATION

T he massive and impassioned campaigns for and against the nomination of Robert H. Bork as associate justice of the Supreme Court in 1987 employed just about every known lobbying tactic and weapon. Strategists on both sides planned carefully, anticipating the opposition and protecting their flanks. Preparation was everything, and information about the nominee and his views became giant ammunition dumps for the targeted and blanket attacks that followed. After the Senate rejected the nomination on October 23, disagreement still existed about whether it did the right thing. But no one could say the Senate or its Judiciary Committee acted in ignorance. Little if anything pertinent about Bork was not brought out by the studies, the mailings, the hearings, and the testimony of Bork himself.

The preparations began immediately after July 1, when President Ronald Reagan nominated Bork to succeed Lewis F. Powell, Jr., who was retiring. They continued through the hearings and until the nomination was buried. In the weeks before the hearings, senators were bombarded with information touting Bork's strengths and weaknesses. Two groups announced national campaigns August 4, urging the Senate to give Bork a critical examination. And a consumer-oriented lawyers' organization, the Public Citizen Litigation Group, released a 123-page analysis of Bork's record showing, the group said, that as a judge on the U.S. Court of Appeals for the District of Columbia since 1982 Bork regularly voted in favor of business and against consumers, environmental groups, and workers.

The week of August 3 a pro-Bork group, Coalitions for America, began airing radio spots supporting the nominee, and a group of Republican House members—who had no formal role in the nomination process—made floor speeches backing Bork.

On August 4 People for the American Way, a liberal lobbying group founded by television producer Norman Lear, announced a national radio and newspaper campaign calling on the Senate to "take a very close look at Robert Bork." One of their newspaper ads said that a Court nominee was supposed to be independent and not a "White House 'team player.' " Then it suggested several things senators should consider, including whether Bork was fair-minded, whether he believed in equal justice, and whether he would protect free speech. In each category the ad criticized Bork. The radio spot said, "Justice may wear a blindfold. But the Senate shouldn't. An active Senate role in the confirmation process is the American way." At a news conference unveiling the campaign, John H. Buchanan, Jr., chairman of the organization, called Bork "a possible if not probable threat to the constitutional rights and liberties of American citizens."

The same day, the Judicial Selection Project, part of the Alliance for Justice, a Washington, D.C.-based civil rights group, kicked off a drive to organize college students against Bork. A booklet handed out to students during a briefing at the Capitol said the purpose of the campaign was "to effectively demonstrate to your senator the massive opposition of the American public to the Bork nomination."

On the other side, the conservative group Coalitions for America and the American Conservative Union began running radio ads in Washington, D.C., supporting Bork. The group ran similar newspaper ads in Washington, New York, Los Angeles, and Chicago. The radio ad said that the Senate's job was "to determine whether Judge Bork is suited by his legal scholarship and experience" to be on the Court. "Judge Bork believes that judges should not overturn laws passed by our elected officials merely because they personally disagree with them," the ad said.

Bork Record

The Public Citizen Litigation Group, a component of consumer activist Ralph Nader's Public Citizen, prepared a report that reviewed the 400 cases Bork had participated in as a federal appeals court judge and his 144 judicial opinions. The lawyers focused on fifty-six "split decisions," which occurred mostly on controversial cases in which one or more judges filed a dissenting motion. William B. Schultz, who directed the study, said that Bork's positions "can be predicted with almost 100 percent certainty simply by identifying the parties to the lawsuit. Judge Bork's votes cannot be explained by the consistent application of judicial restraint or any other judicial philosophy." The study challenged the notion that Bork was a proponent of "judicial restraint," which the lawyers defined as "a judicial philosophy that in administrative law cases requires courts to defer to the executive branch." The study found that "Judge Bork generally adhered to this philosophy only in cases brought by individuals or organizations other than a business."

A Justice Department spokesman, Patrick S. Korten, quickly rejected the group's study. "What we have here is a very clever attempt to skew the statistics by some very careful selection of the cases they chose to study," Korten said. "They chose to look only at divided panels. In doing that, they virtually ignored 86 percent of the cases on which Bork sat." Dan Peterson, executive director of the Center for Judicial Studies, a conservative legal organization headquartered in Cumberland, Virginia, labeled the survey "distorted" because it focused on the split cases. Even in those cases, Peterson said, Bork voted with the majority about two-thirds of the time. Peterson said that when all of Bork's cases were considered, he voted with the majority 94 percent of the time.

But Paul Alan Levy, another litigation-group lawyer, defended the focus on the split cases. He said that the appeals court, unlike the Supreme Court, could not pick and choose which cases it wanted to hear. The bulk of its cases, he said, either were not controversial or dealt with well-settled law. (Bork resigned from the appeals bench after his Supreme Court bid failed.) "You can always point out and say he was in the mainstream, he joined the majority. That's the nature of the job," Levy said. "But it's not a fair way to judge the way he is going to behave on a different court ... where they select their cases."

The stakes in the Bork fight were considerable. Both sides believed he could be a crucial vote in moving the Court to the right, because Powell was a key swing vote perceived to be more moderate than the conservative Bork. Reagan had put his prestige behind the appointment, calling it his top priority. For Bork's opponents—the traditionally liberal community of civil rights, civil liberties, labor, and religious organizations—the stakes were equally high. They wanted to preserve hard-fought judicial victories that expanded the privacy rights of citizens and the rights to employment, housing, schooling, and other benefits for women and minorities.

Opponents got a boost September 9 when it was disclosed that members of a special committee of the American Bar Association (ABA), which regularly reviewed nominees' credentials, dissented from a report giving Bork the highest possible rating—"well-qualified." Four ABA committee members were reported to have dissented and a fifth issued a "not opposing" rating. Orrin G. Hatch, R-Utah, a member of the Judiciary Committee who led the Bork supporters, charged at a news conference September 10 that the ABA was playing politics with the nomination. He contended that no substantive grounds existed for opposing Bork and that philosophical differences, which he said had no place in the nomination fight, were responsible for the dissenting votes.

Heavy-Duty Lobbying

That so much fuss would be made about Robert Bork at first seemed surprising. On the surface Bork looked like an ideal candidate: top law student, law professor, established legal theorist, former solicitor general, and judge. But Bork's views on topics from antitrust to free speech to privacy rights, and his often pungent manner of expressing them, prompted the most vigorous opposition to a judicial nomination in nearly two decades. A panoply of civil rights and civil liberties groups, including the American Civil Liberties Union, Common Cause, the AFL-CIO, and the Leadership Conference, an umbrella group of some 180 organizations, joined forces to keep him off the Court.

Bork supporters were led by Reagan and the White House staff, whose members, including Chief of Staff Howard H. Baker, Jr., and spokesman Marlin Fitzwater, regularly spoke out in his favor. On September 11 the Justice Department released its own study of the Bork record, criticizing the reports of groups that attacked the nominee. Conservative organizations, such as the Free Congress Foundation and Phyllis Schlafly's Eagle Forum, and conservative legal analysts, such as former Justice Department official Bruce Fein, worked on Bork's behalf. The nominee also received enthusiastic and well-organized support from antiabortion groups, which saw his presence on the Supreme Court as critical to reversing the landmark 1973 decision *Roe v. Wade*, making abortion legal nationwide. Bork had criticized the decision as unwise and unconstitutional, but he had not said specifically that he would vote to overrule it. Nor had he publicly stated his views on abortion.

Both sides geared up grassroots campaigns that peaked as the full Senate prepared to consider the nomination. For example, by September 11 North Carolina Democrat Terry Sanford, a key undecided senator, had received 1,080 letters on Bork—600 for, 480 opposed. According to the Senate postmaster, the Bork controversy drew more mail than any issue in recent memory.

Analyzing Bork

The central questions leading up to the confirmation fight were, "Who is Robert Bork?" and "What will he do on the Supreme Court?" Each side answered the questions differently. Supporters contended that Bork adhered to a close and careful reading of the Constitution and practiced judicial restraint. Opponents said he was a judicial activist who went out of his way to insert his philosophy into the decisions he wrote. Such activism, they contended, was apparent from the beginning, in his speeches and writings as a Yale Law School professor and private practitioner.

The nominee's statements and writings on abortion and privacy rights generated the most emotional and divisive debates on his fitness for the Court. Supporters argued that Bork's views on homosexual rights were consistent with Supreme Court positions in this area. But a study by the National Women's Law Center—the most pointed on these issues—charged that Bork's decisions and writings "demonstrate beyond question that he would allow governmental regulation of the most intimate aspects of sexual and family lives without recourse to the basic constitutional freedoms recognized by the Supreme Court for many decades."

Korologos's Attempted Rescue

As other Republican administrations had done when controversial appointments were in jeopardy, the White House turned to Tom C. Korologos to steer the Bork nomination through the Senate. By one estimate it was the twenty-fifth nomination battle in seven years for the veteran lobbyist, who was then fifty-four years old. But nominations were just a sideline of Korologos's career. His full-time job was as president of Timmons and Company, a top-flight corporate lobbying outfit. His reputation as a rescuer of endangered nominees had been enhanced by the fact that he nearly always prevailed. Until Bork, he suffered his only major nomination battle defeat when the Senate Judiciary Committee rejected the nomination of William Bradford Reynolds as associate attorney general in 1985. With Bork's name on the table, Korologos faced the toughest nomination challenge of his career—the most intensely fought Senate confirmation battle since President Richard Nixon was rebuffed on two Supreme Court nominations nearly two decades earlier.

Despite his extensive experience with such matters, Korologos said he still marveled at the hue and cry raised over Bork. "The ferocity of the opposition and the supporters is remarkable," Korologos said. "I've never seen anything quite like it." Korologos was widely credited with devising the administration's strategy of portraying Bork as a moderate, pragmatic man well within the mainstream of American jurisprudence. "He doesn't really have horns, and he's not a right-wing kook," he said. Korologos insisted the White House portrayal was nothing more than the actual Bork. "Everybody said we're painting him as a moderate," Korologos commented. "But that's Bork. We're explaining who he is, not painting him any particular way."

Before the Senate vote Korologos played down his role in helping to craft administration strategy on the nomination. But he assumed a major role in helping the nominee prepare for the Judiciary Committee proceedings. He coached Bork on how to handle himself and put him through practice sessions, peppering him with a wide variety of questions of the type that came up during the hearings. "I don't know anybody that's done it as he's done it," said Sen. Charles McC. Mathias, Jr., R-Md., who served on the Judiciary Committee and felt Korologos's hand on his shoulder more than a few times. "He's extremely helpful in a variety of situations."

But along with the accolades came questions about his actions. Some of his colleagues expressed concern that Korologos's habit of moving so nonchalantly back and forth between private and public sector lobbying could present conflicts of interest. And because he was not officially employed by the White House, he was not subject to laws that restricted corporate lobbying by members of the administration even after they left office.

Some lobbyists said that it was precisely the practice of moving back and forth between the private and public worlds that accounted for Korologos's success at the nominations game. His position outside the inner circles of the White House gave him added credibility when lobbying on the administration's behalf. "He can say the same thing as the administration, and it's more effective," said one well-placed Republican. "You know it's not just the party line."

Others argued that Korologos's careful attention to the Senate was his most important asset. "He works the Senate exclusively, day in and day out," said Thomas Hale Boggs, Jr., himself a powerful Washington lobbyist, but one more closely associated with the Democratic party. "Not that many people do that as intensely as he does."

Korologos had been involved in GOP politics in Washington since the early 1960s. He began his career as a journalist, working ten years as a reporter for the *Salt Lake Tribune* in his home state of Utah. But in 1961, following a two-year stint with a Salt Lake City advertising and public relations firm, he signed on as press secretary for conservative Republican senator Wallace F. Bennett of Utah (1951–1974). He became Bennett's administrative assistant in 1965 and held that job until 1971, when he became a special assistant to President Nixon. Korologos remained a lobbyist for the Nixon White House until the bitter end; after Nixon resigned in 1974, he assumed a similar position under Gerald R. Ford.

It was not until 1975 that Korologos left the public payroll, joining Timmons and Company, which had been founded by former Nixon and Ford aide William E. Timmons. His job involved lobbying Congress for some of the largest corporate concerns in the country, including Chrysler, Boeing, Northrop, and H. J. Heinz.

Korologos learned the ropes of nominations politics while he was still working for the government; in the early 1970s he helped to oversee administration efforts to win congressional approval of vice presidents Ford and Nelson A. Rockefeller.

Korologos noted that he was not paid for his efforts on behalf of the White House. But some lobbyists said that he derived from his relationship benefits that were far more valuable than any salary or fee. "It gives you an opportunity to renew contacts both within the administration and on the Hill, in a way where you're not hat in hand asking somebody for a favor," said a Republican consultant. "Doing something like that, people expect that at some point in the future their phone calls will be returned and that meetings will be easy to establish."

Others reacted more negatively, arguing that it was inappropriate for Korologos to approach senators for a corporate client one day and then on behalf of a White House nomination the next. "It's outrageous," said Joseph L. Rauh, a longtime Democratic lobbyist who helped to defeat Nixon Supreme Court nominees Clement F. Haynsworth, Jr., and G. Harrold Carswell. "The White House ought to have its own people doing the nominations," Rauh argued. "It's unethical for a guy who lobbies the White House on some things to be the lobbyist *for* the White House on judicial nominations."

"Extra care has to be taken that the conflict-of-interest question has been adequately resolved," added William Taylor, a civil rights lawyer who worked to defeat Bork's nomination. "We're dealing with a judicial nominee who may affect the interests of corporations or other interests that he [Korologos] may lobby for."

Korologos dismissed such concerns, saying he did not stand to gain any more access to the administration then he already had. "I've helped the White House during the other nominations, during the campaigns.... I don't need any more friends in the White House," he said.

The lobbyist's defenders scoffed at the notion that he was engaged in anything unethical. "That's hogwash," said M. B. Oglesby, Jr., former director of the Reagan administration's legislative affairs office. "Everybody has a Kitchen Cabinet.... There's nothing wrong with that.... Tom is just more visible because of the spotlight on the Bork nomination."

Mathias added, "He's perfectly open about it ... and I think perhaps that's his saving grace. He never makes any bones about who he's working for. As long as it's all on the record, nobody can doubt where his particular bias is."

Case Study 6

CATASTROPHIC-COSTS COVERAGE

When two buses from Charter House, a senior-citizens apartment building in Silver Spring, Maryland, rolled up to the Forest Glen Senior Center for Rep. Constance A. Morella's July 31, 1989, town hall meeting, staffers knew what was coming. They were right.

"This is a very bad law," one elderly constituent told the Maryland Republican. "It should be repealed."

"The Congress has shown its contempt for the senior citizens of this country," added another, drawing cheers from the hundred or so seniors in the room. "Congress has us at the very highest tax bracket in the country."

Said a third, "This is tantamount to farmers being asked to be the only ones to pay for farm subsidies."

The object of all the ire, not only at Morella's meeting but at hundreds like it across the country throughout the year, was the 1988 Medicare Catastrophic Coverage Act (PL 100-360), designed to shield thirty-three million elderly and disabled Americans from astronomical hospital and doctor bills. Cleared by overwhelming margins amid much fanfare in June 1988, the law represented the largest expansion of Medicare benefits since the program's inception in 1965. President Ronald Reagan told the audience at an elaborate White House signing ceremony that the measure would "remove a terrible threat from the lives of elderly and disabled Americans."

There was only one problem. As it turned out, Medicare beneficiaries did not believe they were at risk. And they did not want to pay for removal of a threat they did not perceive. Sen. Phil Gramm, R-Texas, compared the program's backers with the "Boy Scout who sees a little old lady standing on the corner who happens to be going the other way, but he decides he is taking her on across the street whether she wants to go or not."

The message from seniors was received—loud and clear. Only sixteen months after the law was enacted, it was repealed. The repeal bill (HR 3607—PL 101-234), signed by President George Bush on December 13, 1989, retained the benefits for the elderly provided under Medicaid, the joint federal-state program for the poor. What prompted the dizzying turnabout that led to repeal was not the new benefits—stop-loss coverage of hospital, doctor, and prescription-drug costs, and expansions of existing coverage of nursing home, home health, and hospice care. What seniors objected to was the program's financing. Under ground rules set by Reagan from the start, beneficiaries alone were expected to pay for the new benefits. That was not the case for the rest of Medicare, which was funded in part by a payroll tax on wage earners, nor for any other social program.

Background

Reagan's original 1987 plan, devised by Health and Human Services Secretary Otis R. Bowen, offered rather modest benefits financed by a small increase in the monthly premium that about 98 percent of the program's thirty-three million elderly and disabled beneficiaries already were paying for Medicare's optional Part B, which covered doctor bills and other outpatient expenses. But the benefits in the Bowen plan were seen as too meager by congressional Democrats, who had just regained control of the Senate. After six consecutive years of budget cuts in Medicare, "many members of Congress felt this was their only chance to put something back," said John Rother, director of public policy for the American Association of Retired Persons (AARP), which became the lead organization backing the bill. And put back they did, adding to the hospital and doctor bill coverage in the Bowen plan new benefits such as prescription-drug coverage, "respite" aid for those who care for homebound Medicare beneficiaries, and payments for mammograms to detect breast cancer. The problem was that, to pay for the added coverage, members would have to raise the monthly premium so high it would have been beyond the means of low- and moderate-income beneficiaries.

One early proposal instead would have required seniors to pay income tax on the insurance value of Medicare. But that was seen as far too radical by those fighting against taxation of fringe benefits in general, and it quickly fell by the wayside.

Sponsors then devised a "supplemental premium," an income surtax to be paid only by the estimated 40 percent of beneficiaries affluent enough to owe more than $150 in federal income tax. In 1989 the supplemental premium was capped at $800 per person, a sum about 5.6 percent of beneficiaries would have to pay. By 1993 the maximum surtax was to rise to $1,050. This was not means-testing for Medicare, sponsors told anyone who would listen. Means-testing, they argued, meant that those with the means did not get the benefits. In this case, everyone would get the benefits, but the affluent would pay more for them. The logic appealed to many members.

"What this is is an asset-protection program. It protects people from being wiped out," said Rep. Jim Moody, D-Wis., a member of the Ways and Means Subcommittee on Health. "To insist ... that everybody pays the same would be like saying everybody should pay the same premium for fire insurance, whether they are insuring a mansion or a shack. That would be unfair."

Sen. Alan K. Simpson, R-Wyo., in response to complaints that the financing represented a radical shift away from traditional financing of social insurance programs, said, "It is a social experiment. It's called pay for what you get, especially if you've got the wherewithal to do it."

But that was not how the elderly saw it. "In effect we've told the American people, 'Don't save for your own retirement needs—because if you do, your savings and pensions will be penalized when you reach sixty-five,' " said Rep. Bill Archer, Texas, ranking Republican on the Ways and Means Committee and a key advocate of repeal.

Seniors also complained that the program's benefits duplicated ones that many people already had through private sector Medigap policies. Especially enraged were about 3.3 million beneficiaries with policies fully paid for by their former employers.

"Seniors are not a group of greedy malcontents who want others to pay the costs of benefits targeted only for seniors," said Sen. Mitch McConnell, R-Ky. "What they resent is paying twice for the same benefits, or paying for benefits they don't want or need."

In hindsight backers pointed to several key miscalculations that led to the program's downfall. "We did too much all at once, and we decided we were going to charge them for it," said Sen. Dave Durenberger, Minn., ranking Republican on the Finance Committee's Medicare Subcommittee. "It is not going to work.... I guess that it a lesson I have learned, and a lot of our colleagues have learned."

One of the biggest problems was the very complexity of the law, particularly layered over an already confusing Medicare structure. "I don't think there are three hundred members of the House who could tell you extemporaneously what Medicare benefits are," said Rep. Pete Stark, D-Calif., chairman of the Ways and Means Subcommittee on Health and a leading architect of the law. "I don't think nine of ten seniors understand their Medicare benefits until they get sick."

AARP's Rother said, "The most prevalent misconception about the bill is that everyone was going to pay the $800. I can't tell you how many calls I've gotten from people who said, 'I live on my Social Security and a small pension, and I can't afford $800.' "

The Lobbying Campaign

Adding to the confusion was misinformation provided by groups that opposed some or all of the new law's provisions. The group most crit-icized by the law's backers was the National Committee to Preserve Social Security and Medicare, often called "the Roosevelt Group." It was headed by former representative James Roosevelt, D-Calif. (1955-1965), son of President Franklin D. Roosevelt. In a series of mailings, the group called on its more than five million members to urge Congress to repeal the "seniors-only surtax." Officials of the organization subsequently conceded that they may have misled members into believing that all beneficiaries would have to pay the $800 maximum.

But the Roosevelt group was hardly the only one stirring the discon-tent. A large number of grassroots organizations also sprang up, urging seniors to oppose the law and to send them money. One such group was United Seniors of America, based in San Diego, California, which urged seniors to join for a $15 membership fee to help underwrite the costs of advertising and mass mailings "to help spread the word to get this unfair law changed."

Existing groups climbed on the bandwagon as well. In a mailing that arrived at the home of Ways and Means Chairman Dan Rostenkowski, D-Ill., the Conservative Caucus asked for contributions to help it "finance a nationwide campaign against the Catastrophic Coverage Tax."

"Your contribution is a good investment," said the letter from Howard Phillips, the group's chairman. "It could help save millions of Americans (including you) from paying an extra $800 per year (and more) in taxes—year after year after year."

It was unclear whether the mailings spurred the grassroots reac-tion or vice versa, but what was clear was that they inflamed the situ-ation.

"The thing that does impress me is the power of the negative message," said AARP's Rother. "It has taken on the ability to overwhelm arguments in favor of something. In this context, the only line you needed was, 'Repeal the seniors-only surtax.' " In the end, said program backer Rep. Sander M. Levin, D-Mich., groups that wanted to keep the benefits but repeal the surtax suffered from their own success. "Opponents unleashed a wind they couldn't control," Levin said.

Front-Loaded Costs

Supporters of the program also were hindered by its very design. A key problem was that it was "front loaded," meaning that premiums were to be collected before the benefits were available, to build up financial reserves in the event costs exceeded initial estimates. That, said Rother, was "fiscally responsible," but it "spread the message that this was a bad deal…. How better do you want to demonstrate to people they're getting screwed" than to collect their money and not provide their benefits?

The phase-in of the benefits also complicated efforts to explain to beneficiaries how the new law would affect their Medigap policies. Because the law forbade private plans to duplicate Medicare coverage, over the long term private insurance companies would have been required either to lower their prices or to provide new coverage. But in 1989 the few benefits of the new law that took effect were far offset by increases in medical inflation and utilization. As a result the premiums for most Medigap plans rose, leading many seniors to complain of government rip-offs.

Duplication of Benefits

The duplication issue was more complicated than anyone appreciated. According to a 1989 Congressional Research Service study, roughly 6.9 million beneficiaries in 1987 had no coverage other than Medicare. For them, the law was a boon. The new benefits would likely have been helpful to another 11.7 million beneficiaries with private insurance, because the law barred duplicate coverage.

Those with duplication problems were the 3.3 million beneficiaries with insurance paid for completely by their employers and another 3.7 million beneficiaries with partially subsidized coverage. Those groups, which accounted for about 23 percent of beneficiaries, would be required to pay for benefits they already had.

While those paying the top supplemental premium would technically have been paying more for the new benefits than they might have paid in the private market, the overall Medicare package remained a bargain. In 1989, according to the Congressional Budget Office (CBO), even those paying the $800 maximum received a subsidy of $405 from general tax revenues for their Medicare coverage—after accounting for both premiums paid and payroll taxes paid in during working life. Those paying the "average" surtax, said CBO, would receive a subsidy from general revenues of $1,050.

But backers failed utterly to convince angry constituents that they were getting a good deal. They were hindered by the fact that among those forced to pay for coverage they already had were federal civilian and military retirees, who had highly sophisticated lobbying operations that were adept at finding and pulling legislative levers.

One critical loss for the program came in the spring of 1989, when organized labor abandoned its support of the law and endorsed legislation that would keep the benefits but pay for them by imposing a 33 percent income tax rate on the wealthiest taxpayers. AARP's Rother said the setback was not completely unexpected. "It's very hard to go back and sell it to people who have very generous pensions and would be paying at the high end of the scale, and who also have very generous benefits," he said.

Legislative Action

On April 20, 1989, Senate Finance Committee Chairman Lloyd Bentsen, D-Texas, reported that new estimates from both the Joint Committee on Taxation and CBO indicated that the surtax would raise nearly $5 billion more over the next five years than needed to pay for the new benefits and maintain the legally required contingency and reserve margins. If that were true, he said, the surtax could be reduced and the new law retained.

President Bush and Rostenkowski concurred that the law should be left alone for the time being. "It would be imprudent to tinker with Medicare catastrophic insurance literally in its first few months of life," said Bush in an April 24 letter to Rostenkowski. "We should not now reopen the legislation." In a statement, Rostenkowski added, "Revenue-estimating is hardly an exact science. I urge my colleagues to carefully consider the points raised by the president before pursuing legislation to amend the act."

Nevertheless, the House Ways and Means Committee in July approved a plan to cut the surtax and to permit Medicare beneficiaries to opt out of the catastrophic coverage if they also agreed to drop their Part B physician and outpatient coverage. The proposal also would cut the value of the prescription-drug benefit by increasing the annual deductible. The only major senior citizens' group to embrace the plan was AARP.

The August recess did nothing to increase support for the 1988 law or the Ways and Means compromise to salvage it. In one of the most vivid political images of the year, Rostenkowski, in his home district of Chicago, was photographed trapped in his car by a crowd of angry, shouting senior citizens. As the recess ended, repeal advocates stepped up their efforts. Congressional Republicans urged Bush to drop his support for the program. Bush did not, but administration officials backed away from their endorsement of the Ways and Means plan.

The biggest problem facing the repeal advocates was that eliminating the program meant adding several billion dollars to the federal deficit in 1989. That obstacle was removed October 4 when Richard G. Darden, director of the Office of Management and Budget, reported that new estimates indicated that the budget-reconciliation bill (HR 3299) would produce enough savings to absorb the effects of repeal without triggering the automatic cuts required by the Gramm-Rudman-Hollings antideficit law. The House, as a result, could scarcely wait to wash its hands of the issue, voting 360-66 on October 4 to repeal the law's new Medicare benefits and to leave only some expanded coverage under the Medicaid program for the poor. Action came on an amendment to HR 3299. Rep. Henry A. Waxman, D-Calif., said members voted for repeal because they felt the elderly "were ungrateful … so let them stew in their own juices."

Although the Senate Finance Committee fought to preserve the law it had written in 1988, committee members conceded that continuing constituent fury over the program indicated that alterations were required. Wrangling over catastrophic costs remained unresolved through the end of September 1989, until John McCain, R-Ariz., forced the leadership to the bargaining table by threatening to append his own overhaul proposal to the fiscal 1990 defense appropriations bill (HR 3072). On October 6 the Senate, by a 99-0 vote, passed a freestanding bill (S 1726) sponsored by McCain. It would eliminate the surtax as well as stop-loss coverage of doctor and prescription-drug bills but would preserve unlimited hospital coverage and several smaller Medicare benefits. Earlier that day, during debate over S 1726, the Senate rejected, 26-73, a repeal amendment, offered by William V. Roth, Jr., R-Del., and John C. Danforth, R-Mo.

How the two chambers would resolve their differences was unclear initially. The agreement governing Senate debate specified that the catastrophic-costs measure would not be attached to reconciliation, as it was in the House. In addition, because the Constitution prohibited revenue bills from originating in the Senate, S 1726 could not move to the House on its own. The House subsequently passed its repeal proposal by voice vote November 8 as a separate bill (HR 3607). Later the same day, the Senate by voice vote passed HR 3607, after substituting the text of S 1726.

The conference committee got off to a rocky start. House backers of the original law hoped to expand on McCain's package, while repeal advocates wanted to either pare it or make it optional. Not helping matters was that, by the time the choice came down to a modified McCain plan or repeal, administration officials indicated that Bush would sign either. That did not play well on Capitol Hill. "I guess they don't have a dog in this fight," said Rep. J. J. Pickle, D-Texas.

After a fifteen-hour meeting November 17, Bentsen seemed to have persuaded the Senate conferees to accept repeal. McCain, who was not part of the conference, vowed to filibuster the conference report. During a closed meeting November 19, a majority of Senate conferees agreed to sign the conference report stipulating repeal but with the understanding that it would be rejected on the floor and the McCain proposal would be reoffered. That same day, when annoyed House members discovered that the Senate had by unanimous consent agreed to "deem the conference report defeated," they adopted, 349-57, the conference report on HR 3607 (H Rept 101-378) calling for repeal. The House on November 21 voted 352-63 to insist on repeal. McCain, meanwhile, dropped plans to filibuster, not wishing to hold up Senate proceedings. Senators made one last-ditch attempt to save the McCain plan, sending the House a slightly modified version. It was rejected November 21 on a 55-346 vote. Subsequently, the Senate quietly conceded to the House position, clearing HR 3607.

Implications for the Future

The impact of the repeal was not very clear for the distant future, particularly for efforts to deal with the costs of long-term care for chronic ailments. Throughout 1989 many senior citizens said that what they really needed instead of catastrophic insurance was coverage for long-term care.

But House Speaker Thomas S. Foley, D-Wash., said that repeal of catastrophic costs "is not going to bode well for an even more expensive program, a more elaborate program, one even more daunting as to how it is to be financed or delivered." Waxman agreed: "This is a tremendous setback for the move to broaden benefits for the elderly. There's a very sour feeling among many congressmen."

Groups such as AARP lost credibility, too. "All of us are entitled to be skeptical when any group purporting to represent the elderly says, 'Our members are willing to pay for this if you give us that,' " said Bill Gradison, R-Ohio, a coauthor of the House's original catastrophic-costs plan. "We've been there."

But others said that while laws can be repealed, needs cannot be. Rep. Brian Donnelly, D-Mass., said, "The political demographics will force us to address" long-term care.

Most observers seemed to agree that the repealed 1988 law would mark the end of fragmented efforts to fix what ails the nation's health-care system. "The old strategy of piecemeal, incremental reform may be coming to an end," said Rother.

"We need to rethink the whole damn program," said Donnelly. "It's an idiotic and indefensible health-care system."

Case Study 7

GRAZING FEES

How much western ranchers should pay to graze their cattle and sheep on public rangelands was perhaps the one issue that most symbolized the controversy over the use of federal lands. The grazing dispute cut largely along regional lines and divided Democrats from western and Northern Plains states where ranching was a way of life. Even with Democrat Bill Clinton in the White House, congressional opposition to raising grazing fees and changing federal land management policies could not be overcome.

Background

Under orders issued by the Interior Department in the Reagan and Bush administrations, federal rangelands are leased at a fraction of what private forage acres cost. The current grazing fee rate, based on a formula established in 1985, is $1.86 per animal unit month—enough forage to feed one cow and calf, one horse, or five sheep for one month. This is about one-fifth the amount charged on private lands, although ranchers say the lower federal fee is justified because they have to pay for improvements such as fences and stock ponds that are normally provided by most commercial range operations. Approximately twenty-seven thousand ranchers hold grazing permits in the West, and the federal government takes in about $27 million annually from herders of cattle and sheep.

Members of Congress have tried since 1976 to force western ranchers—dubbed "welfare cowboys" by Rep. Mike Synar, D-Okla.—to pay market prices for leasing federal lands. Efforts to raise the fees have prevailed in the House by overwhelming margins but have been blocked by strong opposition from westerners in the Senate—both Democratic and Republican. Western ranchers, portraying themselves as the backbone of the Old West, claimed that increased federal fees would drive many of them out of business. Furthermore, western senators saw the grazing fee issue as the first salvo in an attack on the West to overhaul all public lands policy, including laws on hard-rock mining and timber harvests. "We are not going to turn over the West to total federal control," said Sen. Orrin G. Hatch, R-Utah.

The interior and agriculture secretaries have the authority to raise the grazing fees without action by Congress. But environmentalists and some industry representatives prefer that a law be passed to avoid further changes—and economic uncertainty—under other administrations. "We want to codify any change in the grazing fee system. That codification gives us stability," said Bill Myers, executive director of the Public Lands Council and a director of the National Cattlemen's Association. "We don't want the administrative solution." Environmentalists have warned about the damage caused by years of grazing. On many public lands, lush rangeland has turned to stubble and once-verdant areas near streams are almost gone.

Interior Appropriations

In early April 1993 President Clinton, under pressure from western Democratic senators whose votes were considered crucial to the success of his proposed economic package, abruptly dropped plans to overhaul federal land-use policy—including increasing grazing fees—through the budget-reconciliation bill (HR 2264). Instead, the administration vowed to act administratively or seek separate legislation. As a result, western lawmakers were given some legislative advantage, because stalling or blocking action in the Senate on regular legislation is easier than on reconciliation, which operates under special procedures. The move disappointed environmentalists, who said it sent a signal that the administration was willing to cave in to the demands of special interest groups. The White House was quick to play down the magnitude of the shift, maintaining it was only adopting a new strategy for achieving the same outcome.

Many western senators supported a separate bill (S 1326) by Ben Nighthorse Campbell, D-Colo., that would limit the grazing fee increase to 25 percent, or $2.33 per animal unit month. S 1326, written with the help of the cattle industry, was criticized by environmentalists and lawmakers concerned that it would not generate a fair return for public land use. Reps. Synar and Ralph Regula, R-Ohio, introduced a bill (HR 643) to change the formula used to calculate the grazing fees and to eventually increase the fees to more than $5 a month. Neither S 1326 nor HR 643 was acted on.

Regula did succeed in adding grazing fee language June 15 to the fiscal 1994 interior spending bill (HR 2520) during House Interior Appropriations Subcommittee consideration. Under Regula's amendment, the fee would increase by about one-third—from $1.86 to $2.47 per animal unit month. However, lawmakers typically objected to legislating in an appropriations bill. The Regula provision was removed from HR 2520 on the House floor July 14. Synar and Regula subsequently planned to offer the language in HR 643 as an amendment to Bureau of Land Management (BLM) reauthorization legislation (HR 2530), but they held off when the Clinton administration August 9 announced plans to impose tougher environmental standards and more than double the fees levied on western ranchers who graze livestock on public lands.

The proposal outlined by Interior Secretary Bruce Babbitt, scion of an Arizona ranching family and an ardent environmentalist, was aimed at boosting federal revenue and improving rangeland conservation. The grazing fee would increase to $2.76 in the first year, to $3.52 in the second year, and to $4.28 in the third year; after the third year, annual increases or decreases would be limited to 25 percent. Babbitt estimated that about $80 million would be generated annually by the new fee when it was fully implemented by fiscal 1996. Under the proposal the government would no longer allow ranchers to claim rights to water on BLM lands after they installed water facilities. The agency would retain title to any other improvements made by ranchers, although they would be compensated for the cost of such facilities. A national rangeland standard would be drafted to protect the ecosystem. Emphasis would be placed on management of riparian zones, the green strips along rivers and streams. Grazing advisory boards, which were dominated by ranchers and herders, would be replaced with "resource advisory boards" that included ranchers, wildlife managers, fisheries experts, environmentalists, and local business owners. And the duration of a grazing permit would be determined, in part, by a holder's land stewardship record—the better the land management record, the longer the term. New fees would be imposed to discourage permits from being sublet. The proposal would apply to more than 260 million acres of land managed by the BLM and the U.S. Forest Service. It could not become effective until federal rulemaking procedures were completed.

Western lawmakers and grazing interests said the plan would devastate the cattle and sheep industries. "The Babbitt proposal turns the management of our nation's rangeland over to a bunch of inside-the-

Beltway bureaucrats who don't know a good strand of grass from a man-icured lawn," said Sen. Conrad Burns, R-Mont. Added Sen. Max Baucus, D-Mont., "This proposal is not so much about protecting the federal range as it is about jacking up the rate as high as possible." Environmen-talists said that the plan had shortcomings but that they would not fight Congress for higher fees or stricter conservation language. "What we have here may be the best thing we can get," said William Howard, executive vice president of the National Wildlife Federation.

The Clinton administration plan suffered a serious setback Septem-ber 14 when the Senate adopted, 59-40, a Pete V. Domenici, R-N.M., amendment to HR 2520 to block the government from spending money in 1994 to implement higher grazing fees and stricter environmental con-trols on federal rangelands. Western senators—and some from else-where—argued on the floor that the grazing proposals were more than a simple rent increase and were too sweeping to be imposed by executive order without congressional input. "We are saying the government should not do this by fiat," said Domenici. Supporters of the grazing fee increase countered that the existing formula to calculate the fee also was estab-lished by executive branch edict. They called arguments that the adminis-tration's plan was too sweeping merely a smoke screen intended to com-pletely block higher fees. "This happens to be an amendment that stops reform in its tracks," said Sen. Bill Bradley, D-N.J., who voted against the Domenici amendment.

Unlike other issues that often were decided along partisan lines, grazing policy usually fell along regional lines. In all, thirty-eight Repub-licans and twenty-one Democrats supported the Domenici amendment, and twenty-three of them were from the West. Only three of eleven Dem-ocratic senators from western states—Daniel K. Akaka of Hawaii, Barbara Boxer of California, and Patty Murray of Washington—opposed the one-year funding moratorium, overcoming geographic concerns to side with Clinton on a major policy issue. Some senators known as environmental-ists defied conventional wisdom and voted for the Domenici amendment. John H. Chafee of Rhode Island, the ranking Republican on the Environ-ment and Public Works Committee, said he sided with the westerners because he believed the administration proposal was too far-reaching. Democrat Dianne Feinstein of California said she voted with Domenici because the plan would hurt ranchers in her home state.

The dispute over the public lands issue began to escalate between some House and Senate lawmakers. Synar called senators the "doctors of gridlock," who were unwilling to end government subsidies to a small number of ranchers who paid a fraction of private land lease rates. Some senators countered that Clinton's push for change threatened the liveli-hood of small ranching families. House Natural Resourcs Committee Chairman George Miller, D-Calif., said the Domenici amendment was nothing short of a gag order on the public. The moratorium would pre-vent Babbitt from publishing the proposed grazing policy changes and from conducting town meetings, which were required by federal rule-making procedures. "They'll simply shoot this proposal in the crib," Miller said. "This is the interruption of the democratic process in this country." Sen. Malcolm Wallop, R-Wyo., said House members, Babbitt, and the president were trying to kill small businesses in the West. "We have had this arrogant posture that if ranchers can't make it in ranching then maybe they should make cappuccino for tourists," Wallop said.

The House on September 29 agreed, 314-109, to a nonbinding motion by Regula to instruct House conferees on HR 2520 to reject the Senate-approved language providing for a one-year moratorium on graz-ing fee increases. In an attempt to break the logjam that stalled the inte-rior spending bill, the Clinton administration on October 7 struck a ten-tative agreement with key Democrats that would increase the grazing fee, but by less than what was proposed in August. Under the compromise the fee would increase to $3.45 over three years; after fiscal 1996 any increase or decrease in the fee would be limited to 15 percent annually. The Inte-rior and Agriculture departments would be required to wait one year before devising new environmental guidelines for rangeland manage-ment and determining the duration of a rancher's grazing permit by his record of environmental stewardship. Furthermore, only ranchers who gained grazing permits after HR 2520 became law would be required to relinquish ownership of future improvements. And a 20 percent sur-charge would be imposed on ranchers who leased their rights to graze on federal lands to others.

The deal was reached by Babbitt, Synar, Miller, Rep. Bruce F. Vento, D-Minn., and Sen. Harry Reid, D-Nev. Western Republicans in the Senate vowed to fight the compromise, branding it a backroom deal that would devastate the cattle and sheep industries. Domenici and Wallop threat-ened to wage a filibuster to stall the final version of the interior appropri-ations measure on the Senate floor if it contained the grazing compro-mise. But Arizona senator Dennis DeConcini and other western Demo-cratic senators urged regional Republicans to accept the deal to staunch

Case Studies in Lobbying

more aggressive efforts by the administration and Congress to overhaul federal land policies. Grazing fee increase supporters also pointed out that holding up the interior bill would only delay funds that paid for the upkeep and operation of huge swaths of land in the West.

Senate negotiators on October 14 accepted the compromise language, offered as an amendment by Reid, on an 8-7 party-line vote; House negotiators adopted the amendment, 5-2. Domenici had tried to alter Reid's amendment with a proposal to stretch the fee increase over six years instead of three years and to delay the overhaul of rangeland management practices for a year. House negotiators shot down Domenici's amendment 2-5; Senate negotiators, 6-9. The full House on October 20 agreed 317-106 to accept the controversial grazing fee increase language. The House had accepted the conference report on HR 2520 (H Rept 103-299) by voice vote earlier the same day.

Meanwhile, Domenici renewed his filibuster threat. In a letter to Senate Appropriations Committee Chairman Robert C. Byrd, D-W.Va., and Majority Leader George J. Mitchell, D-Maine, Domenici said he had the signatures of forty-one senators—enough to stall HR 2520 on the Senate floor. Two western Democrats had signed the letter: Jeff Bingaman of New Mexico and Campbell of Colorado. On October 21 the Senate failed, 53-41, to muster the necessary two-thirds vote to invoke cloture (and thus limit debate) on the interior spending bill. Domenici said senators would stop the filibuster if the fee increase were phased in over a longer period of time and if Babbitt postponed a sweeping series of changes that determined how ranchers could use federal rangeland. The Senate on October 26 defeated a second attempt to end the filibuster, 51-45. A third vote fell short, 54-44, on October 28. That same day Babbitt raised the stakes, announcing that he would bypass Congress and move ahead under federal rulemaking procedures to charge even higher grazing fees—to $4.28 a month—and implement more rangeland management requirements than contained in the interior bill.

Byrd vowed not to seek another vote to limit debate on HR 2520 until November 10, the expiration date of the continuing resolution (H J Res 283—PL 103-128) that was providing funding for the Interior and Defense departments. He also threatened to try to ship the bill back to conference, which would expose every item to the whims of the members on the joint panel. Byrd went on to suggest that the grazing language be struck from the measure, leaving western interests to duel with Babbitt in the administrative arena. In a scathing speech Byrd said he was "sick and

168

tired" of the grazing issue. "I've had it up to my ears," said Byrd, as he gestured toward the Republican side of the Senate chamber.

On November 9 a somber Reid agreed to drop the compromise language that he had brokered and that was added to the interior spending bill by House and Senate conferees. The bloc of Senate Republicans and five Democrats from western and Plains states ended their filibuster. However, eliminating the grazing amendment did not settle the issue. Senate opponents of the compromise said they could accept a raise in the federal fee, pointing to S 1326. Their differences, they said, revolved around Babbitt's land management proposals, which the lawmakers believed would cripple the ranching industry and alter the long-standing relationship between the federal government and ranchers. Among the most criticized was the plan to transfer ownership of water improvement facilities and the rights to water on BLM-controlled lands from the rancher to the federal government. The administration plan would reverse a policy established by Interior Secretary James G. Watt in 1982 and bring BLM rules governing water facilities in line with those imposed by the Forest Service. Sen. Hank Brown, R-Colo., a vocal opponent, said the proposal threatened to undermine state water rights—an outcome Babbitt disputed.

President Clinton and Babbitt entered the grazing debate needing to improve relations with environmentalists. But the battle ended with no clear gain for the environmental community. The yearlong struggle to get higher grazing fees left some environmentalists weary. "We've been saying all along that it's not enough to elect an environmentally conscious administration," said Peter L. Kelley, communications director of the League of Conservation Voters. "You've got to change Congress."

1994 Action

The Clinton administration planned to unveil a comprehensive grazing package in March 1994. Babbitt took initial steps February 14 toward moderating his stance on federal grazing policy, announcing that he would give ranchers, environmentalists, and other interest groups more input in making rangeland policy. He proposed fifteen-member "multiple resource advisory councils" that would include ranchers and environmentalists to advise the interior secretary on rangeland policy.

Environmentalists and their congressional allies, such as Representative Miller, were already angry about Babbitt's attempts to be more conciliatory to western interests. Jim Baca, a favorite of environmentalists but a nemesis of ranchers, was forced to resign February 3 as director of BLM after complaints were lodged by some western governors and senators about his aggressiveness toward changing land management policies. Babbitt said that Baca's departure would not change administration policy and that he and Baca had "different approaches to management style and consensus building."

The National Wildlife Federation and other environmental groups criticized Babbitt's resource council plan, arguing that the councils would politicize federal lands policies. Each state's governor would nominate the members of a council: five would be from extractive industries, such as ranching, mining, and timber; five would be from environmental, conservation, or sportsmen's groups; and five would be public land users, state or local officials, or other members of the public who did not fit in the other two categories. The interior secretary would make the final appointments. The council's duties would include deciding how many head of cattle should be grazed on federal land and how to spend the portion of federal grazing fees that was returned to states. The council also could petition the interior secretary if its advice was not being followed, and the secretary would be required to respond within thirty days. The resource council plan was the brainchild of a group of ranchers, environmentalists, and other interest groups led by Colorado's Democratic governor Roy Romer. Babbitt also said he would accept another proposal from the Colorado group to keep the length of a grazing lease at least ten years, instead of reducing it to five. Ranchers had complained that the shorter grazing leases would lower market value of their ranching operations and make obtaining loans to stay afloat or expand more difficult.

Meanwhile, Republicans continued to attack Babbitt. For example, Senator Domenici was upset with the revisions because he believed they were aimed only at appeasing certain western lawmakers. House Republicans who had supported the Clinton administration's public lands policies in 1993, such as Regula, decided to stay out of the fray.

Four Democrats—Representatives Miller, Synar, and Vento and Senator Reid—on March 4 sent Babbitt a scathing letter regarding the grazing policy changes that were in the works. Although they agreed that grazing advisory boards dominated by ranchers should be abolished, the four Democrats believed the proposed system would allow local residents to "exercise political muscle" and go over the heads of federal land managers. They were concerned that the plan did not address national standards and guidelines for the maintenance of public lands as well as the contentious issue of water rights on federal rangelands. The Democrats also believed that the proposed new grazing fee of $3.96 per animal unit month, to go into full effect in fiscal 1996, should be higher. Also, they thought that implementing the new rate during a presidential election year, when it could be open to intensified GOP attacks, was a political mistake.

Babbitt presented a new plan on March 17. Grazing fees would be raised over three years to $3.96 per animal unit month by 1997. Babbitt proposed a 30 percent discount on the highest rate for ranchers who met certain environmental standards. The federal government would retain the rights to water on federal lands but would not change existing private water rights or the structure of water law in the West. Ranchers would be required to follow four broad environmental standards: the care of ecosystems; the protection of verdant areas by streams, known as riparian areas; the restoration or enhancement of water quality; and the protection of endangered species' habitat. And a surcharge would be levied when a rancher subleased a grazing permit, but no charge would be made if the lease were handed from one family member to another. Babbitt also proposed abolishing local grazing advisory boards and replacing them with local teams that would include environmentalists, wildlife experts, and local officials.

In a hearing before the Senate Energy and Natural Resources Committee April 20, Babbitt said he would continue to revise his March proposals to reach consensus with wary western senators. Ultimately, however, no understanding could be reached. The Clinton administration announced December 21 that it would defer to Congress on the grazing fee issue. The decision was seen as one in a series of steps Clinton had taken after the November 1994 elections, in which Republicans regained control of Congress, to move to the political center.

Case Study 8

FAMILY AND MEDICAL LEAVE

T he legislative odyssey of the family and medical leave measure
showed that, while a bill can muster enough support to clear Congress, it is doomed to fail without White House approval or sufficient votes to overcome a presidential veto. Republican President George
Bush twice vetoed family and medical leave legislation—in 1990 and in
1992; the Democratic-led Congress was unable to override the vetoes.
Then, less than three weeks after the inauguration of Democratic President Bill Clinton in 1993, a family and medical leave bill again cleared
Congress and was signed into law. Certain workers thus would be allowed
to take an unpaid leave for the birth or adoption of a child or the illness
of a close family member.

Benefit Workers or Hurt Businesses?

Whether family and medical leave would benefit workers or hurt
businesses was a point of contention. Supporters of a national, mandato-
ry leave policy, primarily labor and women's groups, said the country was
overdue for federal minimum requirements to bring business in line with
the changing demographics of the workplace. About 60 percent of moth-
ers worked outside the home, they said, and the United States was the only
major industrialized nation besides South Africa that had no family leave
policy. But the U.S. Chamber of Commerce, the Bush administration, and
conservative Republicans argued that mandated leave was unwarranted
government intrusion into the relationship between employer and
employee and would take away employers' flexibility and lead them to cut
other benefits workers might prefer. Businesses also were concerned that
Congress was heading down a long, slippery slope that could encompass
mandated employee health benefits as well. "What we're fearful of is a del-
uge of these proposals similar to what was enacted in the 1930s," when

Social Security, workers' compensation, and other benefits became law, said John J. Motley, vice president for federal government relations at the National Federation of Independent Business (NFIB).

Supporters and opponents also disagreed over the cost of a federally mandated leave policy. Supporters said that, because employers would have to maintain only health insurance for workers who chose to take unpaid leave, the cost would be less than $5.30 a year per covered employee. In addition, according to a 1989 study by the Family Medical Leave Coalition, working women who had no family leave lost an aggregate of about $607 million a year in earnings. Taxpayers, the study said, dished out $108 million a year because of lost taxes and payments for assistance to women who were unemployed or on welfare because they did not get family and medical leave.

Opponents said the $5.30-a-year estimate of the burden to business was far too low and did not take into account hidden costs, such as litigation and training temporary employees. Estimates by the Chamber of Commerce on the cost to business ranged as high as $23.8 billion a year. But the General Accounting Office, an investigative arm of Congress, said that estimate was based on unrealistic assumptions, including how many employees would take leave and how many would be replaced by temporary workers.

Sen. Edward M. Kennedy, D-Mass., said that the costs of the policy cited by opponents were greatly exaggerated. "Many high-priced lobbyists have been paid exorbitant fees to try to prove that this legislation will impose excessive costs on businesses. It is long past time to put this fallacy to rest," he said. Kennedy cited a survey commissioned by the Small Business Administration (SBA), which argued that the costs to businesses for permanently replacing a worker were significantly higher than for granting leave. The SBA report, released in 1991, was based on interviews with 1,730 small businesses nationwide. One finding was that, although most businesses did not have formal leave policies, between 74 percent and 90 percent used existing programs to meet the needs of workers with sick children or other unanticipated leave needs. The study also suggested that the costs of implementing family leave were less than the business community claimed. "The net cost to employers of placing workers on leave is always substantially smaller than the cost of terminating an employee. Therefore, while there will be costs to firms of mandating leave by the federal government, these costs will be relatively small as compared with the cost of terminating the worker who desires the leave," it said.

Many Republicans contended that mandated leave would result in discrimination against women, reduced benefits, and longer hours for workers. They cited a 1991 Gallup survey of businesses that indicated that if family leave legislation were enacted, companies would be less likely to hire women and would make other workers pick up the slack for another employee on leave. In addition, Rep. Dick Armey, R-Texas, complained that only well-to-do workers could afford to take unpaid leave, forcing lower-paid workers to pick up the slack. This is "yuppie welfare—a perverse redistribution of income" from the poor to the rich, Armey charged.

Family leave opponents repeatedly defined family and medical leave legislation as yet another Democratic effort to regulate industry, increase the bureaucracy, and set the stage for costly litigation. "The House can't even run its own business. How dare we put ourselves in the place of workers and employers who might want to reach different agreements?" said Minority Leader Robert H. Michel, R-Ill. Advocates, meanwhile, invoked the notion of "family values," which had been embraced by the GOP. "If family values are important, and they are, there is no more important piece of legislation than family leave," said House Speaker Thomas S. Foley, D-Wash.

Proponents maintained that the odds were negligible that companies would face chaos because of numerous workers taking unpaid leave. "I think they are going to be surprised at how things are not going to be as difficult as they anticipate," said Dana Friedman, copresident of the Families and Work Institute, a nonprofit research company in New York. The institute looked at businesses in four states that enacted family leave laws to find out how hard it was for companies to comply. The study found that 91 percent did not have difficulty adopting the policy. Of those, 39 percent said the process was "extremely easy." Friedman said the companies that had difficulty adapting to state laws usually had managers who did not want to do it and did not know the rules. "They dug their heels in and made it hard for themselves," she said.

Businesses new to family and medical leave were likely to discover what large companies already knew, as stated by Brad Googins, associate professor and director of the Center on Work and Family at Boston University: "Most people won't utilize it because they can't afford it." Googins said that if the leave were paid, as it is in most European countries, more people would take advantage of it. But, he said, provision for paid leave was not likely to happen in the United States. For most people, Googins said, the unpaid leave policy would do no more than protect them from losing jobs in a short emergency. Googins and Friedman also argued that the policy would not be difficult to put in place in part because many companies already had some sort of plan giving workers time off for a new baby or a family medical emergency.

1990 Veto

George Bush, during the 1988 presidential campaign, endorsed parental leave in concept but opposed forcing companies to provide the benefit. He maintained that position upon taking office. "The administration supports and encourages parental- and medical-leave policies designed to meet the specific needs of individual companies and their employees," Labor Secretary Elizabeth H. Dole wrote in an April 17, 1989, letter to Orrin G. Hatch, Utah, ranking Republican on the Senate Labor and Human Resources Committee. "We strongly believe this can be best achieved voluntarily; therefore, the administration strongly opposes the mandated approach to employee benefits," she continued.

The House on May 10, 1990, passed HR 770 (H Rept 101-28, Parts I-III) on a 237-187 vote, forty-six short of the two-thirds needed for an override. The bill had been scaled back to gain support from wavering Republicans and conservative Democrats. Sponsors said they were confident that Bush would retract his veto threat by the time the bill reached his desk. Marge Roukema, N.J., ranking Republican on the Education and Labor Subcommittee on Labor-Management Relations, said she and other GOP supporters of parental leave would push for a meeting with Bush to convince him that it was a "bedrock family issue worthy of his support." But business lobbyists, who met with White House Chief of Staff John H. Sununu on May 7, said Bush would not change his mind. "I had John Sununu look me straight in the eye and say that the president would veto it," said Mary T. Tavenner, a lobbyist for the National Association of Wholesaler-Distributors.

The Senate on June 14 passed HR 770 by voice vote, clearing the bill. The Office of Management and Budget issued a statement the same day reiterating that the administration "strongly opposes" the measure. As cleared, HR 770 would require businesses with fifty or more employees to offer twelve weeks a year of unpaid medical or parental leave. Only one parent could take parental leave at a time. Medical leave, when certified by a doctor, could be used to care for a sick spouse, parent, or child. Employees who had worked in a job for at least one thousand hours over the course of a year would be eligible. The legislation would give federal workers more comprehensive benefits: eighteen weeks over two years for parental leave and twenty-six weeks a year for medical leave. House workers would get the same protections as private employees; the bill was not amended to include Senate workers.

Bush vetoed HR 770 on June 29. "I want to emphasize my belief that time off for a child's birth or adoption or for family illness is an important benefit for employers to offer employees," Bush said in a veto message. "I strongly object, however, to the federal government mandating leave policies." Bush said the bill would place undue burdens on business. "We must ensure that federal policies do not stifle the creation of new jobs, nor result in the elimination of existing jobs," Bush said in his statement.

Despite intense lobbying by Democrats hoping to score an election-year upset, the House July 25 resoundingly sustained Bush's veto of HR 770. The 232-195 vote fell fifty-four short of the two-thirds necessary to override. Democrats wasted no time trying to capture the political high ground after the failed override attempt. Sen. Christopher J. Dodd, D-Conn., recalled the presidential campaign statement Bush made in support of unpaid leave for workers. In "one of the first opportunities [Bush] had to live up to a campaign pledge, he walked away from it," Dodd said.

1992 Veto

In 1991 some hopeful signs existed for the family and medical leave legislation. For example, Jane O'Grady, a legislative representative of the AFL-CIO, said the American Association of Retired Persons would put its muscle behind the bill; and Lynn Martin, who voted for the legislation in 1990 as a Republican House member from Illinois, had become Bush's new labor secretary in February. However, while bill supporters believed they had enough Senate votes to override a veto, House support was questionable. According to Mary Tavenner the House was likely to sustain a veto. "We've checked every member of the House, including the freshmen, and we're in very good shape over there," she said.

The Senate passed S 5 (S Rept 102-68) by voice vote on October 2, 1991. Minutes earlier members voted 65-32 for a compromise offered by Christopher S. Bond, R-Mo., and backed by bill sponsor Dodd. The measure would mandate that businesses with more than fifty workers give all but their "key employees"—those who were the highest paid 10 percent of a company's workforce—up to twelve weeks of unpaid leave for the birth or adoption of a child or for the serious illness of the worker or an immediate family member. In an October 1 letter to Minority Leader Bob Dole,

R-Kan., Bush wrote, "Should S 5 or any other mandated leave legislation be presented to me, I will veto it." A September 30 White House statement made clear that that threat included Bond's language.

Mary Tavenner, citing the exemption of "key employees," said it was ironic that the bill might not affect the only group able to take advantage of it. "Yuppies are the only people who can afford to take off anyway," she said, adding that most lower-paid workers did not have the resources to take weeks of unpaid leave. A representative of the NFIB, a powerful lobbying force in Washington, said that group also remained opposed to the bill. "It's still a mandate. It doesn't change anything," said the NFIB's Angela Jones. That view was echoed by Thomas A. Scully, an associate director at the White House Office of Management and Budget. "The compromise isn't much of a compromise," he said, predicting that Bush would veto it. "We just don't like to be in a position of mandating benefits, because it imposes economic consequences," Scully said. The Bush administration encouraged businesses to provide flexible family leave policies but did not want to force them to do it, he said.

The House on November 13 passed HR 2 (H Rept 102-135, Parts I and II), 253-177, falling short of the two-thirds margin necessary to override. The House then passed by voice vote S 5, with the language of HR 2. Earlier that day lawmakers, on a 287-143 vote, adopted a substitute, sponsored by Bart Gordon, D-Tenn., and Henry J. Hyde, R-Ill., that embodied the Bond-Dodd compromise. By itself, the House vote on the substitute would have given the House the numbers needed to override a veto that day. But many who voted for the compromise voted against passage of the bill. Tavenner explained the discrepancy between the two votes this way: "Members wanted to be on record voting for something, but they didn't want it to become law."

Business organizations, among them the U.S. Chamber of Commerce and the NFIB, complained strenuously that the bill's mandate that employers provide up to twelve weeks of unpaid leave would hurt small businesses. However, the legislation exempted businesses with fewer than fifty workers, which was 95 percent of all employers in the country. (But the remaining 5 percent employed about 60 percent of all workers.)

The only changes made by conferees on S 5 concerned provisions extending leave rights to congressional employees. The new language included enforcement and grievance provisions that paralleled those in the 1991 civil rights bill (PL 102-166). The bill would extend leave rights to federal civil service employees. The Senate adopted the conference report (H Rept 102-816) by voice vote August 11; the House, 241-161 on September 10.

President Bush on September 16 announced an alternative proposal—providing business tax credits of up to $1,200 per worker if companies gave employees time off for family emergencies. The plan, to be offered to businesses with fewer than five hundred employees, would cost about $500 million, according to the White House. Representative Roukema called Bush's idea "an interesting supplement to the basic bill. But it is no substitute." She said, "To use the tax incentives does not give you the job guarantee." Roukema said she was extremely disappointed that Bush did not try to compromise on the family leave legislation while it was going through the legislative process. "I think his advisers have painted him into a very unfortunate corner," she said. The proposal, she said, was obviously an attempt to give Bush a reason for vetoing the legislation.

Representative Armey, who opposed the family leave legislation, said the timing of Bush's proposal was "unfortunate" but added that he and the administration had been busy fighting the S 5 mandate. "To the extent the president's proposal is political, it's in response to the timing of the Democrats," Armey said. "They thought this is a great time to embarrass the president" by sending him a family leave bill so close to the 1992 election. Democratic presidential nominee Bill Clinton voiced strong support for family and medical leave legislation.

Bush vetoed S 5 on September 22. He objected to mandating how businesses should conduct themselves. Voting 68 to 31, two votes more than the two-thirds necessary, the Senate September 24 voted to override the president's veto of S 5. However, the House voted September 30 to sustain Bush's veto, 258-169.

Bill Becomes Law

Clinton's election changed the political arithmetic on the issue.

The House passed HR 1 (H Rept 103-8, Parts I and II) on February 3, 1993, by a 265-163 vote. Just before the bill went to the Senate floor, the National Retail Federation broke away from the antileave coalition to support the bill. President Tracy Mullin said the bill would no longer pose "an administrative nightmare" for retailers. "This bill has gone through an evolution," she said. The Senate on February 4 passed HR 1, on a 71-27 vote, with the language of its version (S 5—S Rept 103-3). The House, 247-152, accepted the Senate changes the same day, clearing HR 1. Clinton signed the bill on February 5 (PL 103-3).

The measure would allow workers to take up to twelve weeks of unpaid leave during any twelve-month period because of the birth or adoption of a child; the need to care for a child, spouse, or parent with a serious health condition; or the worker's own serious illness. It applied to employees who worked for the same employer for at least one year and for at least 1,250 hours that year. Businesses that employed fewer than fifty people were exempt. And employers could deny leave to a worker who fell among the highest paid 10 percent of workers if that person were considered a key employee whose leave would result in "substantial and grievous economic injury" to the business.

GLOSSARY

Appropriation. Legislation that funds an agency or program by directing the expenditure of money from the Treasury. All such legislation emanates from the Appropriations committees of the House and Senate, each of which has thirteen subcommittees with jurisdiction over all federal spending. Each subcommittee reports spending legislation for the agencies and programs under its purview. By custom, all appropriations bills originate in the House. In general, appropriations bills can fund only programs that have been authorized by other congressional committees. *See* Authorization. Although appropriations bills can contain policy matters under the jurisdiction of the other, authorizing committees, such provisions are subject to the challenge—in the House by the Rules Committee (*See* Rules Committee) and to points of order on the floor, or in the Senate by a vote to appeal a point of order against the policy provision. *See* Point of order.

As the fiscal year for the federal government begins each October 1, it is desirable for all appropriations bills to be passed and signed into law by that date. This, however, is a rare occurrence. If the October 1 deadline is missed (meaning that government agencies and programs not funded for the new fiscal year cannot operate, and must shut down, until funding is provided), Congress can enact legislation known as a "continuing resolution," which provides interim funding for all regular appropriations bills not enacted. The "CR," as it is known, can be a magnet for every proposal that has not made it through the regular legislative process in any given year, including pet projects and special-interest provisions.

Authorization. Legislation that authorizes, or permits, the expenditure of funds for an agency or program, with the actual spending to be approved by the Appropriations committees. All legislative committees, except Appropriations and Budget, process authorization bills. Such legislation generally renews (or establishes) the mandate for an agency, defines the parameters under which it is to operate, and authorizes its funding. Often, the amount of money authorized exceeds the funds actually appropriated for the program. Members can score political points with a program's supporters by authorizing large sums, even if they know that chances for a full appropriation are small. Authorizations generally run for one to three years. If an authorization lapses, the program can be continued through the appropriations process.

Calendar. There are six House calendars: Union, House, Private, Consent, Corrections, and Discharge. In modern practice, calendars are basically lists of certain types of legislation that have undergone certain processes in the House. The Union and House calendars—the two most important—contain legislation that has been reported from committees, has passed the House, has come over from the Senate, or is in conference. In the Senate, placement of a bill on the calendar is a signal of the measure's eligibility for floor consideration.

Cloture. Applies only in the Senate. To break a filibuster, a supermajority of senators—sixty—must vote to invoke cloture, or order the closure of debate. *See* Filibuster. Special procedures apply following a cloture vote. Filibusters and cloture votes are usually associated with the most heated and divisive public policy issues—controversial bills and nominees requiring Senate confirmation. A determined minority will resort to a filibuster to frustrate the majority will on such issues, with votes on cloture read by interest groups and analysts as referendums on the underlying policy issue.

Colloquy. A discussion in committee or on the floor, during debate or markup of a bill. *See* Markup. Colloquies are used by members to define the intent of the sponsor of the bill (or amendment): the meaning or interpretation the legislation should be given by the agencies that will administer it and the courts that will review legal challenges under it. Colloquies are very important in tying down the specifics of a bill's provisions. As they are not a part of the statutory language itself, however, but only a part of the record (or "legislative history") of the bill, they are not binding with the force of law. Colloquies reflect intent: how the lawmakers expect the bill to be interpreted and executed. To have any standing, colloquies must be spoken and their content incorporated in the committee report; if spoken on the floor, the colloquy between the manager of the bill (usually the chair of the committee or subcommittee with jurisdiction) and another member will be printed verbatim in the *Congressional*

Record. (In the Senate, colloquies can be inserted in the *Record* and published, by unanimous consent, as if they were spoken.) Colloquies are generally negotiated in advance between the members (and their staff) involved, scripted, and read during debate. Colloquies are less cumbersome to develop, manage, and execute than amendments. Often colloquies reflect concerns that could not be accommodated in the drafting or approval of a bill in committee, or that have arisen after the bill has been printed and studied by affected interests and lobbyists.

Conference; Conference committee; Conference reports. When the House and Senate pass similar—but not identical—bills, delegations of members, appointed by the leadership of each body and drawn from the committees of jurisdiction over the legislation, will convene as a joint conference committee to reach final agreement on the legislation. The conference committee reports the accord on the final bill back to the House and Senate, each of which must pass the conference report in identical form. The conferees are supposed to agree to provisions in the final bill that do not exceed the scope of the House or Senate bills—but sometimes these boundaries are breached. Such procedures can be challenged, particularly in the House, under the rules, but the Rules Committee can waive such a challenge. *See* Rules Committee.

Formal meetings of conference committees have in recent years become rarer for legislation emanating from the authorizing committees; more frequently, the committee leadership instructs the staff to negotiate and reach compromises, if possible, on all but the most crucial or controversial issues in the legislation, with members themselves meeting directly to thrash out such matters. At other times the conferees engage in a "paper conference"—sending proposals on paper back and forth between the House and Senate delegations until agreement is reached. When time is short late in the congressional session just prior to adjournment, the House and Senate will often dispense with conference meetings altogether and instead pass amended versions of the legislation back and forth until they both approve the bill in identical form.

The appointment of conferees is a crucial political decision by the leadership. Conferees are usually drawn from the members of the committee that wrote the bill. In the House, the Speaker, in consultation with the committee and subcommittee chairs, appoints the majority party's conferees—but he does not have to follow their advice. (The minority's conferees also are formally named by the Speaker, but he follows the decisions made by the minority leader.) Thus, the discretion of the Speaker and the minority leader can decidedly affect the political balance of the conferees, and therefore the potential outcome of their deliberations on key issues. The jockeying for appointment to conference is intense. The appointment power also can be used to reward or punish certain members. Similar procedures and dynamics occur in the Senate.

When conferences are concluded, a report (known as the "statement of managers") is filed, containing both the statutory language and an explanation, which constitutes legislative history, of the final bill—how each provision of the two separate bills was resolved in conference. Conference reports on authorization bills are sent to the floor of the House and Senate for an up-or-down vote on the package as a whole; they cannot, except under the most extraordinary circumstances, be amended in any way. The entire package must be voted down to defeat a single provision in a conference report on an authorization bill.

Conference reports on appropriations bills are treated differently. Where the House and Senate have approved differing amounts for the same program or agency, or where one chamber has passed funding for a program but the other is silent on the matter, the conferees will agree on a compromise amount and state that agreement in the conference report. Sometimes the conferees will be unable to compromise on a specific line item, and their disagreement will be subject to subsequent votes in each chamber. When the conference report is considered on the floor, each such amendment that was originally in disagreement is called up by the manager of the bill (usually the chair of the appropriations subcommittee that originated the bill) and amended to reflect the conference agreement—with each such amendment subject to a separate vote. Thus, specific provisions in appropriations conference reports are open to challenge on the floor without defeating the entire conference report. Before appropriations conference reports are finally cleared by Congress, all such amendments in disagreement must be approved in identical form by the House and Senate.

Continuing resolution. *See* Appropriation.

"Dear Colleague" letters. Letters from one member, or a group of members, to all their colleagues, and are known by their salutation, "Dear Colleague." They can be on any subject that a senator or representative deems worthy of other members' attention, but most frequently members use them to announce the introduction of a bill and to request cosponsorship, or to argue for or against a bill or amendment in committee or on the floor. They also are used to provide substantive information on issues and are an important educational and lobbying tool. Staff and members use Dear Colleagues to track sentiment on an issue; who writes and signs Dear Colleagues are important signals about the degree and quality of support or opposition a given measure has. Dozens, if not hundreds, of Dear Colleagues are sent throughout the congressional office buildings each week. Like mail from constituents, Dear Colleagues are an informal barometer of which issues are hot.

Discharge petition. Applies in the House only. If a committee has not acted on a bill under its jurisdiction, members can sign a discharge petition at the Speaker's desk on the House floor—a motion that discharges the committee from further consideration and places the bill on the appropriate calendar. *See* Calendar. A majority (218 members) must sign a discharge petition before the petition itself is brought to the floor for a vote on its approval—and it must pass before the legislation it addresses can itself be taken up by the House. Discharge petitions are employed, usually by the minority party, for bills where sentiment is high and the committee chair's opposition is entrenched, such as if the chair is effectively killing a bill by refusing to bring it up for a vote in committee (and a majority of the committee declines to force action in the panel). Discharge petitions are therefore a strong rebuff to the chair and to the majority leadership of the House, which almost always defers to the committee chair. Members have to sign the discharge petition on the floor literally under the eyes of the Speaker. It is therefore very hard to get a majority to sign a discharge petition, much less approve it on a floor vote. But if significant numbers of members sign it, all but the most recalcitrant chair will appreciate the political message being sent and will let the committee decide what to do with the bill.

In 1993, Republicans forced the Democratic majority to allow signatures on discharge petitions to be made public—making it harder for leaders to pressure members into removing their names.

Ex parte rules. These originate with regulatory agencies in the executive branch. In general, when a policy issue or adjudicated matter has been set for decision by a regulatory agency, ex parte rules limit the nature and form of communications on the issue between any outside parties and the agency officials who will make the decision on the pending matter. Whether ex parte rules apply to members of Congress varies from agency to agency and the nature of the proceeding involved. For lobbyists this distinction is crucial because—if the ex parte curtain has come down on a given matter, barring or limiting the parties to a proceeding from continued advocacy before the agency—their concerns can still be voiced through official correspondence, or telephone calls, between members (and their staff) and the agency's officials.

Filibuster. Applies to the Senate only. Each senator, under the rules, has the right to engage in unlimited debate, on any matter (although budget reconciliation bills are subject to a time limitation). Such unlimited debate or filibuster is subject to a cloture vote. *See* Cloture. A filibuster is the ultimate delaying tactic, the last resort if all other attempts to stop a bill have failed. Rarely used in the past, filibusters and cloture votes have become increasingly common in the Senate since the 1970s, to the frustration of many senators. From the 91st Congress, beginning in 1971, through the 101st Congress, effectively ending in 1990, there were 248 attempted cloture votes, or an average of 22.5 per two-year session. Of these, 95, or an average of nearly 9 per session, were successful. In 1995, only 4 of 21 cloture votes were successful.

The filibuster's very endurance, and senators' resistance to changes in the rules to limit their utilization—notwithstanding the glare of nationwide television coverage of the Senate's proceedings—is a tribute to the overriding value senators place on the protection of their individual rights. Filibusters are used especially for political leverage. The threat of beginning one is so unpalatable that senators will go to great lengths to compromise to avoid its initiation. As much as senators hate it when a filibuster is employed against their bills, it is more tolerable to them than relinquishing their ability to resort to it themselves. There is little doubt the Senate will remain the world's greatest deliberative body.

Germane amendments. The House and Senate have extensive rules, and innumerable precedents, that govern whether an amendment is germane (or relevant) to a bill. In the House, germaneness rules are more restrictive, so that a bill amending particular sections of existing law is not open to amendments that would modify other, unrelated or unaffected provisions of the broader underlying law. The Rules Committee can nevertheless waive points of order against such nongermane amendments, making them eligible for debate and vote. *See* Rules Committee; Points of order. In general, appropriations bills cannot contain authorizing legislation. Similar restrictions on funding bills exist in the Senate but are more easily circumvented in that chamber. *See* Appropriation. Germaneness is critical because it determines whether a bill can be used as a vehicle for a given amendment.

Hold. An informal but powerful tool that applies in the Senate only. Any one senator can prevent floor consideration of a bill (or nomination requiring senator approval) by notifying the majority leader that he or she has a "hold" on the matter and does not want it to come up without the senator's permission. Although the leadership makes known that a hold has been placed on a bill, the senator responsible is not publicly identified. Members have to find out from the leader, or committee sources, and try to remove the hold. Holds are powerful negotiating tools. They are most often used to get concessions on a bill the leadership wants to schedule. A hold also can be used to influence the House; one can, for example, be placed on a bill that a House chair wants in order to get concessions on that bill or another bill that the House may want to send to the Senate. Except in unusual circumstances, such as consideration of a cabinet appointment that has been approved by the responsible committee for a vote on the floor or at the end of a session, the leadership will honor the hold until the senator who has made it removes it.

Legislative counsel. Both the House and Senate have an Office of the Legislative Counsel: cadres of lawyers whose responsibility is to draft legislation—bills that are introduced, and amendments for committee and floor consideration. Legislative counsels work exclusively for the members and are scrupulously nonpartisan in that they do not favor members of the majority over those in the minority. The writing of legislation is a sensitive task politically no less than substantively. The same legislative counsel can be asked by different members to write conflicting bills or amendments to the same bill. Confidentiality and trust are therefore essential, and legislative counsels and members establish a lawyer-client relationship in the development of legislation.

Legislative counsels are (or become over time) experts in their respective fields. The body of American law is so extensive and complex that Congress could not function without their expertise in writing legislation. Legislative counsels are generally assigned by committee and come to master the statutes within the committee's jurisdiction. What legislative counsels require to perform their work are precise specifications for the bill or amendment: what the proposed bill does and how it is to work. These instructions are then translated into legislative language. The counsels, who are experts on parliamentary procedure, draft bills and amendments in ways that can best withstand any anticipated challenges under the rules. Bills also can be drafted, within limits, to ensure referral to a certain committee—either because the sponsor sits on the panel and wants personal jurisdiction or to avoid referral to a committee known to be hostile to the measure. Legislative counsels are therefore not political—they do not make policy choices—but are substantive technicians of the legislative process. Legislative counsels are not lobbied by outside interests; concerns lobbyists might have with a bill or amendment are expressed to its author, who makes the decision whether and how such concerns might be accommodated.

Markup. When a subcommittee or committee meets to consider a bill and amendments to it, the meeting is known as a "markup" session. The term dates from days when bills were literally marked up, by hand, with changes approved by the members. Each committee has its own style of conducting markups, generally set by the chair and ranging from the very formal, with strict adherence to the letter of the rules (such as requiring all amendments to be provided in writing), to the more informal, with members casually arrayed around a table, engaging more in discussion.

Lobbyists have to be attuned to these differing committee styles to ensure their effective participation in the markup. Few experiences are more frustrating than not having an amendment prepared in time for consideration. In most markups the printed bill is before the members, with written amendments considered in an orderly fashion. In some committees, however, particularly on tax bills, the panel works from an outline of legislative provisions, and not statutory language. Once the committee has made the policy decisions, the staff, working with legislative counsel, are instructed to write the legislation. *See* Legislative counsel. In such instances lobbyists have to ensure that the language drafted pursuant to instructions in fact reflects the intent of the committee's instructions. Well-intended but poor drafting can create more problems than the original issue that prompted the amendment.

Oversight hearing. A hearing held when a committee oversees the activities of an agency or program or issues within its jurisdiction. Oversight hearings are not legislative sessions. Generally they are investigatory or status checks on how officials in the executive branch are performing their responsibilities pursuant to law on the books. The oversight hearing is one of the most effective tools available to a committee, in part because it poses the threat of legislative action to remedy a public policy issue.

Exercising their authority to rewrite an agency's statutory mandate, committees use oversight hearings to call to account agencies and the private sector interests affected by them. By documenting shortcomings in government, oversight hearings can be a precursor to new legislation. But they also are effective substitutes for legislation. A vigorous oversight hearing can be used to jawbone agencies, industry, and other constituencies into taking action themselves to avoid passage of a law requiring them to do so. Indeed, most executive branch agencies have, under their statutory charters, large reservoirs of residual legal power that permit them to regulate broadly in their field (this generally falls under the rubric of a "public-interest" standard in the law). Oversight hearings can encourage an agency to exercise that power—or, alternatively, to curb the zeal of an agency head whose aggressive actions in testing the limits of an agency's authority have caused concern. Oversight hearings also serve the interest of more junior legislators—members other than the chair or ranking minority member. *See* Ranking Member. By studying the issues to be covered and preparing an incisive line of questioning, a member can make a dramatic impression before his or her colleagues and the media.

As they do with legislation, lobbyists seek to protect their interest in oversight hearings. Primarily, this involves either testifying or lining up sympathetic members to ask questions, or cajole witnesses, in ways helpful to their issue. Oversight hearings can take on a trial-like atmosphere, with the committee acting as both advocate and jury. Lobbyists must therefore be aware of the rules governing these sessions, such as whether legal counsel can be present, or whether a witness has the right to bar the presence of television cameras. Witnesses also may be sworn during oversight hearings—raising the potential of prosecution for perjury if untruthful testimony is given. Oversight committees also can, by subpoena, compel the presence of witnesses and the submission of requested documents. The best defense in an oversight hearing, therefore, is to canvass the committee and its staff beforehand to understand the purpose of the hearing, the areas of inquiry, what is expected of witnesses, and the objective the committee is seeking.

Point of order. Under parliamentary procedure, a point of order, which is directed to the presiding officer, raises a question of whether the matter under consideration, such as a bill or amendment, is in order under the rules. The presiding officer (the committee or subcommittee chair; on the House floor, the Speaker or the designated presiding official; in the Senate, the vice president, or, more usually, the president pro tempore or a designee) rules on the point of order after consulting the rules and precedents that apply. If the point of order is sustained, the bill, or portions of the bill (for example, authorizing language contained in an appropriations bill), or the challenged amendment are ruled out of order and barred from further consideration at that time. Points of order can be appealed by the members, and the chair's decision can be overturned by a majority vote of the members present and voting. (In the Senate, rulings by the chair on certain points of order under the Budget Act can be overturned only by sixty votes instead of a simple majority.)

In the House, such challenges are exceptionally rare and usually involve partisan pique by the minority party, with a vote on the chair's ruling used as an effort to embarrass the chair for political purposes. Appeals of the ruling of the chair are much more common in the Senate, where they are not viewed as setting important precedents, and they are most often employed to add amendments involving policy issues to appropriations bills.

Points of order are essentially defensive tactics. Regardless of whether there is overwhelming sentiment for an amendment, a point of order, if properly lodged, can defeat it. Care must therefore be taken in drafting amendments to make sure they withstand such parliamentary challenges. *See* Legislative counsel. The key aspect of a point of order is that, in most instances, it must be made on a timely basis—that is, immediately when the matter is presented for consideration. If a point of order is not made at that time, and debate begins unchallenged on procedural grounds, the point of order comes too late and will not be sustained.

Political action committee (PAC). Under the campaign finance laws, political action committees (or PACs) are voluntary associations of individuals who contribute personal funds (not corporate or organizational funds) into a pool that is used for political contributions to candidates for public office. The activities and operations of PACs, and their contributors, are limited by law. Individuals can contribute no more than $5,000 to any one PAC. PACs can donate up to $5,000 to any one candidate in each of the primary and general elections. Contributions to PACs must be voluntary; management cannot coerce employees to participate, and corporate PACs cannot solicit from lower-level employees but only from professional staff and senior managers. Labor PACs can solicit from all union members. PAC contributions must be reported to the Federal Election Commission in Washington, and the records are available to the public.

There are nearly thirty-nine hundred PACs, and they are playing a greater and increasingly controversial role in the election process. In the 1994 congressional elections, PACs contributed $178.8 million to candidates for office (better than a threefold increase from 1980), with 71 percent of the funds directed to incumbents. Because PAC contributions favor incumbents, regardless of party, it is arguable that they tend to perpetuate the majority party's control in both the House and Senate. Critics inside and outside Congress believe PACs permit special interests to wield inordinate influence, through financial contributions to legislators responsible for their issues, over public policy questions.

Ranking member. The most senior member of the minority party on a committee or subcommittee. The ranking member usually exercises great authority over his party's colleagues on the panel by setting strategy for the minority's amendments in committee and on the floor and by controlling the minority's committee staff appointments. In the absence of control of a majority of the votes, the greatest asset the minority has is its rights under the rules. The ranking member helps ensure that his colleagues can exercise, to the limits, their ability to participate in the legislative process. Disregard of the minority, even if the majority's votes are well in hand, is extremely dangerous. Concerted action by the minority can create endless delay and political obstacles, such as the filing of numerous, contentious, and dilatory amendments and, in the Senate, the threat of a filibuster. *See* Filibuster. Prudence dictates that lobbyists not only elicit the minority's support whenever possible, but also keep the minority fully informed of all relevant developments.

Reconciliation. The legislative procedure, under the Budget Control and Impoundment Act of 1974, in which the committees are instructed by the House and Senate Budget committees to report, for floor consideration, bills that comply with the spending targets for each fiscal year, as established in the annual budget resolution. Pursuant to the Budget Act, Congress establishes overall spending, revenue (taxes), and deficit limits by specifying permissible expenditures for broad governmental categories and activities. These targets are then reconciled by the committees with jurisdiction over these activities through changes in the law that will meet the requisite budget reduction instructions. The Appropriations committees are not reconciled. Reconciliation attacks direct spending programs and tax provisions emanating from the authorizing committees and the Finance and Ways and Means committees. The budget resolution further specifies the date by which the committees are to complete action on such legislation, and may state preferences for the policy decisions the committees should implement. The reconciliation instructions from the Budget Committee are only dollar amounts of required savings; they cannot force any committee to adopt any particular proposal to achieve them.

In the late 1980s, with annual budget deficits, absent reconciliation, in the $150-$200 billion range, the yearly required deficit reductions amounted to tens of billions of dollars, instigating a frenzy of lobbying activity to protect favored programs from the budget ax. As the budget has become an increasingly high-profile issue, the reconciliation process has assumed greater importance, and it lasts for months, involving passage of the budget resolution each spring, committee action to implement its provisions through the summer, and floor debate and House-Senate conference agreement lasting into the fall. Some of the most important legislation is therefore wrapped into the reconciliation bill, with the final measure totaling hundreds of pages of changes in existing law. Special parliamentary rules apply, under the Budget Act, to floor consideration of the legislation. Maintaining the amount of money for a program, or even increasing it, may require finding an offsetting cut in another program. Points of order or, in the Senate, supermajority voting requirements (sixty votes) must be hurdled for proposals that would exceed the spending ceilings established by the budget resolution. *See* Point of order.

As "must" legislation, the reconciliation bill, depending on the issue involved, can be either an unparalleled opportunity to obtain a change in existing law or a mortal threat to a program's funding. Because it is so huge, the reconciliation bill is an ideal vehicle for amendments that might not withstand scrutiny as stand-alone proposals. (The so-called Byrd rule in the Senate bars certain types of extraneous provisions from the bill; amendments containing extraneous provisions require sixty votes to prevail.)

The budget process also has unleashed great tensions between the Budget committees and the authorizing and appropriating committees— who often resist, if not resent, the Budget panels' instructions and definitions of spending and tax priorities. It also has created conflict between Congress and the president, whose budget can be completely rewritten by the budget resolution and the reconciliation bill. (Several budgets of Presidents Ronald Reagan and George Bush were deemed "dead on arrival" on Capitol Hill by House Democrats in the 1980s and early 1990s.) These differences are ultimately resolved by votes on the House and Senate floors, and tests of will with the president over a threatened veto of the final reconciliation bill—as in 1995, when President Clinton vetoed a massive reconciliation bill intended to balance the budget within seven years. The "winners" in reconciliation are those who understand its intricacies and the political dynamics surrounding the process in any given year. Success in reconciliation can be measured by the political support that has been marshaled for a program or expenditure in the months before it is subject to the reconciliation process. Constituencies not heard from to defend their interests are sacrificed under the relentless pressure (due to the size of the federal budget deficit) to make substantial cuts in spending. Even then, a victory may well be escaping with a minimal spending reduction relative to other programs.

Record vote. A recorded vote in subcommittee, committee, or on the floor. Any member can ask for a record vote, but it is granted only if a sufficient number of members agree to the request. (In the House, an automatic recorded vote is held if a quorum is not present.) Recorded votes are important for tactical reasons. Where there is overwhelming support for a measure, recorded votes can demonstrate such sentiment, ratifying the consensus a bill or amendment enjoys. Record votes on controversial issues on the floor often become tests of whether there is sufficient support to override a threatened veto by the president. Members (and interest groups) may want a record vote on an issue so that it can be used for political purposes during election campaigns (for example, "Your representative voted for gun control."). If a member (or interest group) is going to lose a vote on a bill or amendment, it may be more desirable to avoid a record vote in order to understate the degree of opposition that exists; it is tougher to overturn a provision on the floor if a committee has voted to approve it by a decisive margin. Record votes also are used by the leadership of both parties to demonstrate party loyalty and discipline on controversial issues.

In past years members of both the House and Senate could cast their votes in committee without being present. The procedure, known as proxy voting, permits a legislator to give a colleague—usually the committee chair or ranking member—the right to cast his or her vote during a markup session. *See* Ranking member; Markup. Use of the proxy was abolished in the House at the beginning of the 104th Congress but remains in effect in the Senate, though the rules for its application are complex and can vary from committee to committee. Where permitted, proxies can be of two sorts: general (permitting the member exercising the proxy to vote it as he or she sees fit) or with instructions (specifying that the proxy be voted a certain way on specified amendments and on final committee action of the bill.)

Proxies are important to lobbyists: they can mean the difference between winning or losing a key committee vote. Not uncommonly, lobbyists will join forces with friendly staff in determining which members are not planning to attend a markup, and the lobbyists will encourage these members to give their proxy to a colleague who will then vote it in the "right" manner.

Registration. In December 1995, Congress enacted legislation substantially expanding the requirements under which lobbyists must register. Under the 1946 Federal Registration of Lobbying Act, lobbyists were supposed to register, but over the years it had been derided as "more loophole than law." A 1991 General Accounting Office report found that fewer than 4,000 of the 13,500 individuals listed in a directory of Washington lobbyists were registered. Under the new law, anyone who received at least $5,000 in a six-month period from a single client would be required to register with the clerk of the House and the secretary of the Senate, listing the congressional chambers and federal agencies they contacted, the issues they lobbied on, and how much money was spent on the effort. The reporting requirements also applied to organizations that used their own employees to lobby and spent at least $20,000 in a six-month period on that effort.

Report language. When a committee completes action on a bill, clearing it for floor consideration, it files a document, know as the committee report, to accompany the legislation. The report is an explanation of the bill's provisions and includes the justification for the legislation, the meaning and authoritative interpretation of the statutory language, a cost estimate for the legislation (important for budgetary reasons, particularly compliance with the budget resolution), and supplemental supporting or dissenting views by committee members. (From time to time, particularly on high-priority legislation requested by the president or, in the Senate, on presidential nominees, the legislation or nomination will be reported to the floor even if it has been defeated in committee, with the report explaining the committee's actions. This usually occurs if the president is exerting enormous political pressure on the issue or nomination, or if the vote in committee was extremely close.)

The committee report is the decisive statement of the panel's views on the legislation. Report language is a critical substantive and political tool. It will be relied upon by the government agency in developing the regulations and administering the bill's programs and policies. Report language also can be used (especially in appropriations bills) to direct an agency to undertake specified activities. Although these instructions do not have the force of law (only the statutory language itself does), they are a strong signal of congressional intent than an agency disregards at its peril, and for which it might be held accountable in a future oversight hearing. *See* Oversight hearing. To a lesser extent, the courts may turn, in cases arising under the law, to the report language to discern the meaning of the legislation. In the course of committee markup a member may decide not to offer an amendment to a bill, but instead to develop report language to address the concern. *See* Colloquy; Markup. Report language is most appropriate in fleshing out small, but important, details about how the legislation should be implemented. Members also can file supplemental, additional, or dissenting views at the end of the committee report. These are statements on the bill, and they are used to help frame the debate on the legislation when it reaches the floor.

Rules Committee. In the House, the Rules Committee controls the flow of legislation to the House floor. All major bills and resolutions reported from other committees must pass through the Rules Committee before being eligible for floor consideration. (The major exception is bills from the Appropriations Committee, which are privileged and do not require Rules Committee clearance, unless protection is sought for legislative language in the appropriations measure, which otherwise would be subject to a point of order.)

The committee is an arm of the Speaker and the majority leadership, with its members appointed by the Speaker and with its party ratio artificially inflated in favor of the majority in disproportion to the partisan ratio of the House as a whole. For each bill, the committee specifies procedures, known as rules, by which the bill will be debated on the floor: how long the debate will last, who controls the debate time, the precise measure to be considered for amendment, the amendments that may be offered, and the procedures leading to a final vote. After the Rules Committee approves a rule for a bill, the rule is itself reported to the floor, and the rule must be approved by the House before the bill it controls can be brought up. If the rule is defeated, the bill is dead for the moment. The Rules Committee can make in order amendments that would otherwise be subject to a point of order to be nongermane, and it can bar specific amendments that would otherwise be eligible (this occurs under what are known as "modified rules," in which only specified amendments can be offered). *See* Point of order; Germane amendments. Most bills are given "open" rules, which permit members to offer any amendment in order under the House rules generally.

The Rules Committee, particularly just prior to adjournment for the year, sometimes approves rules for bills which, if approved by the House, simultaneously execute passage of the underlying legislation. The Rules

Committee is, accordingly, extremely powerful, partisan, and controversial. On difficult or divisive legislation that is a priority of the House leadership, the committee, dominated by the majority, and at the behest of the leadership, will craft rules that severely limit the minority's opportunities to amend the bill—resulting in angry, partisan floor debate on the rule. At times the controversy will be so great that the rule is defeated by a coalition of a united minority and disaffected members of the majority; the rule is then sent back to committee for reworking into politically acceptable form.

As the arbiter of floor procedure, the Rules Committee is often turned to as the last resort of lobbyists and interest groups who have been defeated in earlier (legislative) committee action; they will seek support from Rules Committee members for a rule making their amendment in order on the floor, or barring an amendment sponsored by their opposition. Before writing the rule for a bill, however, the Rules Committee, unlike all other committees, receives testimony only from other members; outside witnesses usually are not heard. Thus, it is members from the committee that wrote the bill, and other members who want the chance to offer amendments, who go before the Rules Committee to state their case and lobby their colleagues.

Some bills fall under the jurisdiction of more than one House committee, each of which will report separate (and often differing) versions of the same legislation. The Rules Committee can choose the version of the bill it will send to the floor, and permit the other committee(s) to offer its version as an amendment to the bill. The Rules Committee also can withhold a decision and encourage the two (or more) committees to develop a compromise they can take to the floor together. The House Rules Committee has no say as to when a measure is taken up on the floor—only that it will be at some time after Rules acts. The scheduling power belongs to the majority leadership. The Senate also has a Rules and Administration Committee, but it does not parallel the authority, nature, or responsibilities of the House Rules Committee. The Senate panel is simply another legislative committee, with jurisdiction over the administration of the Senate, ethics and campaign laws, and other matters. The Senate leadership, through less formal processes, exercises for the Senate the duties assigned to the House Rules Committee. *See* Time Agreement. The Senate leadership controls the scheduling of legislation on the floor.

Suspension of the rules. Applies in the House only. Many bills considered by the House are noncontroversial or enjoy broad bipartisan support. Such legislation can receive expedited floor consideration, either after being reported by committee or by bypassing the committee entirely and being presented to the floor for a vote, under a procedure known as suspension of the rules. Under this process, the normal rules that apply to floor consideration are set aside, with debate limited to forty minutes (as opposed to the normal one or more hours) and no amendments permitted (as opposed to the normal process of amendments made in order under the rule for a bill). *See* Rules Committee. In exchange for this expedited consideration, the bill, to be approved, must pass by a two-thirds majority of those present and voting (as opposed to the normal simple majority).

Obviously, bills "under suspension" place a special premium on consensus, as they can be blocked by the "nay" votes of only one-third of the members. Usually, for a bill to be brought up under suspension, it has to be cleared by the bipartisan leadership of the committee with jurisdiction; if the minority objects, the bill will almost always be defeated. (The majority sometimes tries to bring up a bill under suspension regardless of the minority's views.) Opposition by the administration to a bill under suspension also is usually sufficient to prevent attainment of the supermajority needed for passage.

If the House leadership is not enamored of a particular bill reported by the committee, or if time pressures are great late in a session, the leadership has been known to permit a bill to come to the floor, but only under suspension—placing the burden for securing the needed two-thirds majority on the committee chair and advocates for the bill. If a bill is defeated under suspension, it can be brought up under the regular procedures, with a rule from the Rules Committee—but the bill might then be subject to unwanted amendments on the floor. Indeed, a chair may bring a bill to the floor under suspension precisely because adoption of a hostile amendment could be more unpalatable than having the bill defeated outright. In general, approval of a bill under suspension indicates excellent prospects for ultimate enactment.

Time agreement. A time agreement effectively does for the Senate what the Rules Committee does for the House in terms of framing consideration of a bill on the floor. *See* Rules Committee. It is, in effect, a contract between the majority leader, the minority, and all senators to govern consideration of a bill on the Senate floor. All time agreements are approved by unanimous consent of all senators; the objection of one senator whose interests are not served by the time agreement can scuttle it. In the absence of a time agreement, a bill can be considered indefinitely, and be subject to unlimited debate (*see* Filibuster) and amendment. Time agreements are negotiated between the majority and minority leaders (or their designees), the chair and ranking member (*see* Ranking member) of the committee with jurisdiction, all senators who want to offer amendments to the bill, and any senator who has indicated an intention to place a hold (*see* Hold) on the bill.

Negotiating such an agreement can be a painstaking process, particularly if a significant number of senators, or a determined minority, do not want to see the bill approved, much less considered. The majority leader, by propounding a time agreement, can flush out the opposition to a bill by announcing the leadership's intention to take the bill up; other senators, to protect their rights, have to come forward and state what they want or the provisions to which they object. This precipitates negotiations that will ultimately lead to a time agreement or "extended debate" or filibuster. In final form, a time agreement resembles a rule from the House Rules Committee: it lists the amendments that can be offered, the sequence of amendments, the time that can be spent debating each amendment (and how the time is divided between senators), and procedures leading to a vote on the final passage (including the day and hour of a final vote). In the Senate, the time agreement is the ultimate form of comity between senators, because it permits the Senate to function through the concurrence of the members. The majority leader, in securing approval of a time agreement, always thanks all senators for their cooperation.

Transition rules. When omnibus legislation, such as a major tax or banking bill, is considered, private interests placed at a disadvantage by the bill's provisions will seek exceptions, or transition rules, from the legislation. Transition rules are among the most significant favors that members can bestow on private interests. Transition rules can be general in nature (such as exempting entire classes of people from compliance with the new law, or exempting all transactions completed before a certain date from the bill's new changes in tax or regulatory treatment), or very specific (separate language carving out a benefit for only one company, interest, or constituent).

If a request for a transition rule is based on a compelling argument, with several parties seeking the same type of relief, a generic transition rule may be developed by the committee staff and incorporated in the bill. The strongest case for a transition rule is when it can be demonstrated that, in previous changes in law, similar legislative treatment was previously granted to another, similarly placed party. Members will generally sponsor transition rules only for their constituents. Thus, a lobbyist representing a client who needs a transition rule but is not represented by a legislator on the committee writing the bill is at a distinct disadvantage. Lobbyists will often go to "their" member to ask their intercession with members on the committee writing the legislation. Members not on the committee often resent that their colleagues on the panel can protect their constituents with transition rules—and they may demand similar opportunities for amendments when the bill reaches the floor on in conference. *See* Conference. A committee chair may often use his or her discretion to support a requested transition rule in order to obtain a member's vote for the overall bill; this is a very powerful bargaining tactic.

Transition rules, by their nature as special breaks for very small numbers of corporations or individuals, are extremely sensitive and at times controversial. Transition rules are usually artfully drafted to avoid the ready identification of the beneficiary (for example, one transition rule from the 1986 Tax Reform Act begins, "A facility is described in this subparagraph if it is a domed stadium which was the subject of a city ordinance passed on September 23, 1985....."). The disclosure of the beneficiary, particularly if the transition rule involves substantial amounts of money (such as in taxes that would otherwise be paid), can cause political embarrassment. Especially egregious transition rules are often the subject of floor amendments to delete them. Nevertheless, transition rules are the only way to secure relief from a bill if the underlying policy provision is locked in concrete in the legislation. As long as members represent constituents, and as long as there are committee chairs, there will always be transition rules.

INDEX